THE RISE OF THE PRESIDENT'S
PERMANENT CAMPAIGN

THE RISE OF
THE PRESIDENT'S
PERMANENT
CAMPAIGN

Brendan J. Doherty

 University Press of Kansas

For my parents, John and Wendy Doherty,
to whom I owe everything

Published by the University Press of Kansas (Lawrence, Kansas 66045), which was
organized by the Kansas Board of Regents and is operated and funded by Emporia
State University, Fort Hays State University, Kansas State University, Pittsburg State
University, the University of Kansas, and Wichita State University

Library of Congress Cataloging-in-Publication Data
Doherty, Brendan J.
The rise of the president's permanent campaign / Brendan J. Doherty.
   p.   cm.
Includes bibliographical references and index.
ISBN 978-0-7006-1859-0 (cloth : alk. paper) — ISBN 978-0-7006-1860-6 (pbk. : alk.
paper)
1. Presidents—United States—History—20th century. 2. Presidents—United States—
History—21st century. 3. Political campaigns—United States—History—20th century.
4. Political campaigns—United States—History—21st century. I. Title.
JK511.D65   2012
324.70973--dc23

                                                                          2012016765

British Library Cataloguing-in-Publication Data is available.

Printed in the United States of America

10 9 8 7 6 5 4 3 2 1

The paper used in this publication is recycled and contains 30 percent postconsumer
waste. It is acid free and meets the minimum requirements of the American National
Standard for Permanence of Paper for Printed Library Materials Z39.48-1992.

CONTENTS

PREFACE

The seed for this book was planted in 2003 when much was being made of the extensive amounts of time that George W. Bush was spending in the states of Florida, Pennsylvania, and Ohio. The media's focus was based on the assumption that political concerns were driving decisions about how the president allocated his time and where he bestowed his attention. This emphasis was reminiscent of press coverage of Bill Clinton's presidency, with its focus on the purportedly political nature of his White House. While one could certainly find examples of presidential actions that had electoral implications, I wondered whether the so-called permanent campaign would be evident if I examined its key indicators systematically and objectively.

As I considered the many potential ways to approach the question of whether the permanent campaign did or did not exist, I was first drawn to presidential travel. When it comes to presidential elections, geography is a paramount factor. At both the nominating and general election stages, certain states are critically important to an aspiring or incumbent president's prospects, while others offer little or no electoral reward. As the president's time is arguably his, and someday her, scarcest resource, how he allocates it and where he chooses to travel can reveal a great deal about his priorities. Naturally, the incentives of our electoral system structure candidate strategies. Do they relate to the ways presidents behave in office too?

Thus, this study began with painstaking efforts to build an original data set on presidential travel, which led to many hours spent poring over the *Public Papers of the Presidents of the United States*. As I did so, I was struck by how often recent presidents had headlined political fundraisers and thought that this was an important and understudied part of the story, since most research on campaign finance is based on contribution data, which campaigns are required by law to provide to the Federal Election Commission. The extent to which presidents commit themselves to raise political funds had not yet been examined, in part because of the effort involved in collecting the data, which would involve not only examining the *Public Papers* but also reviewing thousands of newspaper articles on presidential fundraising to capture the substantial number of fundraisers that were conducted out of public view and did not end up in the *Public Papers*. Additionally, in the course of writing this book, I conducted archival research at several presidential libraries and drew on accounts by presidents and their aides in an effort to understand how decisions about electoral matters are made, and the ways in which the role of White House staff in these matters has changed over time.

I seek to address four principal questions in this book. To what extent do presidents respond to electoral incentives and tend to electoral concerns throughout their terms in office? How have these dynamics evolved over time? Why have these changes come about? And what are the implications of these dynamics for presidential leadership? My goal is not to disparage any particular president for a focus on electoral matters but instead to better understand the ways in which political actors respond to the institutional incentives of our electoral system. No political system is neutral. Each sets up a series of rules that help to structure the behavior of goal-oriented politicians. It has long been understood that the behavior of presidential candidates is shaped by the incentives established by the American campaign finance regime, the presidential nominating process, and the Electoral College. The evidence presented here demonstrates that these incentives relate to the way presidents behave throughout their terms in office as well.

I would like to make clear what I do and do not focus on in this book. The *permanent campaign* is a term that is often used broadly to refer to a president's ongoing efforts to win public approval, to sell his policies once in office in the same manner in which he marketed himself as a candidate in the campaign, or to measure public sentiment through extensive use of public opinion polling. The extent to which presidents bring these techniques of a political campaign to the practice of governing is important and worthy of study, but this is not the subject of this project.

To give this book a clear focus, my study examines the president's efforts that are related to electoral concerns and the ways in which decisions about these matters are made in the White House. The first area of focus is presidential fundraising, which is an unambiguously electoral activity that reveals the extent to which a president devotes time to financing his own reelection campaign and to supporting the electoral efforts of his fellow party members. The second is the president's disproportionate attention to states that are strategically important in both the nominating process and the Electoral College. I then examine the evolving roles of key players in and out of the White House who help to make decisions about these matters. I advance an argument about why we see these changing dynamics, and what they portend for the nature of presidential leadership. Readers may agree with or contest my interpretation of these elements of the presidency, but the heart of the book is the clear and important empirical evidence of the growing focus by American presidents on electoral concerns throughout their terms in office.

I am deeply grateful for the support and advice that many people have generously provided me as I have worked on this project. As thanking them all properly might require doubling the length of the book, I hope that these brief words of gratitude will suffice instead. I owe special thanks to Nelson Polsby and Bruce Cain of the University of California, Berkeley. Both did much to teach me about conducting scholarly research with practical political implications, and their leadership of Berkeley's Institute of Governmental Studies provided me with an academic home that was a vibrant hub of collaborative scholarship. Nelson, who passed away shortly after I completed graduate school, often claimed that he left no fingerprints on the work of his advisees. I respectfully beg to differ, as my research is infused with the thoughtful advice he offered me and is inspired by the example of his own carefully crafted scholarship. Bruce worked diligently to support my research on the West and the East Coast, providing me with invaluable feedback on my work as well as enlightening opportunities to collaborate with him on research and engage with other scholars both in the United States and abroad, all of which greatly aided my professional and personal development.

At Berkeley, a number of other people kindly lent their time and assistance. Gordon Silverstein helped to frame my research in light of the all-important "so what?" question, and Terri Bimes taught me by example how one can conduct rigorous and systematic research on the presidency. I am also grateful to Eric Schickler, Ray Wolfinger, Sandy Muir, Bob Kagan, Jack Citrin, Judy Gruber, Laura Stoker, Henry Brady, John Ellwood, and Jerry Lubenow, as well as my then fellow graduate students Melissa Cully Anderson, Dave Hopkins, Matt Grossmann, Iris Hui, Casey Dominguez, Darshan Goux, Megan Mullin, and Jill Greenlee, all of whom helped to shape this project at its early stages by providing specific feedback and general support.

I owe an even earlier debt of gratitude to George Demko, who helped spark my fascination with political geography when I was an undergraduate at Dartmouth College. His example as a teacher and scholar inspired me to pursue a career as a professor. When I moved to the East Coast near the conclusion of my graduate studies, the University of California Washington Center and the American Political Science Association's Centennial Center for Political Science and Public Affairs each provided a warm and welcoming community in which to do my work, for which I thank Bruce Cain, Jeff Biggs, Sean Twombly, and Veronica Jones. For the past five years, my colleagues at the U.S. Naval Academy have provided a supportive environment in which both teaching and research are valued. I owe particular thanks to my three department chairs, Ellie Malone, Gale Mattox, and Priscilla Zotti, as well as my colleagues in American politics, Howard Ernst and Steve Frantzich.

Other people from across the country have generously shared their expertise at conferences, over coffee, and in various other venues. Jessica Gerrity kindly read the entire manuscript with a keen and skillful eye, providing me with insightful advice for which I am tremendously grateful. Dorie Apollonio, Hal Bass, David

Brady, Lara Brown, Gary Bugh, Dan Carpenter, Jeff Cohen, George Edwards, Victoria Farrar-Myers, Fred Greenstein, Simon Jackman, David Karol, Mark Knoller, Martha Joynt Kumar, Ray La Raja, Burdett Loomis, Scott Long, Tom Mann, Bruce Miroff, Rich Powell, Doug Rivers, Brandon Rottinghaus, Mary Stuckey, Henry Tom, Danielle Vinson, Shirley Anne Warshaw, and Martin Wattenberg all shared valuable feedback on a wide range of questions through the years as I worked on this project. George Elsey kindly provided me a firsthand perspective on political decision-making in the Truman administration.

I have benefited greatly from the efforts of the dedicated librarians at Berkeley's Institute of Governmental Studies and the Naval Academy's Nimitz Library. I am grateful for the guidance of skilled archivists at the Truman Library in Independence, Missouri; the Eisenhower Library in Abilene, Kansas; the Johnson Library in Austin, Texas; the Carter Library in Atlanta, Georgia; the Reagan Library in Simi Valley, California; the Bush Library in College Station, Texas; and the Clinton Library in Little Rock, Arkansas. Additionally, I owe a debt of gratitude to John Woolley and Gerhard Peters, whose American Presidency Project is an invaluable resource that enabled me to compile much of the data used in this book.

I would like to express my gratitude for financial support for my research provided by three Seed Grants from the Naval Academy Research Council; the Harry Middleton Fellowship in Presidential Studies from the Lyndon Baines Johnson Foundation; an O'Donnell Research Grant from the George Bush Presidential Library Foundation; a Small Research Grant and Presidency Research Fund Fellowship from the American Political Science Association; as well as several grants and fellowships from the University of California, Berkeley's Travers Department of Political Science, Institute of Governmental Studies, and Graduate Division.

While this book is almost entirely composed of new analysis and prose, in several instances I have used wording or anecdotes from my previously published research in *Presidential Studies Quarterly* and in my chapter in Gary Bugh's edited volume, *Electoral College Reform: Challenges and Possibilities* (Ashgate, 2010). I thank those editors for their earlier support of my work.

I have been fortunate to work with my thoughtful and supportive editor, Fred Woodward, and his talented colleagues at the University Press of Kansas, especially Kelly Chrisman Jacques and Susan Schott. I am also grateful to Richard Ellis and Michael Nelson, whose careful reviews of the manuscript improved and strengthened this book.

I have saved for last my thanks to my wonderful family. I dedicate this book to my parents, John and Wendy Doherty, who have taught me to love learning and teaching, and whose unstinting support, hard work, dedication to their family, and love have opened up a world of opportunity to me. I love and thank them more than words can properly convey. I also thank my sister, Kate, and her husband, Sean, whose encouragement and faith in me have been boundless, as well as Rowan and Patrick. I am grateful as well to my family by marriage, Gene, Shelley, Eric, and Lisa Altman, as well as Paul Knowlton, who have supported my endeavors on both coasts and are always up for a conversation about politics.

My wife, Robyn Altman, supported me when I first considered graduate school in political science more than a decade ago, moved west with me to sunny California so that I could work on my degree, and then back east again as we both pursued our careers. Her love, friendship, and laughter have been an inspiration and a source of strength. I am fortunate to have married a skilled writer and editor who read every word of this manuscript and improved it substantially. I thank her for her unwavering support and her genuine interest and belief in my chosen profession. I am so lucky to have her. Most of all, I thank her for Eva and Asa, both of whom spent substantial time napping on my lap as I worked on this manuscript. They may have had no idea what their daddy was writing about, but I could not have been happier to have them there with me.

1. Presidents and the Permanent Campaign

> Since he is President, he *cannot be politically active* until well after the July Convention. The people are inconsistent and capricious but there is no argument that they feel deeply on this—: He must be President of *all* the people and not merely the leader of a party, until the very last minute.
>
> *Clifford-Rowe memorandum to Harry S. Truman, November 19, 1947*

In a famed 1947 memorandum, White House aide Clark Clifford and former FDR adviser James Rowe proposed a reelection campaign strategy for President Harry S. Truman.[1] Its counsel that the president refrain from engaging in overtly partisan political activity before the Democratic National Convention tapped into fundamental dynamics of American politics and the tension between unifying presidential leadership and divisive partisan activity that remain instructive in the present day. President Barack Obama did not heed Clifford and Rowe's advice more than six decades later when he took the stage in a packed hotel ballroom in Indianapolis and declared to a boisterous crowd of Democratic supporters:

> It's a pleasure to be with your outstanding representatives in Congress, Andre Carson, Joe Donnelly, Brad Ellsworth, Baron Hill. . . . We're here to make sure they can stay right where they belong, in the United States Congress, representing your hopes, representing your dreams, carrying your voices to Washington, DC. . . . That's why all of you are here tonight. That's why you're digging deep again, even when times are a little tight, why I know you're going to make those calls and knock on those doors and get to the polls again next November, because we've got to make sure these four leaders continue their devoted service to Indiana and to America.[2]

The appeal that Obama made at this fundraiser was not unusual in its substance—presidents often ask the party faithful to give generously and volunteer their time to help reelect members of Congress and other officials. But its timing and location make this event noteworthy. The president did not make this pitch in the weeks, months, or even year leading up to a congressional election. This event took place on May 17, 2009—just over six months after the last election and almost a year and a half before these four members of Congress would again submit their fate to the voters. Indeed, it would have been more accurate, if a bit rhetorically clunky, had the president called on his audience to work to get out the vote in the November *after* next November. He most certainly was not heeding the advice given to Truman more than sixty years earlier to avoid the role of party leader until the months immediately preceding Election Day.

Location is the second noteworthy element of Obama's three events that day—in addition to raising money for four Democratic House members, he headlined another fundraiser in Indianapolis, this one for the Democratic National Committee, which followed a commencement speech at the University of Notre Dame in nearby South Bend. While the speech at Notre Dame was an official presidential event, observers noted that it happened to take place in one of the states that Obama had narrowly carried in 2008, when he became the first Democratic presidential nominee to win Indiana in forty-four years. This was a return visit, as Indiana had also been the site of his first trip outside of the nation's capital region in February 2009. The early focus on a key electoral state was the rule for Obama, not the exception. Of the eleven states outside of the Washington, DC, metropolitan area that Obama had visited at that point in his term, eight were states in which he had won or lost the two-party vote by under 10 percent in 2008—in descending order of closeness, Missouri, North Carolina, Indiana, Florida, Ohio, Arizona, Colorado, and Iowa. Of the other three states Obama had visited, one was the electorally secure but cash-rich state of California, another was the battleground state of New Mexico, and the last was his home state of Illinois.

Obama's early travel bore two of the hallmarks of what has been commonly dubbed the permanent campaign—travel to key electoral states, even with Election Day several years away, and political fundraising events. According to the logic of the permanent campaign, electoral concerns are assumed to be central to decisions throughout a president's term in office, and the techniques and strategies of presidential campaigning are applied throughout the course of a president's term. In this school of thought, the conventional idea that a presidency can be clearly and neatly divided into periods of governing and of campaigning, with the latter occurring only as an election draws near, no longer holds.

This book examines the strategic choices that presidents make, what those choices reveal about presidential priorities, and the evolving relationship between campaigning and governing. It draws on extensive empirical evidence to analyze the causes, indicators, and implications of the permanent campaign and argues that while the presidency has always been a political office, the distinction between campaigning and governing has become increasingly blurred as electoral concerns and patterns of behavior have become central to the operation of the White House. Presidents since the mid-1970s have devoted more and more time to their role as fundraiser-in-chief, jetting around the country to fill their campaign coffers and those of their political allies. As they have done so, they have also traveled more to key electoral states, disproportionately targeting those states that are important to their political prospects, while largely neglecting those without electoral payoff.

This study contends that the increased blurring of the lines between campaigning and governing that characterizes the permanent campaign is primarily the consequence of the interaction of the rising costs of campaigns and the institutional rules of the game created by the evolving campaign finance regime; the tendencies of the presidents produced in recent years by the rules structuring presidential nominating and general election campaigns; competitive presidential elections and narrow margins of party control of Congress that raise the stakes of all federal elections; changes in the organization and role of the White House staff; and evolving norms of presidential behavior. These dynamics work against and often overcome the formal rules that are meant to separate the president's governing activities from his, and one day her, campaigning efforts. The institutionalization of some of these changes means that each new president inherits a White House where the path of least resistance is one that facilitates the perpetuation of the permanent campaign. Pursuing electoral interests can strengthen a presidency by helping to secure another term in the White House and electing more fellow party members to Congress and offices across the country. But doing so also leads to trade-offs, as allocating a president's time to electoral concerns by necessity means less time devoted to other pressing concerns. Perhaps most problematic, a president focused on electoral gain can heighten public cynicism and limit prospects for bipartisan compromise and effective presidential leadership.

THE PRESIDENT AS A DIVISIVE AND UNIFYING LEADER

The tension over the proper ways in which the president is to balance the duties of his office and his electoral aims flows from the dual nature of the office of the presidency that was established by the Constitution. As several scholars have discussed, the framers created a presidency that combines the roles of head of state and political leader, embedding tensions in the office that do not exist in other democracies in which these roles are carried out by two people. As a result, our president serves as an image of national unity in certain instances, carrying out the role that a constitutional monarch plays in many countries, while his responsibilities as the head of his party require him to advocate for a partisan political agenda in pursuit of his and his party's policy and electoral objectives that is sure to divide the country into supporting and opposing factions.[3]

Aggressive pursuit of one role can compromise a president's effectiveness in the other. Presidents who place their primary focus on being a unifying national leader might be less effective at leading their party and building the electoral and popular support necessary to enact their legislative agenda. At the other end of the spectrum, presidents who devote much of their efforts to their role as head of their party might become polarizing figures with limited ability to reach across the aisle to work on a bipartisan basis when needed.

It is important to note that the presidency is an inherently and intentionally political office. When the framers of the Constitution gathered in Philadelphia in the steamy summer of 1787, they forged the office of a chief executive for the nation who would serve renewable four-year terms without limit. Alexander Hamilton, writing in *The Federalist* No. 72, contended that the political nature of the office and a president's eligibility for and desire to win reelection would lead to better, not worse, governance:

> One ill effect of the exclusion [of the president from eligibility for reelection] would be a diminution of the inducements to good behavior. There are few men who would not feel much less zeal in the discharge of a duty when they were conscious that the advantages of the station with which it was connected must be relinquished at a determinate period, than when they were permitted to entertain a hope of OBTAINING, by MERITING, a continuance of them. This position will not be disputed so long as it is admitted that the desire of reward is one of the strongest incentives of human conduct; or that the best security for the fidelity of mankind is to make their interests coincide with their duty.[4]

In this view, electoral objectives would incentivize, rather than compromise, effective presidential leadership. The motive for reelection would lead presidents to serve the nation's needs, not their own, by holding the president accountable to those who elected him. Nineteenth-century British writer James Bryce expanded on this point, remarking in *The American Commonwealth* that the president of the United States would be "apart from and *above political parties*. He was to represent the nation as a whole. . . . The independence of his position, with nothing either to gain or to fear from Congress, would, it was hoped, leave him free to think only of the welfare of the people."[5] The president's position as a nationally elected leader who would not be dependent upon the Congress would allow him to serve the public good, though of course how to define the public good would be a matter of much contention.

Presidents dating back to at least Andrew Jackson have publicly laid claim to the mantle of national leadership, declaring that they, in stark contrast with the Congress, represent the national interest, instead of particularistic local and regional concerns.[6] Harry Truman, speaking at Columbia University seven years after he left office, declared, "The president is the representative of the whole nation, and he's the only lobbyist that all of the 160 million people in this country have."[7] George H. W. Bush, addressing an audience at Princeton University on

May 10, 1991, articulated this view when he remarked, "Consider the President's role. Thomas Jefferson once noted that a President commands a view of the whole ground, while Congress necessarily adopts the views of its constituents. The President and Vice President are the only officials elected to serve the entire Nation."[8] Presidents consistently contend that the electoral process that elevated them to office incentivizes them to focus on the national interest.

Many scholars, particularly in studies of pork barrel politics, have echoed the claims that the president is the only elected official who truly represents the national interest, arguing that the president has a universal constituency, in contrast with members of Congress, who favor their respective regions.[9] According to their logic, the president makes decisions with the national interest in mind because his electorate is national, whereas members of Congress naturally respond more to the needs of their own states and districts.

These arguments certainly have merit, but they do not take into account the incentives of the Electoral College system, in which not all votes are equally important. Due to the unit rule used by forty-eight of the fifty states, under which a state allocates all its Electoral College votes to the winner of the statewide popular vote, presidential candidates devote disproportionate attention to the largest states that offer the greatest electoral payoffs. States that are electorally safe for either party provide no incentive for campaign attention because additional effort invested there will not affect the prospects of winning and losing. Instead, the focus becomes the so-called battleground or swing states, with the most attention devoted to the most populous of these electorally competitive states. Thus, Florida, Ohio, and Pennsylvania have been three of the most hotly contested states in recent presidential elections. In the study of pork barrel politics, Nolan McCarty is a rare scholar who takes these dynamics into account, contending that presidents do indeed use policy decisions to favor certain parts of the country over others in pursuit of political goals.[10]

Several scholars have investigated how the incentives of the Electoral College structure the allocation of campaign resources.[11] The logic of the permanent campaign suggests that these incentives not only would structure campaign activity but also would help to guide actions throughout a president's term in office. According to this school of thought, presidents would not always act as unifying national leaders, but at times would instead favor certain states throughout their first term in office according to the incentives of the Electoral College. Additionally, the disproportionate influence of Iowa and New Hampshire in the presidential nominating process would make them the object of particular attention throughout a presidents' first term in office.

While the president often serves as a unifying national leader, the idea that the presidency can be apolitical is a fiction. Politics is the process through which we fight out disagreements over national priorities. The president is elected following a campaign in which he advocated certain policy prescriptions, and many members of Congress in his party share his political perspective. They work to enact those policy priorities, and to do so the president supports his fellow party members, helping to raise funds and framing his positions in contrast to those of the political opposition. Presidents often devote much effort to winning the next election, for themselves or for their co-partisans, knowing that doing so will strengthen their ability to win much-desired political victories.

Political leaders on both ends of Pennsylvania Avenue have recognized the tension between the institutional incentives that make the presidency a political office and the need for a president to be above the political fray in many ways. In response, they have crafted rules that attempt to draw lines between the president's campaigning and governing activities. Presidents and presidential staff are not permitted to engage in campaign activities in most parts of the White House, a fact of which Vice President Al Gore became painfully aware in the 1990s when he controversially made fundraising calls from his White House office.[12] Presidential aides involved in both campaign and official business now have two Blackberries, computers, and email accounts so that electoral activities are not carried out on official government equipment. Laws require that many of the costs of presidential travel for overtly political events be borne by the responsible political organizations. The taxpayers, however, do subsidize these political trips, as the president's campaign or political party does not have to pay for the substantial costs of Secret Service protection, advance logistics, the provision of secure communications technology, a medical team on standby, and other expenses that are incurred whenever the president leaves the White House.[13] It has become quite common in recent years for presidents to pair an explicitly political event on a trip with an official nonpolitical event nearby, which leads the taxpayer to support even more of a trip's costs.[14] The White House counsel provides extensive legal guidance to the president's aides so that those who need to can fulfill their dual roles as government employees and political operatives within the constraints imposed by the law.[15]

The behavior that these lines between campaigning and governing are supposed to wall off from the official business of government has become all the more prevalent. As the president's staff has grown, as more political functions have been placed within the White House itself, and as presidents devote more and more of their time to fundraising and other electorally related activity throughout their term in office, the formal separations of the overtly partisan and supposedly nonpolitical elements of a presidency have come to be both more necessary and less effective.

STUDYING THE PERMANENT CAMPAIGN

The *permanent campaign* is an often-used term that encompasses many types of presidential behavior. Pat Caddell, a top aide and pollster to then president-elect Jimmy Carter, is often credited with authoring the concept of the permanent campaign in a 1976 transition memo, titled "Initial Working Paper on Political Strategy." In it he recommended, "In devising a strategy for the Administration, it is important to recognize we cannot successfully separate politics and government. . . . Essentially it is my thesis that governing with public approval requires a continuing political campaign." He also called for the creation of a group that would start to prepare for Carter's reelection campaign four years later.[16] The term was popularized by Sidney Blumenthal's book *The Permanent Campaign: Inside the World of Elite Political Operatives* (1980) and has taken on a broad meaning that includes a range of activities for electoral ends that involve employing the techniques and strategies of campaigning throughout a president's term in office.[17]

Many scholars who have investigated elements of the permanent campaign have built upon Samuel Kernell's theory of "going public," as this work does as well. Kernell argues that presidents take their case to the American people with much greater frequency than they once did in hopes of building public support for their legislative agenda.[18] Subsequent works have focused on whether these efforts to move public opinion and pressure Congress actually work, and if not, then why presidents continue this practice.[19] One scholar has argued that going public is actually a signal to the Congress rather than an attempt to motivate an inattentive public.[20] Other studies have examined whether presidents lead or follow public opinion.[21] These works all examine questions related to the premise that presidents' efforts to reach the public are part of an ongoing campaign-like effort throughout their term in office that is tied to their role in the legislative process and the bargaining environment in Washington.

The concept of a permanent campaign for the presidency has been much discussed, and while many scholars have examined certain aspects of it, few have set out to grapple systematically and empirically with these important dynamics. Only three book-length academic studies have addressed directly the question of the permanent campaign. Norman Ornstein and Thomas Mann's edited volume on the subject provides a number of illuminating essays on different elements of the permanent campaign, but it does not advance one common argument and was written before the presidency of George W. Bush.[22] George Edwards's *Governing by Campaigning: The Politics of the Bush Presidency,* in contrast, is a revealing study of a single presidency but does not address the question of the evolution of the permanent campaign over time.[23] Kathryn Dunn Tenpas's *Presidents as Candidates:*

Inside the White House for the Presidential Campaign examines how presidential campaigns have come to be run from within the White House itself and offers insights into the ways the presidency changes when it gears up for a reelection bid. This informative book focuses on one important element of the permanent campaign, but it was published in 1997 and thus does not cover these dynamics subsequent to Bill Clinton's first term.[24]

Few studies have attempted to examine empirically the extent to which electoral incentives relate to the ways sitting presidents govern. One notable exception is Scott James's historical study of Democratic regulatory policy and Electoral College incentives, in which he argues that geographic electoral incentives were tightly tied to the regulatory policies of Democratic presidents from 1884 through 1936. Through analysis of the political dynamics surrounding the Interstate Commerce Act of 1887, the Federal Trade Commission Act of 1914, and the Public Utility Holding Act of 1935, James makes a powerful case that electoral concerns driven by the desire to hold onto the White House led Democratic presidents to abandon their party's long-held positions on the nature of the regulatory state. While he does not frame his study around the concept of the permanent campaign, his effort to relate the ways in which presidents govern to electoral incentives is instructive.[25]

Much good scholarship has been dedicated to the evolving nature and structure of the White House staff, as it has become a more complex, hierarchical, and political organization,[26] and the evolution of White House polling practices.[27] Only one academic book-length study examines the evolution of presidential travel, though its focus is not on presidential campaigning.[28] Several popular books by political actors have examined some of the dynamics of the permanent campaign,[29] but their perspectives are quite different from the systematic, empirical approach employed by political scientists. These are important elements that are related to the presidency and the permanent campaign, but they do not tell the entire story. There is no book that advances a single argument about the causes, indicators, and implications of the rise of the permanent campaign. This work aims to do so.

The few scholarly works that do directly address the concept of the permanent campaign are exceptions to the convention in political science that has long kept most scholarship on presidential campaigns separate from the study of the presidency. One of the long-held assumptions in the study of American politics is that the time when a sitting president campaigns for reelection can be separated from the time when he governs. One notable example is Samuel Kernell, who, in his study of presidents "going public," justified studying speeches over a president's first three years but not the fourth by asserting, "To eliminate public activities inspired by concerns of reelection rather than governing, only the first three years have been tabulated."[30] Can we legitimately assume that activities in the first three years of a president's term are inspired by governing but not reelection? The logic of the permanent campaign would say that the answer is no.

The scholarly practice of dividing a presidency into periods of governing and campaigning is grounded in long-standing political tradition. An undated and unsigned memo from the files of White House aide Ken Hechler found in the Harry S. Truman Library's archives reviewing the 1948 campaign begins by stating that the "campaign extended from September 6, Labor Day, to November 2."[31] Similarly, many studies of presidential and congressional campaigns begin their analysis at Labor Day of the election year, which was the traditional kickoff of the fall campaign.[32] The logic of the permanent campaign suggests that focusing a study of presidential campaigning only on the months immediately preceding Election Day would miss much important and relevant activity.

This study builds on this premise to ask what certain presidential actions throughout a term in office can tell us about presidential priorities and the evolving nature of the presidency itself. The idea of a permanent campaign is nothing new to the study of Congress, but it has played relatively little role in research on the presidency. If, following the logic that David Mayhew applies to members of Congress, we assume that presidents are single-minded seekers of reelection, strategic presidents, as rational actors, would be expected to favor key states in ways that reflect the institutional incentives of the Electoral College in order to maximize their chances of reelection.[33] They would also work to accumulate the financial resources that would bolster both their own electoral fortunes and those of their political party. Additionally, they would organize the White House staff to facilitate the achievement of their political goals.

Winning elections is the sine qua non of American politics. A president must be reelected to have additional time to advance his agenda, and he needs a sufficient number of fellow party members in Congress to have hope of enacting his will via the legislative process. As Mayhew explains, assuming that politicians are single-minded seekers of reelection "necessarily does some violence to the facts."[34] A number of motivations explain certain elements of presidential resource allocation. Presidents travel to certain states to advance their own reelection interests, to raise funds, to support their fellow party members, to exert pressure on recalcitrant legislators, to promote their policy agenda or achievements in a setting outside the nation's capital, to attend ceremonial events, to respond to natural disasters or other crises, to influence public opinion, or simply to get out of Washington. Although presidents engage in many more activities than the pursuit of reelection and party building, the question remains whether this simplistic assumption explains well a substantial portion of presidential actions.

Drawing systematic conclusions about presidential actions is complicated by the individual nature of the presidency. Each president is indeed unique and brings to the presidency his own agenda, strategic plan, personal background, age, proclivity for public activity, and so forth, all set against the political context of the era. One can quite naturally expect to see different patterns of behavior from Ronald Reagan, our oldest president, who came to office in the latter years of the Cold War, and Bill Clinton, our third-youngest president, who was inaugurated just over three years after the Berlin Wall was torn down. Even genetics is not necessarily a reliable predictor of presidential activity, as George W. Bush governed in ways markedly different from those of his father. Nevertheless, it is fruitful to engage in systematic studies of presidential actions over time and across presidencies. For in spite of the differences in presidential characteristics and circumstances, each chief executive responds to the institutional and contextual incentives of the world in which he is situated. All recent presidents have faced similar rules of the game when it comes to being elected and seeking reelection, and all have an interest in accumulating the financial resources to advance their own electoral fortunes and those of their party.

The term *permanent campaign* is often used broadly to characterize a president's efforts to gain the public's approval, the frequent use of public opinion polling by presidential aides, and the employment of the techniques of campaigning throughout a president's term in office. The aim of this book is to focus on presidential actions that relate directly to questions that are electoral in nature and not simply political—presidential fundraising, targeted travel that corresponds to the incentives of the Electoral College and the presidential nominating system, and the evolving roles of key players in and out the White House who help to make these decisions.

OVERVIEW OF THE BOOK

This book is primarily a study of the strategic choices of the presidents who first came to office via the plebiscitary nominating process, which came into being following the McGovern-Fraser Commission's recommendations in 1971, and who have governed during the campaign finance regime established by the Federal Election Campaign Act of 1974 (FECA). It is certainly the case that earlier presidents tended to electoral concerns throughout their terms in office. Indeed, one could examine the political machinations of presidents from George Washington onward, and at various points in this book I make comparisons to earlier presidents to highlight the manner in which recent practices represent a continuation of or departure from earlier dynamics. But focusing on the actions of the six presidents who have served during the almost thirty-five years from Jimmy Carter's inauguration in 1977 to the midpoint of 2011 sheds light on the ways in which similarly situated political actors respond to institutional and contextual incentives.

The plebiscitary nominating process has produced presidents for whom extended campaigning has been the key to their political success, and once in office, many continue to rely on the political practices that have served them well in the past. The campaign finance requirements of the regime established by FECA provide unprecedented institutional rules that shape the way presidents raise funds and mandate remarkable transparency, providing political observers with a much fuller picture of the ways in which presidents fill their electoral coffers and those of their fellow party members. And during this period, the White House staff was reorganized in a way that institutionalized the making of many electoral decisions within the walls of the White House itself. This period saw dramatic changes in my areas of principal focus—presidential fundraising, strategic travel, and the organization and role of the White House staff, which I examine in the following chapters. I focus on what the actions of our chief executives reveal about both presidential priorities and the relationship between campaigning and governing.

In chapter 2, I examine a particularly salient element of the permanent campaign—presidential fundraising. Drawing on newly compiled data, I systematically analyze the volume, timing, and nature of presidential fundraising and show how this indisputably electorally motivated presidential activity has become increasingly prevalent throughout a president's term in office. While much research on political fundraising is based on data from the Federal Election Commission that details contributions to candidates, political parties, and political action groups, this study examines the other side of the coin—what do presidents do in search of political funds? After laying out the empirical case that recent presidents have increasingly focused on their role as fundraiser-in-chief, I argue that these trends are largely the result of the intersection of the rising costs of campaigns and the rules of the game created by the evolving campaign finance regime established by the Federal Election Campaign Act of 1974.

In chapter 3, I explore the beneficiaries of presidential fundraising to shed light on the president's role as party-builder-in-chief. I find that the overwhelming majority of presidential fundraising is done not for the president's own reelection campaign but for his co-partisans and argue that presidential party building is on the rise in large part because competitive presidential elections and narrow margins of party control of Congress have raised the stakes of all federal elections. The beneficiaries of presidential fundraising have varied over time, revealing where presidents place their political chips and how they see their role as party-builder-in-chief. The dynamics revealed here challenge some long-held beliefs about the nature of the president's relationship to his party.

In chapter 4, I turn to the geography of strategic presidential travel. Because a president's time is his most precious commodity, these patterns reveal a great deal about the priorities of our nation's chief executive. Detailing the rise of targeted presidential travel illustrates that especially in recent presidencies, the incentives of the Electoral College and the presidential nominating process are reflected in patterns of travel throughout a president's term in office. I contend that the increasing prevalence of targeted travel is largely the consequence of the type of president produced in recent years by the rules structuring presidential nominating and general election campaigns, as, once in office, presidents and their aides continue to employ the same strategies that secured them the White House in the first place.

Chapter 5 examines the source, rather than the manifestations, of the decisions that shape the permanent campaign by focusing on who is involved with making decisions about electoral considerations. To focus on changing dynamics within the White House itself, I draw upon archival research at presidential libraries and the commentaries of presidents and their aides to illustrate that decisions about electoral concerns that were once made by the Democratic and Republican National Committees are now often made by White House staff. I contend that these changes and evolving norms have increasingly blurred the lines between campaigning and governing. Because these changes in the White House staff have been institutionalized, each incoming president arrives at a White House where the path of least resistance is one that perpetuates the permanent campaign.

In chapter 6, I discuss my findings on the changing dynamics of the permanent campaign, emphasizing the importance of evolving contextual factors and institutional incentives in this developing narrative. I address my findings from a normative perspective and discuss the implications of the permanent campaign for presidential leadership. I conclude by arguing that the permanent campaign yields a presidency that is at times more powerful and at others more vulnerable and fragile. While success in advancing the president's and his party's electoral prospects can strengthen his political hand and enable him to enact his policy priorities, I contend that the permanent campaign can lead to increased public cynicism and reduce the prospects for bipartisan cooperation and effective presidential leadership.

2. The President as Fundraiser-in-Chief

On August 11, 2003, almost fifteen months before the next presidential election, President George W. Bush took the stage at a museum in Denver, Colorado, and earnestly declared to the crowd, "The political season will come in its own time. For me, now is not the time for politics. You see, I've got a job to do. I'm staying focused on the people's business."[1] It was an odd message for the president to send, given that he was addressing a Bush-Cheney 2004 reelection fundraiser, the eleventh such event he had headlined since beginning his reelection fundraising efforts two months earlier. The message was a typical one for Bush—a review of the *Public Papers of the Presidents of the United States* reveals that Bush used the phrase "the political season will come in its own time" while addressing eighteen different Bush-Cheney fundraisers that year. Bush headlined forty-one fundraisers to benefit his reelection bid in 2003 alone, which suggests that the political season had indeed already begun, in spite of the president's protestations to the contrary.

The question of when the electoral season begins during the course of a presidency is of interest to presidents, journalists, and scholars alike. Academic studies of elections often focus on the traditional campaign season, which commences on Labor Day in the year of the election.[2] This makes logical and practical sense. Labor Day is seen as the long-established kickoff of the fall campaign and is the natural starting point for a political scientist seeking a beginning date in a study of campaign activity. Some studies have acknowledged the reality that campaign activity is under way well before Labor Day by examining political activity in the summer months of an election year as well, especially given that much campaigning takes place during the extended congressional recess in August of even-numbered years. This approach gives a broader picture of electoral activity but still not a complete one.[3] As discussed in the previous chapter, other studies follow the practice of Samuel Kernell, who explained his decision to analyze speeches over a president's first three years but not the fourth this way: "To eliminate public activities inspired by concerns of reelection rather than governing, only the first three years have been tabulated."[4] This broader view of campaign activity still assumes that the electoral action takes place during the election year itself and not before.

Two examples of rare exceptions to the practice of limiting campaign studies to all or some of the year of election drew on data provided by journalist Mark Knoller, who has carefully chronicled presidential activity since the early 1990s. Both Herrnson and Morris, in their study of President George W. Bush's efforts on behalf of House candidates leading up to the 2002 midterm elections, and Jacobson, Kernell, and Lazarus, who examined President Bill Clinton's fundraising in 1999 and 2000, analyzed presidential campaign efforts throughout the entire electoral cycle. Additionally, Sellers and Denton relied on the *Public Papers of the Presidents of the United States* in their study of presidential efforts in midterm Senate campaigns in the twenty-two months leading up to each midterm election from 1982 to 2002.[5] The *Public Papers* are an excellent resource, but they provide an incomplete record of presidential fundraising, since many fundraisers are not recorded there—a deficiency that I seek to correct in this book.

George W. Bush's actions, and not his words of protest as he spoke at reelection fundraising events in 2003, illustrate that examining activity throughout an entire presidential term yields a more complete picture of presidential electoral efforts, as the nation's politician-in-chief does not wait until Labor Day of an election year or even until the election year itself to direct his political efforts toward his or his party's electoral success. This broader time frame seems most illuminating in an era in which more and more discussion in both popular and academic circles is focused on the notion of the permanent campaign.

Looking at presidents' campaign efforts far in advance of Election Day raises the complicated question of just which presidential activities should be considered electorally connected. How can we seek to understand presidential actions without improperly imputing electoral considerations to everything a president does? This chapter addresses this dilemma by focusing on a type of presidential activity that is clearly and unambiguously electoral in nature—political fundraising. While we may not know definitively if a presidential visit to a factory in Ohio far in advance of an election is related to the upcoming campaign, if the president raises funds for a candidate or for a political party while there, he leaves no doubt about the electoral nature of his activity. In this chapter I examine patterns of fundraising efforts throughout a president's term in office to illuminate the president's increasing focus on his role as fundraiser-in-chief. Because a president's time is his most precious commodity, these electoral efforts reveal a great deal about the priorities of our nation's chief executive. I then advance an argument that the rise in presidential fundraising chiefly results from the intersection of the rising costs of campaigns and the institutional rules of the game created by the evolving campaign finance regime established by the Federal Election Campaign Act of 1974.

STUDYING PRESIDENTIAL FUNDRAISING

Most research that has focused on political fundraising is based on data from the Federal Election Commission that detail contributions to and expenditures by candidates, political parties, and political action groups or studies the politics of campaign finance reform efforts. Recent works have analyzed the geography of political contributions by examining where donors live.[6] This study looks at the other side of the coin—what do political actors, in this case presidents, do in search of political funds? I build on research on the role of money in politics by analyzing the dynamics of campaign finance from another angle through a focus on presidential fundraising. What do these trends reveal about presidential priorities, the relationship between campaigning and governing, and the evolving nature of the presidency?

To investigate the extent and nature of presidential fundraising efforts, I constructed an original data set of political fundraisers presidents attended both in Washington, DC, and around the country from 1977 through June 2011 by first examining the *Public Papers of the Presidents of the United States* at the American Presidency Project and the presidential library web sites of the Ronald Reagan, George H. W. Bush, and Bill Clinton, as well as the White House web sites of George W. Bush and Barack Obama. While many presidential fundraisers are recorded in the *Public Papers,* the substantial number that take place in private residences are often closed to the press or do not involve a speech by the president and thus are routinely excluded from the public record. To account for these private fundraisers, I conducted LexisNexis searches of Associated Press articles that contained each president's name within twenty-five words of the word *fundraiser* or one of its variants over the thirty-five-year period of this study and checked the resulting news stories against my data set, often cross-referencing what I found with the discussion of the president's schedule by the White House press secretary in his or her daily gaggle with the press corps.

This endeavor yielded substantial results. In addition to the 1,256 fundraisers found in the *Public Papers* for this thirty-five-year period, these efforts revealed an additional 233 fundraisers that were not referenced in the *Public Papers.* Almost one in every six fundraisers that presidents held in this period went unreported in the *Public Papers.* This practice was particularly common in certain years. For example, in 2007 and 2008 combined, President George W. Bush headlined twelve open fundraisers that were recorded in the *Public Papers;* combing the journalistic record uncovered an additional sixty-one closed fundraisers for his fellow Republicans in these two years. An observer relying just on the *Public Papers* would conclude that Bush did not invest much time in fundraising for his fellow Republicans in his final years in office, when in fact he did. Relying on these new data in addition to the official presidential record provides a much more complete accounting of presidential fundraising efforts.

This chapter examines the period from 1977 onward, beginning with Jimmy Carter's inauguration, because he was the first elected president to govern during the campaign finance regime established by the Federal Election Campaign Act of 1974 (FECA). Carter and his five successors all made strategic choices that took into account the restrictions, requirements, and incentives established by FECA and thus operated within a common, though evolving, institutional environment. My focus is on how a president allocates his most precious resource—his time. While I sometimes discuss the amount of money raised at a certain presidential fundraiser in this study, I do not do so for each of the 1,489 fundraisers over this thirty-five-year period. FECA requirements compel candidates for federal office to disclose information on contributions by donor, not by event, so it is not possible to know how much a specific presidential fundraiser generated unless the sponsoring campaign released that information to the press, which sometimes happened but often did not. While I note these numbers at times, it is impossible to do so as systematically as one would like. My primary aim is to analyze what the allocation of our chief executive's time reveals about both presidential priorities and the relationship between campaigning and governing in a way that sheds light on the ways in which similarly situated political actors respond to institutional and contextual incentives.

THE RISE OF PRESIDENTIAL FUNDRAISING

Presidential fundraising efforts have increased substantially over the third of a century since Jimmy Carter became the first president elected under the campaign finance regime established by FECA. The rise in first-term fundraising has been remarkably steady, as depicted in table 2.1. After a slight dip from Carter's 85 fundraisers to Reagan's 80 in his first term, George H. W. Bush, Bill Clinton, and George W. Bush headlined 137, 167, and 173 first-term fundraisers, respectively. Barack Obama's 121 fundraisers in his first two and a half years in office put him on pace to surpass the first-term totals of both George W. Bush and Clinton. Because he will be the first sitting president not to accept public funding for the general election and thus the first during the FECA regime to fundraise for his own re-election campaign after his party's national convention, his first-term fundraising efforts will likely far exceed those of his predecessors.

The frequency of first-term presidential fundraising has steadily increased. Carter attended a fundraiser every 17.2 days on average, while Reagan did so every 18.3 days on average during his first term—both presidents averaged just under two fundraising events per month. George H. W. Bush picked up the pace, taking

Table 2.1: Presidential Fundraisers by Term, 1977–June 2011

President	First Term	Second Term
Carter	85	
Reagan	80	100
GHW Bush	137	
Clinton	167	471
GW Bush	173	155
Obama (through June 2011)	121	

Source: Data compiled by the author from the *Public Papers of the Presidents* and from Associated Press articles.

part in one fundraiser every 10.7 days of his presidency on average, or about three per month. The three most recent presidents devoted far more time to fundraising in their first term—Clinton averaged one fundraiser every 8.7 days, George W. Bush one every 8.4 days, and Obama one every 7.5 days. In the thirty-five years covered by this study, the frequency of first-term presidential fundraising has increased from an average of under two fundraisers per month to over four per month, or about one per week.

The three presidents in this study who each served two terms varied widely in their second-term fundraising activities, when their own reelection was no longer at stake. While Reagan's total jumped from 80 to 100 fundraisers, averaging 1 every 14.6 days of his second term, and George W. Bush's number dropped slightly from 173 to 155, an average of one every 9.4 days of his second term, Bill Clinton turned in four years of record-breaking fundraising activity, attending 471 events over his last four years in office, as compared with 167 in his first term. In his second term, he took part in a fundraiser, on average, every 3.1 days—more than two fundraisers each week. This unprecedented effort is due at least in part to four key factors—his efforts to help retire the substantial debt of the Democratic National Committee left over from the 1996 election season; a push to retake control of the House and Senate from the Republicans; his raising money in hopes of electing Vice President Al Gore to succeed him in the Oval Office; and the unprecedented run by First Lady Hillary Clinton for a U.S. Senate seat in New York. To a greater and greater extent, the president is indeed the fundraiser-in-chief and party-builder-in-chief, and that activity is by no means confined to the traditional campaign season.

Timing of Fundraising Efforts

Can we understand well the dynamics of presidential fundraising if we focus on the traditional few months before Election Day? Figure 2.1 presents evidence that

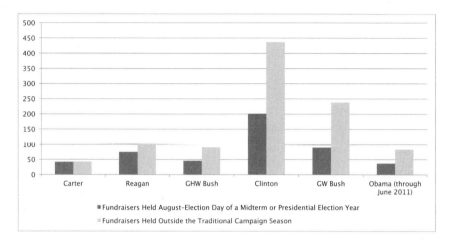

Figure 2.1: Presidential Fundraisers Within and Outside the Traditional Campaign Season, 1977–June 2011
Source: Data compiled by the author from the *Public Papers of the Presidents* and from Associated Press articles.

the notion that electoral activity does not begin until the three months leading up to the election has not been accurate throughout the FECA campaign finance regime. In this figure, fundraisers that each of the past six presidents have headlined are divided into those that took place in the three months from August through Election Day of a midterm or presidential election year, and those that were held outside the traditional campaign season. Even using this slightly expanded definition of the formal window for campaigning that begins on August 1 instead of on Labor Day, every president in this study attended more fundraisers outside of the traditional campaign season than during it. The differences are least pronounced for Carter (42 fundraisers in the three months leading up to Election Day and 43 at other times) and most evident for Clinton (201 and 437, respectively) and George W. Bush (90 and 238, respectively). Obama, who held 37 events in the traditional three months of preelection campaigning and 84 at other times through June 2011, has attended fundraisers with such frequency throughout the first half of his third year in office that he is on track to continue the trend of substantial presidential fundraising well outside of the traditional campaign season.

Altogether, these six presidents held 491 fundraisers from August to November of a midterm or presidential election year and 998 at other times. Clearly, one cannot get a full picture of presidential campaign efforts without taking into account fundraising activity throughout a president's term in office. In the era of the

Table 2.2: Timing of First Fundraiser and Number of
Fundraisers in First Year

President	Date of First Fundraiser	Number of Fundraisers Held in First Year in Office
Carter	June 23, 1977	5
Reagan	July 7, 1981	10
GHW Bush	May 13, 1989	18
Clinton	February 1, 1993	16
GW Bush	April 25, 2001	6
Obama	March 25, 2009	24

Source: Data compiled by the author from the *Public Papers of the Presidents* and from Associated Press articles.

permanent campaign, it is difficult to draw the line at where governing stops and campaigning begins.

Indeed, presidents raise money early and often. Each of the six presidents in this study headlined his first fundraiser between February and July of his first year in office. As table 2.2 illustrates, Carter's first was June 23, and he attended five fundraisers in 1977. Reagan's first was on July 7, but would have been on April 7 had he not been shot in late March by John Hinckley; Vice President Bush attended a party fundraiser in early April in Reagan's place at the very hotel where Reagan had been shot just over a week earlier. Reagan attended ten fundraisers in 1981, a total that would have been higher had he not missed several fundraisers in the wake of the assassination attempt. While he convalesced, Bush stood in for him as the headliner of at least two additional fundraisers in April 1981 in Los Angeles and Hartford, Connecticut. When Bush was asked if he also would give the bride away at the upcoming wedding of Reagan's daughter Maureen, the vice president replied, "I am not going that far in my stand-in responsibilities."[7]

George H. W. Bush's first fundraiser as president took place on May 13, the first of eighteen he would take part in during 1989. Clinton's initial fundraiser was on February 1, a mere twelve days after taking office, and the first of sixteen he would participate in during 1993. George W. Bush first attended a fundraiser on April 25 and headlined a total of 6 in 2001—a lower total than it otherwise might have been, as he attended none after the terrorist attacks on September 11 of that year. Obama's first fundraiser was on March 25, on his way to a total of 24 in 2009—more first-year fundraisers than for any other president in this study. Not only does presidential fundraising begin early in a president's term, but the trend has been toward an earlier kickoff to presidential fundraising and toward more and more presidential efforts devoted to raising money during the first year in office.

Presidents are often hesitant to take on the overtly partisan role of political fundraising early in their term. When Carter headlined a party fundraiser in New York City on June 23, 1977, it was the first explicitly political event he had taken part in as president. Up until this point, Carter had not even consented to having fundraising appeals mailed to supporters in his name, as he had requested that the Democratic National Committee not involve him in any political efforts so early in his term.[8] Reagan was similarly hesitant to appear at fundraisers near the beginning of his term. One Reagan aide explained the president's lack of fundraising in his first year and a half in office by saying that it would be problematic to appear at upscale fundraisers in a tuxedo in a time of economic distress in many parts of the country, contending that "there's no question that if the only time grass-roots people get to see the president is at a $1,000-a-plate dinner, that does not help with the overall picture."[9]

Obama faced comparable concerns when he attended his first political fundraisers as president in March 2009 in the midst of the worst economic downturn since the Great Depression. One reporter asked White House press secretary Robert Gibbs whether he was "worried about the tone that [a fundraiser with a $30,000 per couple admission price] sets in a time when Americans are struggling." Gibbs defended the president's decision to headline the partisan fundraiser, arguing that Obama "fully understands the hardships and the troubles that the American people are undergoing in their lives each day. . . . [W]e haven't seen politics by either party stop in this period, though I think the President fully understands the situation the American people face."[10]

Following on the heels of Bill Clinton's record-setting fundraising, George W. Bush took pains to convey that he wanted to limit his involvement with fundraising early in his term. In April 2001 he gave his first speech at a fundraiser as president, declaring, "I hope people realize that good public policy means good politics and we don't need to be spending all our time on politics in Washington." In an interview, he explained that when it came to political fundraising, "I've committed to help when asked on a limited basis."[11] At a June 2001 dinner that generated $20 million in support of Republican candidates for the House and Senate, Bush held photo sessions with major contributors at the start of the event, delivered an eighteen-minute speech during the salad course, and departed before the main course was served, claiming, "We've got to go home and feed Barney, the dog." Congressman Tom Davis of Virginia, head of the National Republican Congressional Committee, reasoned that Bush "didn't want to be there for the dinner when we announced the [amount raised that] evening. I think that's the bottom line." Davis added that the president wanted to send the message that "he's not the fundraiser in chief."[12]

Former Democratic senator J. Bennett Johnston noted the difference between Bush and his predecessor: "Clinton was famous for shaking every hand in a room and having something to say and remembering the names of and something about almost everyone there. You go to George W. and it's the other end of the spectrum. He makes his appearance, he shows up on time, he says the appropriate things and he's out of there." Later that summer, a journalist pointed out to a spokesperson for the National Republican Congressional Committee that President Bush had few fundraisers scheduled for the fall, whereas former president Clinton was traveling the country to raise money for various Democratic groups. The spokesperson responded by repeating a refrain of Bush's from the 2000 campaign trail and applied it to fundraising: "When President Bush said he was going to restore dignity to the office, part of that was not being fundraiser-in-chief." A member of the Republican National Committee tried to frame the contrast between Bush and Clinton in a flattering light, contending, "For this president, [fundraising is] an obligation. For the former president, it was a joy," an assertion that Democratic officials would likely dispute, especially given that Bush would go on to headline more fundraisers in his first term than Clinton did during his first four years in office.[13] Presidents' initial reluctance about and averred distaste for political fundraisers consistently give way, to varying degrees, to the imperative of raising money for the national party, a president's fellow party members, and his own reelection bid.

Fundraising Records Are Made to Be Broken

It is natural to look at presidential fundraising since 1977 and focus on the most recent record-setting efforts to raise campaign cash. But it is more illuminating to view this rise over time as those witnessing it did—one president at a time. Only in this way can we appreciate how each president's fundraising was viewed at the time he undertook it and the succession of fundraising records that were deemed impressive and unprecedented at the time, only to be shattered by a president's successors.

As discussed earlier, Carter was reluctant to engage in too much partisan political activity early in his term and took part in only 5 fundraisers during his first year in office, only 2 of which benefited the Democratic National Committee (DNC). When John White was named the new chief of the DNC in December 1977, he touted President Carter's commitment to aid the national committee in retiring its $2.5 million debt and support Democrats in the next year's midterm elections. As evidence, DNC aides cited Carter's plans to attend 5 fundraisers to benefit the national committee in 1978. Such a small number contrasts remarkably with the party fundraising efforts of Carter's successors. At the other end of the spectrum, Bill Clinton would average 29.8 fundraisers per year for the DNC over his eight years as president. But the fact that Carter's relatively modest commitment in 1977 was considered newsworthy merits noting in and of itself.[14] His 29 total fundraisers in 1978 fell far below the money-raising activity in a midterm election year of any of his successors, and his total of 85 fundraisers during his four years in office was less than for all but Reagan during his first term.

In each of Reagan's first three years in office, he attended more fundraisers than did Carter, headlining 10 money-raising events in his first year, compared with Carter's 5; 36 in his second year to Carter's 29; and 25 in his third year to Carter's 15. But in his reelection year, Reagan took part in only 9 fundraisers to Carter's 36. Indeed, the Reagan campaign's direct mail fundraising solicitations and the fundraising efforts of Vice President George Bush were so successful that this author found no record of Reagan's personal participation in any fundraising events for his 1984 reelection bid, though he did attend fundraisers in support of other Republicans that year. This followed Reagan's strategy in the 1982 midterm elections, when he engaged in little fundraising himself and instead delegated many of these duties to his vice president. By July 1982, in just over a year and a half in office, Bush had traveled to forty-two states and headlined fundraisers that generated more than $12 million for the GOP. Bush would handle most of the money-raising duties, while Reagan concentrated on other matters.[15] In Reagan's first term and Carter's only term, both presidents spent relatively little time fundraising.

Reagan would pick up the pace in his second term, however, when he headlined 100 fundraisers in an effort to help his fellow Republicans. In 1986 he took part in 47 fundraisers, more than he or Carter had participated in during a single year to that point. Reagan's increased commitment to fundraising led to financial takes from these events that made headlines. One Reagan aide told reporters that each of the 11 fundraisers that the president attended for Senate candidates between May 1985 and June 1986 was the biggest fundraiser in the history of the state in which it took place. The largest of these raised $1.7 million for Senator Alfonse D'Amato at the Waldorf-Astoria Hotel in New York City, and in total these 11 events yielded $7.86 million to support the Republicans' efforts to retain control of the Senate. Such record-breaking totals were characterized at the time as being "big money."[16]

When Reagan prepared to head to New Orleans in 1988 for the Republican National Convention that would nominate his vice president to succeed him in the White House, a newspaper account noted that the president was poised to campaign for his potential successor in an unprecedented fashion. "No modern president has conducted a parting campaign to match the one Reagan has promised Bush and the Republicans. He expects to appear at least twice a week in behalf of the ticket and Republican fund-raising efforts from Labor Day to Election Day."[17] True to his word, Reagan headlined 18 fundraisers for the GOP between the convention and the election in a testament to his commitment to electing George Bush to the presidency and to supporting other Republican candidates for office.

While Reagan's fundraising efforts were record-setting at the time, those of his successor soon eclipsed them. When President George H. W. Bush headlined a fundraiser for Senator Phil Gramm of Texas in December 1989 that generated $2.4 million for the senator's campaign, the chair of the Republican National Committee (RNC), Lee Atwater, called it the largest political fundraiser ever. This event was part of a three-day trip in which the president held fundraisers for Republican Senate candidates in Iowa, Colorado, and Texas. The Iowa event yielded a far smaller $250,000, a sum that campaign officials declared the largest from a single event ever in that state, illustrating the variation in successful presidential fundraising.[18]

Bush continued his record-breaking fundraising in 1990. In April of that year, a White House spokesperson described plans that called for the president to headline 50 fundraisers between April and August of that year and indicated that Bush would ramp up his electoral efforts even more after Labor Day.[19] That summer, one RNC official attested, "This is the type of thing the president will do a lot of. The best thing the president can do now is to provide material resources for these candidates."[20] One Associated Press news account that summer described the president as "a traveling cash register for GOP candidates." A White House spokesperson said of the president's fundraising drive, "You can call it unprecedented."[21]

The Bush White House estimated that Reagan had raised $33 million for GOP candidates in 1986, the previous midterm election year, while Bush's efforts in 1989 and 1990 yielded approximately $90 million for his fellow party members in an effort that a newspaper account at the time called "a methodical, unmatched off-year election campaign."[22] Bush headlined a record 69 fundraisers that year, following 18 in his first year in office, and followed by another 18 in his third year as president. At the close of 1991, as Bush headed to Texas in an effort to raise $2 million over two days for the GOP, a newspaper report called him "the most successful political fund-raiser in history."[23]

The superlatives describing Bush's fundraising kept on coming when in April 1992 he starred at an RNC gala called the President's Dinner that was described at the time as "the biggest political fund-raiser in history, a glittering dinner that brought in $9 million as contributors paid top dollar to rub elbows with the administration's elite." Donors anted up between $1,500 and $400,000 to attend the event, as the RNC capitalized on so-called soft money donations, which were not subject to federal contribution limits or to the ban on contributions to federal candidates by corporations and labor unions. Both parties used this loophole in campaign finance law, explained in more detail later, to accept contributions in un-limited amounts for party building and get-out-the-vote activities until the practice was prohibited in 2002.[24]

These successive record-breaking developments highlight the importance of not discounting George H. W. Bush's fundraising as being off the pace of the three presidents who would succeed him. Instead, we must appreciate that Bush, a former chair of the Republican National Committee who was committed to helping his fellow GOP candidates as well as his own reelection prospects, devoted unprecedented time to raise unprecedented sums during his four years as president. As a consequence, he deservedly received much attention for being a record-setting fundraiser-in-chief.

After an initial two years in which Bill Clinton's fundraising efforts were substantial but did not eclipse those of his predecessor, he would eventually go on to shatter the records that George H. W. Bush had set, for both the amount of time he devoted to fundraising and the amounts of money he raised. When Clinton headlined the Democratic National Committee's own President's Dinner in June 1993, it brought in $4.2 million, which a DNC spokesperson called the highest yield from a Democratic Party fundraising event ever.[25] While this event's take was smaller than some that Bush had headlined, it was a precursor of fundraising records to come. In 1993 and 1994, Clinton took part in 63 fundraisers, far more than the 34 and 46 that Carter and Reagan attended, respectively, in their first two years in office, but shy of the first President Bush's total of 87 for his first two years as president.

Clinton's fundraising efforts picked up substantially after the midterm elections of 1994, as his own date to face the voters approached. A former DNC aide recounted that in the first two years of Clinton's term, "it took months to get the White House to schedule a reception for the party's Business Leadership Council, comprising major corporate contributors. But by mid-1995, Clinton was attending White House receptions with donors and prospective contributors almost weekly." These efforts sprang from Clinton's approval of a $1 million per week television advertising campaign early in 1996, even before the Republicans had chosen a nominee to face him in the general election. This aggressive undertaking created pressure to raise substantial sums of money early in the campaign season.[26] Clinton went on to headline 104 fundraisers in 1995 and 1996 combined, which would eclipse Carter's total of 51 in the two years leading up to his reelection bid, 1979 and 1980, Reagan's 34 in 1983 and 1984, and George H. W. Bush's 50 in 1991 and 1992.

As the total numbers of presidential fundraisers grew, so did the amount of money raised at party affairs, where soft money donations fueled unprecedented fundraising. In one example, Clinton was the star attraction at a DNC gala dinner in Washington, DC, on May 8, 1996, that set a new Democratic Party record for a fundraiser, bringing in $12.3 million. At the dinner, Clinton praised Peter Knight, who had planned the dinner and would manage Clinton's reelection bid, by declaring, "Any man who can pick your pocket and still earn your applause deserves to be the campaign manager." The 51 DNC fundraisers that Clinton attended in 1995 and 1996 helped the national committee to raise a record $207 million that election cycle, more than twice the $83 million it raised in 1993 and 1994, when Clinton headlined only 12 DNC fundraisers. As Clinton's commitment to party fundraising increased, so did his party's ability to raise unprecedented funds.[27]

Clinton's second-term fundraising drive would soon make both his own first-term efforts and George H. W. Bush's unprecedented devotion to raising political funds seem modest. Clinton headlined 77 fundraisers in 1997, 111 in 1998, 89 in 1999, and a staggering 194 in 2000 and the first 20 days of 2001. Each of these was greater than the number of fundraisers attended in any individual year by Carter, Reagan, and George H. W. Bush, and Clinton's totals in each of his last three years in office were greater than the number of fundraisers attended by Carter throughout his entire four years in office and by Reagan during his first term. An Associated Press review of party fundraising efforts near the end of 1998 indicated that the various national Democratic Party committees had raised a record-breaking total of almost $79 million over the previous two years. DNC chair Roy Romer declared, "The president, the vice president and the first lady have done more than any team in history to raise money and raise issues."[28]

As Clinton neared the end of his time as president, his fundraising efforts set new record after new record. In May 2000, a tribute dinner in honor of Clinton and Gore would set a new record for a single political fundraiser when it raised more than $23 million—almost doubling the record for a single party event Clinton had set four years earlier.[29] His dedication to raising political funds earned headlines like this one from September 1999: "Clinton's King of Presidential Fund-raising, Analysts Say." The director of the government watchdog group the Center for Public Integrity declared, "No one has ever seen anyone do more to raise money than this man at the state or federal level in our lifetimes."[30] In his final year in office, Clinton headlined 194 fundraisers. To put this record in perspective, eight years earlier news accounts called George H. W. Bush the greatest fundraiser in history for taking part in a total of 137 fundraisers throughout his entire four years in office. Clinton attended almost one and a half times that many fundraising events in just his last year as president. Clinton's unprecedented party-building efforts in his second term will be discussed in much greater detail in the next chapter.

The first two years of George W. Bush's term as president were the last in which parties could raise soft money, and in spite of limiting his fundraising efforts in

2001 due to the terrorist attacks on the United States that September, Bush set a series of new records. The 173 fundraisers he headlined during his first term almost equaled Reagan's two-term total and were an even larger number than Clinton's 167 in his first term, though Bush did not come close to Clinton's astounding second-term fundraising pace. After attending only 6 fundraisers in 2001, Bush's 70 in 2002 were more than Carter, Reagan, George H. W. Bush, and Clinton took part in during their second year in office. A press account described Bush's 2002 efforts as "an unprecedented White House fund-raising campaign that channeled more than $180 million to GOP candidates."[31] As George H. W. Bush and Bill Clinton had done before, George W. Bush set new records for the single largest fundraiser in history, first at a 2002 gala that yielded about $30 million and then at an event that brought in more than $38.5 million two years later, in 2004.[32] Bush attended 97 fundraisers in 2003 and 2004 and raised a record-setting $270 million for his reelection campaign as the first sitting president who did not participate in the public funding program for the nominating process, as discussed later.[33] Bush's 155 fundraisers in his second term did not set a new record, but they still exceeded by far the four-year totals of Carter, Reagan, and George H. W. Bush.

Two and a half years into Barack Obama's presidency, the new president was far ahead of the fundraising pace of his five immediate predecessors in the Oval Office. Obama had attended 121 fundraisers through June 30, 2011; at a similar point in their presidencies, Carter had attended 44 fundraisers, Reagan 63, George H. W. Bush 90, Clinton 74, and George W. Bush 84. He started his reelection fundraising earlier than any other president in the campaign finance regime created by the Federal Election Campaign Act of 1974, and many analysts and political operatives predict that he will raise an unprecedented $1 billion for his 2012 reelection bid.

While it is natural to look at the astounding fundraising of the last three presidents and see their efforts as dwarfing those that came before, a president-by-president review shows that the rise in presidential fundraising is best appreciated by understanding that new records have been set by almost every president in this study, only to be broken by their successors. Over time, presidents have become more and more committed to their role as fundraiser-in-chief. The next section advances an argument about why this is the case.

WHY THE RISE IN PRESIDENTIAL FUNDRAISING?

Presidents are goal-oriented political actors who respond to the institutional and contextual incentives that result from the rules of the game in which they operate. The dramatic increase of the president acting as fundraiser-in-chief over the past three and a half decades is in large part a function of the interaction between the

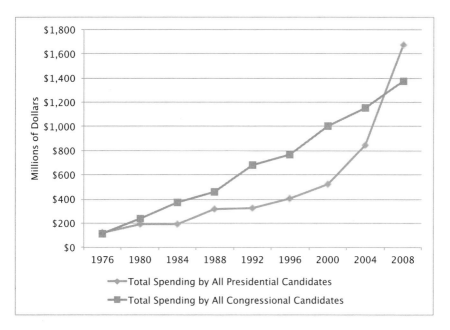

Figure 2.2: Total Spending in Presidential and Congressional Elections, 1976–2008
Source: Nelson W. Polsby, Aaron B. Wildavsky, Steven E. Schier, and David A. Hopkins, *Presidential Elections: Strategies and Structures of American Politics,* 13th ed. (Rowman & Littlefield Publishers, 2011).

rising costs of campaigns and the evolving campaign finance regime established by the Federal Election Campaign Act of 1974.

The costs of both presidential and congressional elections have risen dramatically over the past three and a half decades. Figure 2.2 displays the total amount spent in presidential election years by all candidates in presidential and congressional elections from 1976 through 2008. The trend is clear for both types of contests. In presidential elections, we first see a steady and substantial rise in money spent through 1996, followed by a dramatic increase in 2000, 2004, and 2008 at a pace that far exceeded the rate of inflation. These higher totals resulted in large part from the winning candidates opting out of first the public funding regime during the nominating process in 2000 and 2004, and then both the nominating and general election stages in 2008. If the 1976 total of $118 million spent by all presidential candidates had risen at the rate of inflation, the amount for 2008 would have been $447 million, but the actual total was almost four times higher, with total spending reaching $1.68 billion. The total amount spent in congressional campaigns rose substantially between 1976 and 2008 as well, though the increase over this period was far steadier than for presidential races. The total grew from $115 million in 1976 to $1.38 billion in 2008, an almost twelvefold increase. Had money spent in these races risen at the rate of inflation, the 2008 total would have been a mere $435 million, less than one-third of the actual amount spent.[34]

As was the case with the numbers of presidential fundraisers described earlier, the dramatic increase in the amount of money spent in presidential elections between 1996 and 2008 can obscure the magnitude of the increases before that point, as totals increased from $118 million in 1976 to $188 million in 1980, $194 million in 1984, $316 million in 1988, $323 million in 1992, and $405 million in 1996. While the increase between 1976 and 1996 might look gradual in figure 2.2 compared with the subsequent rise of much greater magnitude, the money spent in 1996 was almost three times that spent in 1976. The total amount spent in 1996 would more than quadruple by 2008, as presidential election spending rose at even greater rates. The 2008 totals were more than fourteen times the amount spent in 1976.

Campaign spending levels have increased in a ratchet-like fashion, moving only in one direction. As each sitting president and presidential candidate looks at the amount of money it took to win the last election, the assumption is that the total the next time around will be higher. Similar dynamics apply to congressional races. One principal reason that campaign costs have risen so greatly is what political scientist Herbert Alexander calls "the professionalization of politics." Alexander argued in the mid-1980s that "any serious candidate for any major office today has to hire an outside campaign consultant, has to hire a pollster, has to hire media specialists—time-buyers, production people for advertising and the rest—and is likely to hire a computer expert to do either targeting or direct mail."[35] David Eichenbaum, who served as communications director for the Democratic National Committee, explained the rising costs of campaigns in the mid-1990s, saying, "Pressure has been exerted on the entire system by all the parties to do more and more media spending, which means raising increasing amounts of money. Until the system is changed in some way, to ease the pressure, it will continue to be a problem."[36]

Raymond La Raja, who has written extensively on the evolution of campaign finance rules, expanded on these arguments when he made the case more recently that the dramatic rise in campaign costs results from technological developments in the way campaigns are run. Television advertising, public opinion polling, and direct mail outreach and fundraising solicitations all depend upon expensive political consultants and campaign professionals who devise and execute the appropriate strategy in each area for a campaign.[37] Recent advances in technology—the rise of the Internet and social media—have only made Alexander's, Eichenbaum's, and La Raja's words all the more applicable as campaign costs have continued to rise.

The Impact of Fixed Contribution Limits and
Rising Spending Caps

Understanding how the rising costs of campaigns have interacted with the rules of the game created by evolving campaign finance rules established by the Federal Election Campaign Act of 1974 is central to the analysis of the president's role as fundraiser-in-chief. FECA set ceilings on political donations in order to limit the potential that elected officials would be beholden to large contributors or any particular special interest and prevent corruption or the appearance of corruption. The act limited contributions to candidates for federal office by individuals to $1,000 per election cycle, an amount that did not change for almost three decades until it was raised to $2,000 and indexed to rise with inflation with the passage of the Bipartisan Campaign Reform Act of 2002 (BCRA), which was more commonly known as the McCain-Feingold bill, after its two principal sponsors in the U.S. Senate, John McCain, a Republican representing Arizona, and Russell Feingold, a Democrat from Wisconsin. Because this cap did not rise between 1974 and 2002, the amount of money that a presidential or congressional campaign could raise from an individual fell in real terms over time due to inflation. One scholar calculated that a contribution of $1,000 in 1976 was equivalent to a donation of $363 in 1996 dollars.[38] Thus, presidents campaigning for themselves and their co-partisans needed to reach out to greater numbers of donors over time as campaign costs rose and the individual contribution limit did not.

While individual contribution limits remained constant over the course of almost three decades, the spending caps associated with candidates accepting public funding during the presidential nomination process rose. The campaign finance regime of the 1970s established a system of voluntary public financing of presidential campaigns in which qualifying candidates would receive money from the government in exchange for limiting their campaign spending. To qualify for funding during the nominating process, the candidates needed to raise a total of $5,000 in each of twenty states in contributions of $250 or less. Contributions larger than $250 could help a candidate to meet this threshold, but only the first $250 of each contribution counted toward the requirement to qualify for the program, and candidates who qualified would have only the first $250 of any contribution matched by federal funding. In exchange for receiving public funding, candidates would agree to campaign spending caps, both by state and overall. The program was designed to incentivize candidates to rely on a broad base of small donors and to limit overall spending. The caps on the spending of candidates who accepted public funding during the nomination stage rose from $10.9 million for the 1976 race to $40.5 million for the 2000 campaign, the last year in which contributions were limited to $1,000.[39]

The combination of rising spending caps and fixed contribution limits led to a system in which presidents spent more of their time raising money, since they needed to solicit contributions from greater numbers of donors to keep pace with the rising costs of campaigns. A candidate relying entirely on individual donations would have needed to find 109,000 people who would contribute the maximum amount of $1,000 in 1976 to reach that year's spending limit. In 2000, a candidate would need to reach out to 405,000 contributors who would each give the maximum donation of $1,000 in order to raise enough money to reach that year's cap—almost four times as many donors than were needed in 1976. While presidents and presidential candidates also raise money through events featuring other officials who stand in as surrogates for the president, direct mail solicitations, and now the Internet, for most presidents, raising money in person for their own reelection bid is a political necessity. Even with the increased individual contribution limits enacted by the BCRA in 2002, presidents spend more and more of their time soliciting funds, both for themselves and for their fellow party members.

Early in the FECA regime, presidential campaigns were able to meet their need for campaign cash without requiring too much personal participation by the president, but over time the political imperative to raise greater sums of money in relatively small increments has led presidents to spend more of their time on fundraising even earlier in their term in office. Jimmy Carter did not attend a fundraiser to benefit his own reelection bid until May 29, 1980, just over five months before Election Day, and attended a total of only 4 fundraisers for his own reelection campaign. As described previously, the Reagan reelection campaign's direct mail fundraising solicitations and the in-person efforts of Vice President Bush were so successful that this author found no record of Reagan's personal participation in any fundraising events for his 1984 reelection bid, though he did attend fundraisers that year in support of other Republicans.

Carter and Reagan were the last presidents to have limited personal involvement with reelection fundraising; the last four presidents have headlined increasing numbers of fundraisers in support of their reelection bid, beginning increasingly earlier in their term in office. George H. W. Bush headlined his first fundraiser for the Bush-Quayle '92 committee on October 31, 1991, with just over a year to go until he would face the voters in November 1992. A Republican who was involved in Bush's reelection fundraising efforts explained the situation this way in September 1991: "We've got to raise $25 million with $1,000 limits [on each individual contribution]. So it's a huge undertaking no matter how popular you are."[40]

Four years later, Bill Clinton got an earlier start, holding his first fundraiser for the Clinton-Gore campaign on June 22, 1995, almost a year and a half before Election Day. The next sitting president to campaign for his reelection started raising money even sooner in his term, when George W. Bush held his first reelection fundraiser on June 17, 2003. Barack Obama continued the practice of outdoing his predecessors' early starts, kicking off his reelection fundraising on April 14, 2011. When he sent an email to supporters announcing his reelection campaign on April 4, 2011, he wrote, "So even though I'm focused on the job you elected me to do, and the race may not reach full speed for a year or more, the work of laying the foundation for our campaign must start today."[41]

The foundation Obama referred to was monetary. Campaign finance rules designed to limit the influence of money in politics by limiting contribution amounts have at the same time incentivized presidents to begin their reelection fundraising earlier in their term, as they anticipate needing more time to hold a sufficient number of events to accumulate the financial resources they believe they need to secure their reelection to the White House. Raising a big political war chest early also has the salutary effect of scaring off prospective challengers for renomination, as political science research on the Congress has demonstrated.[42] These same dynamics apply to presidential efforts to support their fellow Democrats and Republicans by headlining fundraisers in down-ticket races. Candidates for the House and Senate must raise money in the same small increments as presidents; as costs for congressional campaigns have risen as well, members of Congress must start their fundraising earlier and earlier in their term, and the demand for presidential help in raising campaign cash is all the greater, as I will discuss in more detail in the next chapter, which focuses on presidential party-building efforts.

A Giant Loophole: The Proliferation and Banning of Soft Money

The proliferation of soft money in the 1990s and its subsequent ban in 2002 provide an illuminating example of how presidents respond to the institutional rules of the fundraising process. Presidents spend much time raising funds not only for themselves but also for national and state parties and for fellow party members running for elected office. In the 1990s, the ways in which they raised money for their national parties changed dramatically. The Federal Election Campaign Act was amended in 1976 to set a $20,000 limit on individuals contributing to national party committees, an amount that would not rise with inflation.[43]

By the late 1970s, many state party officials argued that FECA had limited the ability of state parties to mobilize voters because of its constraints on aiding presidential candidates who had accepted federal public funds. In 1979, Congress responded by amending FECA to exclude party-building activities such as voter registration and get-out-the-vote efforts from the contribution limitations imposed by the act. The Federal Election Commission then issued an advisory opinion

allowing state parties to use nonregulated funds not subject to contribution limits, known as soft money, to fund electoral efforts related to state, but not federal,
campaigns. Because state parties worked on behalf of both state and federal candidates, this opinion authorized the use of a mix of soft money (unregulated funds,
which could be raised in unlimited amounts) and hard money (regulated funds,
raised under the FECA constraints) to fund state campaign efforts. Subsequently,
the FEC ruled that national party organizations should also be able to raise soft
money to finance their efforts related to state elections.

National parties were also allowed to use soft money, which was not subject
to FECA contribution limits, to run general issue advertisements that were not
tied to a particular candidate, though in practice it was easy for most viewers to
connect a supposedly independent issue advertisement to a specific candidate for
office. These legislative and regulatory decisions opened the door to massive national party efforts to raise soft money in unlimited amounts to be used for party-
building activities. Many of these efforts would be at the state level, but in practice
this fundraising would become a powerful tool in federal elections that created a
gigantic loophole allowing for large, unregulated contributions to political parties
that far exceeded FECA limits.[44]

While soft money contributions went to political parties and were nominally
not tied to any campaign by a candidate for federal office, many donors chose to
make such contributions because of their desire to support the president or a party's nominee for the presidency. One such supporter, Herbert McAdams II of Arkansas, explained the motivations behind his $100,000 contribution to the DNC
in 1992 by saying, "I even wrote Bill Clinton a note telling him the contribution
was from one native Arkansan to another."[45] The premise that soft money would
fund only party-building activities that were separate from specific campaigns for
federal office quickly became a legal fiction.

Both parties began to take advantage of the soft money loophole with vigor in
the 1990s. Table 2.3 shows the rise of party fundraising over time, in both hard and
soft money. In the 1993–1994 election cycle, the national Democratic Party raised
$49.1 million in soft money, while the national Republican Party raised $52.5 million in such funds. The totals jumped to $123.9 million and $138.2 million, respectively, in 1995–1996, a presidential election cycle. Soft money fundraising dropped
a bit in the following midterm election cycle but jumped to a then-record $245.2
million for the Democrats and $249.9 million for the Republicans in the 1999–
2000 election cycle. Even though the following election cycle was not a presidential election year, totals in the midterm cycle of 2001–2002 topped the amounts
raised in the preceding election cycle, with Democrats raising $246.1 million and
Republicans $250.0 million in unregulated soft money.

Table 2.3: Soft and Hard Money Raised by National Parties,
1993–2006 (millions of dollars)

Type of Funds Raised	Party	1993– 1994	1995– 1996	1997– 1998	1999– 2000	2001– 2002	2003– 2004	2005– 2006
Nonfederal, "soft" money	Democrats	49.1	123.9	92.8	245.2	246.1	—	—
	Republicans	52.5	138.2	131.6	249.9	250.0	—	—
Federal, "hard" money	Democrats	132.8	221.6	160.0	275.2	217.2	678.8	483.1
	Republicans	244.1	416.5	285.0	465.8	424.1	782.4	602.3
Total, "soft" and "hard" money	Democrats	181.9	345.5	252.8	520.4	463.3	678.8	483.1
	Republicans	296.6	554.7	416.6	715.7	674.1	782.4	602.3

Source: "Table 2.9," CQ Press Electronic Library, Vital Statistics on American Politics Online Edition, originally published in Harold W. Stanley and Richard G. Niemi, *Vital Statistics on American Politics 2007–2008* (Washington, DC: CQ Press, 2008), http://library.cqpress.com/vsap/ (accessed May 15, 2009).

In each year, hard money contributions exceeded soft money contributions, but soft money totals became successively larger. For example, a study by the group Common Cause examining soft money contributions from July 1992 through March 1994 found that Time Warner was the leading donor to the Democratic Party, contributing $508,333 over a period of under two years. The National Education Association topped the list of union donors with $339,950 in contributions, while the chief executive officer of American Financial Corporation gave $250,000, making him the most generous individual donor.[46] Donations on this scale made a farce out of FECA contribution limits and the ban on donations to federal campaigns by corporations and labor unions.

These remarkable totals resulted in part from active participation in soft money fundraising by both Democratic and Republican presidents, who would headline large galas and small dinners with high-dollar party donors. Throughout the 1990s, the largest contribution either party solicited was $250,000, but for a May 2000 gala, the Democratic National Committee asked its biggest donors to make a $500,000 soft money contribution. Those who gave this unprecedented amount would receive front-row seats at the gala and would be invited to a small dinner with President Clinton the preceding night.[47]

The growth in the role of soft money was one of several factors leading to the Bipartisan Campaign Reform Act of 2002, since the ability to make limitless contributions to political parties cut directly against FECA's goal of making political actors rely on many small donations to reduce corruption or the appearance of corruption. The act effectively banned soft money contributions to national parties by mandating that their activities had to be funded with hard, or regulated, money, subject to contribution caps. In an acknowledgment that the fixed contribution limits that had not risen since the 1970s had placed more and more pressure on elected officials and candidates to devote increasing amounts of time to fundraising, the act also raised contribution limits and indexed them to rise over time with inflation. The maximum individual contribution in 2002 was $1,000 per candidate per election and $20,000 to a national party committee per year. The act raised the amount for candidate contributions to $2,000 per election and for party committee contributions to $25,000 per year for the 2004 election cycle, and by the 2012 election cycle, they had risen according to the law's formula to $2,500 and $30,800, respectively.[48]

After BCRA, unregulated soft money did not disappear from the American political scene. While it no longer flowed to national parties, in the 2004 election, so-called 529 groups on both ends of the political spectrum, the most prominent of which was the anti–John Kerry organization called Swift Boat Veterans for Truth, raised funds in unregulated amounts and ran advertisements designed to influence federal elections. In the wake of the Supreme Court's 2010 decision in the *Citizens United* case that overturned the prohibition on direct spending in federal elections by corporations, in the 2010 and 2012 elections outside groups that have come to be called Super PACs played and, at this writing, intend to play a similar role to that of the 529 groups in 2004.[49] BCRA reduced the possibility that national parties would be corrupted by large, unregulated contributions. In doing so, it pushed these contributions to other, less accountable actors.

BCRA changed the rules of the game in ways that affected presidential fundraising in several ways. First, the larger individual contribution amounts meant that in 2004, a president could tap half as many donors as he had in 2000 who were willing to contribute the maximum legal amount in order to raise the same amount of money for his or a fellow party member's campaign. Alternatively, if a president and his political team could convince all of their deep-pocketed contributors to give the new maximum amount, they could generate twice as much money from the same number of political donors. These higher contribution limits certainly contributed to George W. Bush's unprecedented reelection fundraising in 2004. Parties focused by necessity on hard money donations and did so successfully, as table 2.3 indicates. Both parties raised more in hard money in the 2003–2004 election cycle, the first after the implementation of BCRA, than they had in hard and soft money combined four years previously in the prior presidential election. The annual GOP House-Senate gala dinner in 2003, the first year under BCRA, yielded $22 million in hard money from 7,500 attendees, a substantial total that fell short of the $30 million that party raised at the same event from about 5,000 attendees who contributed both hard and soft money the previous year. In short, the new law meant that fundraisers had to work harder to raise money in smaller amounts from more people.[50]

Mark Knoller of CBS News highlighted how changing campaign finance laws can affect the fundraising activities of presidents. In July 2010, he reported that Obama had taken part in 49 fundraisers to date as president, compared with the 38 fundraisers that George W. Bush had attended at the same point in his presidency. But Obama's greater number of fundraisers had yielded less money than Bush's efforts had, due to the BCRA's soft money ban. Obama's 49 events had raised more than $46 million for his fellow Democrats, while Bush's 38 events had brought in $145 million.[51] Arguably, the ban in soft money donations to national parties led to presidents spending even more time fundraising to help parties fund their activities under the new institutional rules of the game.

Opting Out of Public Funding—
Political Incentives and Self-interest

The rules of the game governing public financing of presidential campaigns have also shaped the ways presidents raise money for their own reelection bids. Between 1976 and 1996, the campaign finance regime established by FECA succeeded in holding down overall candidate campaign spending, as every major-party nominee over this twenty-year period chose to participate in the federal matching funds program and accept the accompanying limits on campaign spending. In 2000, then Governor George W. Bush became the first major-party nominee to not take part in the federal matching funds program during the nominating process. He did so because, as a self-interested political actor, he concluded that it would be more advantageous for him to forgo the public funding provided through the program so that he could raise greater amounts of money and spend it without the constraints of the spending caps that accompany public funds. Bush did so again in 2004, and several leading Democratic candidates that year followed suit. In 2008, the principal contenders for the nomination of both parties forwent public funding during the nominating process and raised much more money than they would have been able to do had they participated in the public funding program.

Bush's decision to opt out of public funding during the nominating process allowed him to bring many more resources to bear on his campaign than otherwise would have been possible. If he had participated in the public funding system, he would have had to limit his spending until the time of the Republican National Convention to the $40.5 million spending cap proscribed by law. In exchange for abiding by this spending limit, Bush would have received the maximum allowed amount of $16.9 million in matching funds, which seems like a substantial incentive for taking part in the public system, until one learns that Bush raised more than $95 million for his campaign committee during the nominating season leading up to the 2000 general election. It was clearly in Bush's self-interest to opt out of the public funding system during the nominating process in 2000. The difference four years later would be even more dramatic. The cap on 2004 nomination spending by those candidates who accepted public funding was $44.8 million. In return for accepting this spending limit, candidates could receive up to $18.7 million in federal matching funds. Bush raised almost $270 million for his campaign committee in 2004, when he was unopposed for renomination.[52]

In 2004, Senator John Kerry, the Democratic Party's nominee for the presidency, responded to the institutional incentives of the campaign finance regime and the contextual incentives provided by Bush's decision to opt out of public funding when he followed the president's lead and decided not to take part in the public funding program during the nominating process. He did so with an eye on the plight of the last nominee to face a sitting president, Bob Dole, who was the Republican standard-bearer aiming to defeat Bill Clinton in 1996. Dole accepted public funding that year and spent almost all of the $37 million allowed under the spending cap by April of that year in the course of winning the Republican nomination. As a result, he had very little money to expend until he received the general election public funding available to him once he officially became his party's nominee at the Republican National Convention in August. Clinton, on the other hand, who had no primary opposition, had also participated in the public funding program and stood ready to launch a barrage of advertisements targeting Dole using the approximately $20 million he had in his campaign account for the nominating stage. Kerry sought to avoid Dole's strategic disadvantage eight years later by forgoing public financing for the nomination stage and the spending caps that went with it. While he was not limited in the amount he could raise and spend before the Democratic National Convention, he did emerge from his nominating fight at a severe financial disadvantage. By the end of March 2004, Kerry had raised $60 million to Bush's $170 million. Had both taken part in the public financing system during the nominating process, they would have had to abide by the $44.8 million spending cap, something neither candidate was willing to do.[53]

Kerry's financial disadvantage continued during the general election because of another choice made by the Democratic Party following Bob Dole's experience with the campaign finance regime in 1996. While Kerry opted out of public funding in the nominating process, he did accept $75 million in public funding for the general election, which he could access once he was officially nominated at the Democratic National Convention in late July. Candidates who accept public funds for the general election agree to raise no additional private money for their campaign after their national convention. The Democrats in 2004 scheduled such an early convention in part so that their nominee could access general election funds earlier in the summer than did Dole, who had to wait until an August convention to receive his general election funding and was financially overmatched by Bill Clinton that summer.

Because the Republicans held their convention a month later, Kerry had to make his $75 million last over more than three months, whereas Bush could spend his general election money over just two months. Thus Kerry found himself financially outgunned in August, when he limited his spending of public funds to conserve resources for the final months of the contest while Bush spent the last of the private funds he raised during the nominating process. Kerry's financial disadvantage continued into September. When Bush received his $75 million in public funding after his convention, Kerry had only $62 million left to spend.[54] Holding a convention substantially earlier than the other party came with both the benefit of receiving general election public funds earlier and the drawback of having to make those funds last over a substantially longer period than did the opposing party. The strategic choices made by both nominees and parties were structured by the campaign finance regime created by the Federal Election Campaign Act of 1974 and lessons learned from previous candidates navigating the incentives created by that system.

Those incentives created by the institutional rules of the game would affect the amount of time that George W. Bush would spend raising funds for his own reelection bid. Bush's 2004 campaign marked the first time a sitting president had opted out of public financing for the nominating process. Not coincidentally, he also began his reelection fundraising earlier than any other president in the era of the FECA regime. While he chose not to be part of the public financing system, his fundraising was still subject to caps in individual donations, which had been raised to $2,000 per person for the 2004 elections by the Bipartisan Campaign Reform Act of 2002. He headlined 57 fundraisers for the Bush-Cheney reelection campaign, compared with Clinton's 14, George H. W. Bush's 19, Reagan's 0, and Carter's 4 fundraisers for their own campaigns. His overall fundraising goal was higher than that of any president in history, and he would need to devote record time to raising campaign cash due to the limits on individual contributions.

Bush was not the first sitting president who considered opting out of the public financing system during the nominating process. Twenty years earlier, Ed Rollins, who ran Ronald Reagan's 1984 reelection bid, discussed the possibility that the president would choose not to take part in the public system. Speaking in late January 1984, Rollins talked about the rate at which the campaign had raised funds, even in advance of Reagan's official declaration that he was a candidate for reelection: "We've raised more money in the last quarter than any of the other candidates," citing more than $4 million in contributions. "If the money continues to roll in, we may just make the choice not to take [matching funds]." Rollins emphasized, however, that even if the campaign did not participate in the matching fund program and was therefore not bound by its spending limits, it would not seek to exceed those limits. "We certainly have no intention of raising any more than we talked about in the budget figures—$26 million. We certainly don't want to get into a 'shades of '72 campaign' with more money than you could spend."[55] In 1984, the Reagan campaign's behavior was constrained by the specter of the Watergate scandal, which had unfolded just over a decade earlier, and thus aimed to limit its own spending. In 2004, when Bush became the first sitting president to not participate in the federal matching fund program during the nomination stage, his almost $270 million raised was about six times the spending limit he would have been bound by had he taken public money. Clearly, the ghosts of Watergate were not as significant a factor in 2004 as in 1984, nor would they be eight years later as Barack Obama geared up to break the younger Bush's reelection fundraising records.

The Reagan-Bush '84 campaign did end up participating in the matching funds program, and its fundraising efforts were so successful that this author found no record of Reagan himself headlining a fundraiser to benefit his own campaign organization. Additionally, his campaign ceased its fundraising efforts in May 1984, having already raised all the money it could spend under the voluntary spending limits that go along with the acceptance of public funds for the nominating process. Reagan was unopposed for the nomination and would take public funding in the general election, so he had plenty of money but little to spend it on. Donations continued to arrive after the campaign stopped soliciting them, resulting in a surplus of more than $1.5 million above what the campaign could legally spend throughout the nominating process.[56] If the public financing system is designed in part to reduce the amount of money presidential candidates raise and thus the amount of time they spend fundraising, it certainly succeeded in this respect in 1984. Reagan's lack of personal involvement in his reelection fundraising would not be emulated by his successors, who devoted more and more time to raising political cash.

The Federal Election Campaign Act of 1974 also established a public financing regime for the general election under which major party candidates for the presidency would receive a set amount of public funding to be used from their party's national convention through Election Day, and in return they would agree not to raise any additional funds for their own campaign. The amount rose each year from $21.8 million in 1976 to $84.1 million in 2008, and every candidate of both major parties from 1976 through 2004 took public funds for the general election.[57] Barack Obama broke new ground in 2008 when he opted not to participate in the public financing system at either the nominating or the general election stage and proceeded to raise $745 million. Had he participated in the public financing system, he would have been limited to spending only $50.5 million during the nomination process, in addition to the $84.1 million he would have received for the general election.[58] It was clearly in his self-interest to opt out of the public financing system. John McCain opted out of public funding at the nominating stage but accepted public money for the general election in 2008, which left him with far fewer financial resources than his Democratic opponent in the final months of the campaign.

With Obama poised to become the first sitting president to not participate in public financing at either the nomination or the general election stage in 2012, the eventual Republican nominee is expected to do the same. One Republican strategist predicted, "I would be shocked if [leading Republican candidates] took matching funds. I don't think that it's a successful model this time, or in the future." Qualifying for matching funds during the nominating contest was once seen as a sign of political viability. A candidate who could raise at least $5,000 in increments of $250 in twenty different states had demonstrated a broad base of political supporters and in return received federal matching funds that would help fill his or her campaign coffers. In contrast, in 2012 it is likely that only the candidates who are long shots for the nomination will take part in the public financing program. With Obama raising funds earlier and more ambitiously than any president in the FECA era, the pressure on GOP contenders to opt out of the public financing system will be enormous.[59]

CONCLUSIONS

There is no clearer indicator of the permanent campaign than the rise of presidential fundraising. The increasing amounts of time presidents devote to seeking financial support throughout their time in office make it hard to draw a line between when governing ends and campaigning begins. Presidents spend increasing amounts of their time raising money in large part because campaign finance rules and the rising costs of campaigns lead them to do so. A system that was designed to reduce corruption or the appearance of corruption by limiting contribution amounts, and to limit the amount of money in campaigns by incentivizing candidates to accept the spending caps that come with public funding, has led to a situation in which presidents have devoted increasing amounts of their most precious resource, their time, to political fundraising throughout their term in office.

The rules of our campaign finance regime structure candidate behavior. Contribution limits mean that presidents must seek funds from many donors to raise enough funds to keep pace with the rising costs of campaigns. Public financing systems during both the nominating stage and the general election stage largely achieved their goal of limiting the rate of growth of candidate spending until winning candidates began to see that it was in their own self-interest to opt out of the systems in the 2000s. Successful presidential candidates no longer see participating in public funding at both the nominating and general election stages as being in their best interest. Without the limiting effects of the spending caps during the nominating process and the ban on private campaign fundraising during the general election, the amount of money raised has skyrocketed.

In order to raise the funds they believe are necessary to wage a successful campaign and to help fellow party members do so as well, presidents have devoted increasing amounts of their time earlier and earlier in their term to raising political cash in the relatively small contributions mandated by the campaign finance regime. This chapter began with George W. Bush declaring at a fundraiser for his own reelection bid fifteen months before the election that the political season would come in its own time, even as he was helping his campaign to raise money hand over fist. His statements reflected his desire to adhere to the traditional norm of acting as a president and not as a partisan campaigner so far in advance of the election. Nevertheless, political reality dictated that he needed to begin reelection fundraising early in order to build up his campaign coffers using donations in small increments.

This substantial rise in fundraising by presidents throughout their time in office has important implications for governance. Because the president's scarcest commodity is his time, how he allocates it tells us a great deal about his priorities. And more and more, presidents prioritize political fundraising. As over 80 percent of the 1,489 presidential fundraisers over the thirty-five-year period since Carter's inauguration took place outside of Washington, DC, a substantial amount of time, effort, and planning went into each presidential fundraising journey. More time spent on such efforts could mean less time spent on the people's business on a day-to-day basis. A newspaper article reported that in 1996 White House Deputy Chief of Staff Evelyn Lieberman suggested that White House aides make their Oval Office briefings with Clinton shorter so that he could spend more time at events to reward political contributors.[60] The extent to which this actually happened is not known, but the more time a president spends fundraising, the less time he has for his other priorities.

In 1998, Republicans tried to hammer this point home when Clinton attended his record-setting 100th fundraiser that year. The Republican National Committee put out a press release calling Clinton "the part-time president" and "fund-raiser in chief," declaring, "Instead of doing his job and negotiating with Republican leaders to finalize the 1999 budget, President Bill Clinton is threatening to shut down the federal government and hopping aboard 'Fund-Raiser One' to New York City to raise campaign cash."[61] Democrats have similarly railed against the fundraising efforts of Republican presidents.

Politicking is tied to governing. Presidents campaign and raise funds for themselves and others so that they can achieve their policy goals. Obama made this link explicit when he addressed an audience of supporters at a fundraiser for Democratic House and Senate candidates in Miami Beach on October 26, 2009, and said, "The reason you're here tonight is you have more to do. . . . Governing is even harder than campaigning."[62] A president hopes that these efforts help elect enough members of his party to office so that he is better able to enact his agenda, and do the people's business as he sees it. But because the president must juggle the dual expectations of being both a unifying national leader and an effective head of party, his growing efforts in the latter role could contribute to the cynicism with which much of the public views our political leaders, as I discuss in more detail in chapter 6.

In the next chapter, I explore what the rise of the president's role as fundraiser-in-chief says about his relationship with his political party. Conventional wisdom has long held that presidents elected under the plebiscitary nominating system have weak ties to political parties. Is this the case? For whom do presidents raise funds, and what does this say about their political priorities and their relationship with the parties of which they are the head?

3. The President as Party-Builder-in-Chief

Bill Clinton caused a stir within the Democratic Party in January 1996 when he said in an interview with the *Washington Post*, "The American people don't think it's the president's business to tell them what ought to happen in the congressional elections." One reporter summed up the common interpretation of his remarks when he asked if Clinton was saying that getting "Democratic candidates elected is not going to be one of his priorities in the [president's upcoming reelection] campaign," an assessment that White House press secretary Mike McCurry emphatically denied.[1] At that point in his term, Clinton had headlined eighty-nine fundraisers, only thirteen of which had been for the Clinton-Gore reelection campaign, demonstrating a substantial commitment to aiding the electoral efforts of his fellow Democrats. Because presidents have increasingly devoted more time to political fundraising throughout their term in office, Clinton's remark prompts the question of just who benefits from this element of the permanent campaign. To what extent do presidents fundraise to help their own electoral prospects, how often do they raise money for fellow party members, and whom within the party are they trying to help? Patterns of presidential party building can reveal a great deal about a president's political priorities and his role as party leader.

Several scholars have argued that presidents produced by the plebiscitary nominating process, in place since the early 1970s, would have weak ties to their political parties. Nelson Polsby contended that the rules of the nominating process would reward candidates who could mobilize factions of like-minded party supporters instead of building broader coalitions within the party, as was necessary under the previous nominating system. Before 1972, party leaders at national conventions chose presidential nominees with limited input from the public, as expressed through primary elections and caucuses. To be nominated in such a system, a candidate needed to appeal to enough party members to assemble a majority coalition at the convention. In the current plebiscitary nominating system, in which voters in primaries and caucuses determine presidential nominees, a candidate might win the Iowa caucus with the support of just over 30 percent of caucus-goers, as Jimmy Carter did in 1976, and then capitalize on the momentum of an early victory to raise money, garner media attention, win subsequent contests, and roll to the nomination. Candidates in the current system build a personal following and can be nominated even if they do not have the support of a majority of their fellow party members. Nominees chosen through such a system, Polsby argued, will have weak ties to party elites, which, if they then win the general election, will complicate their relations with Congress and leave them less able to build the coalitions that they need to govern effectively. According to this line of thinking, recent candidates who win the presidency by mobilizing a faction of personal support among the public instead of a broad coalition of support within the party will continue to have weak ties to their parties once in office.[2]

Samuel Kernell built on Polsby's argument, contending that the plebiscitary nominating process advantages candidates who are Washington outsiders and are not tied to the unpopular political elites who occupy the seats of power in the nation's capital. According to Kernell, "A candidate achieves his outsider status less by his non-Washington residency than by his standing within the party or governmental establishment." In this view, it is an electoral advantage to have weak ties to one's political party. Outsider candidates who would have been quite unlikely to be nominated under the old system in which strong party ties were essential can now take their case to the people and be elected without the support of the party establishment. Those weak party ties help a candidate to get elected, and when in office, Kernell argues that those same weak ties help lead presidents to eschew closed-door bargaining with Congress in favor of taking their case directly to the American people, urging them to put pressure on their elected representatives to support the president's position.[3] According to both Kernell and Polsby, the way we have chosen presidential nominees since the 1970s produces presidents likely to have weak ties to their party who arrive in office due to the support they have mobilized among the people. Once in office, their tendency is to continue to employ as president the strategies that got them to the Oval Office in the first place.

Until recently, most research concluded that modern presidents have done very little to build their political parties. Indeed, Sidney Milkis argued that the growth of executive power has actually weakened both national political parties. As presidents have taken more unilateral action, the result has been a lesser role both for the national and state legislatures and for political parties.[4] Daniel Galvin summed up the conventional wisdom that presidents have "disengaged from their parties, transcended them, subordinated them, exploited them, or ignored them." To test whether this has been indeed the case, Galvin studied presidents from Eisenhower through George W. Bush. Employing extensive archival research, he examined to what extent presidents work to strengthen their party organization. To do so, he studied presidential efforts to "provide campaign services, develop human capital, recruit candidates, mobilize voters, finance party operations, or support internal activities." He argues that whether presidents behave as "party predators" or party builders depends on whether they view their party as the majority or minority party in the nation, and the strength or weakness of the existing party organization. Presidents who see their party as being in the minority tend to invest in party building to help achieve majority status, while presidents who see their party as an entrenched majority either neglect the party or are more predatory, using the party's resources to advance presidential interests with little concern for party building. The weaker the party organization a president inherits, the more challenging party building is, while presidents who inherit a healthy party organization are advantaged when it comes to party building.[5]

Throughout most of the period that Galvin examines, he contends that Republicans were party builders and Democrats party neglecters or predators, due in large part to their long majority status in Congress. However, after the Democrats lost control of both chambers of Congress in 1994 and Bill Clinton secured his own reelection two years later, the president embarked on an extensive party-building effort in his second term, as he recognized that his party's long-held majority status would not necessarily return of its own accord. Galvin concludes by conjecturing that the end of the Democrats' long-held majorities on Capitol Hill signaled an era in which both parties would be incentivized to focus on party building. With both parties convinced that control of Congress is either within reach or at risk, we should see consistent presidential efforts to strengthen their party organizations in an effort to win a lasting political victory.[6]

PRESIDENTIAL FUNDRAISING AND PARTY BUILDING

The purpose of this chapter is to analyze who benefits from the permanent campaign and what patterns of presidential fundraising reveal about whether presidents have weak ties to their parties, as the work of Polsby, Kernell, and Milkis would suggest, or, as Galvin argues, whether there are clear patterns by party of predation and party building up until 1996, with a bipartisan focus on party building afterward. It is important to note that Galvin's focus is exclusively on party as organization—the formal apparatus of the national, state, and local Democratic and Republican parties—which is one of the three elements of a political party laid out by political scientist V. O. Key, along with party in the electorate (partisanship among voters) and party in government (the party's elected officials).[7] When presidents raise money for their co-partisans, they focus primarily on party in government, as they aim to elect more party members to office. At times their efforts also support the party as organization, as the party can use these funds to hire staff, launch voter registration drives, and more.

To examine who benefits from the permanent campaign, for each of the 1,489 presidential fundraisers from 1977 through June 30, 2011, I coded for whom the president raised money, noting the name of the individual or group that was the beneficiary and whether the fundraiser was for the president himself; the Democratic or Republican National Committee; candidates for the House, Senate, or a governor's race; a state or local party; the vice president; multiple beneficiaries; or another type of political campaign. I focus not on money raised but on the allocation of what is arguably the president's scarcest resource, his time, as an indicator of his commitment to aiding his fellow party members to build up the financial resources they need to run campaigns and win elections. Only a few studies have examined the question of whom within the party the president works to assist, but their focus has been on which specific candidates he aids for a certain elected body, such as the House or Senate, or which states have drawn the president's attention.[8] These works reveal much about the kinds of candidates whom presidents support and the effects of their efforts. What I aim to do is address the broader question of which parts of the party the president focuses on.

I build on Galvin's work and contend that a president's fundraising priorities are a function of perceived threats and opportunities. Presidential party-building fundraising is on the rise in large part because competitive presidential elections and narrow margins of party control of Congress have raised the stakes of all federal and many state elections. In an era without long-lasting congressional majorities, presidents and their parties have more to gain and lose in any particular election. Given rising campaign costs and federal contribution limits, presidents have correspondingly devoted more of their resources to helping their party raise the financial resources required for electoral success. Carter, who was president at a time when Democrats had controlled both chambers of Congress for more than two decades, was the only president elected via the plebiscitary nominating system who was not an aggressive party builder. As a president with weak party ties, little sense of electoral threat, and a personal disdain for fundraising, Carter did relatively little to help his fellow Democrats. But the subsequent five presidents have devoted increasing amounts of their time to fundraising for their fellow party members, with the efforts of recent presidents dwarfing those of earlier occupants of the Oval Office.

The thirty-five years since Carter's inauguration have seen a clear nationalization of presidential fundraising, with a decline in fundraising for state parties and a concomitant increase in national party fundraising. Table 3.10, later in this chapter, which highlights the relative fundraising priorities during each presidential term, illustrates that state and at times local parties were a consistent fundraising priority for Jimmy Carter, Ronald Reagan, and George H. W. Bush but have become far less important for Bill Clinton, George W. Bush, and Barack Obama. As attention to state parties has diminished dramatically, presidents have made the Democratic and Republican National Committees top beneficiaries of their fundraising. While the national committees often transfer funds to state parties and individual campaigns, it is quite significant that the national party has become the predominant focal point of and funnel through which presidential campaign fundraising flows.

Presidents have consistently made fundraising for Senate races a top priority, which is understandable due both to the importance of the Senate and to relatively frequent changes in party control over the past few decades. Senate races tend to be more competitive than House contests, as they draw high-quality challengers and take place in states, whose lines cannot be redrawn for electoral advantage as is done for House seats.[9] Because the Senate is critical to presidential nominations and treaties, presidents have added incentive to influence the balance of power in the upper chamber. Additionally, the Senate's smaller size means that winning one race in the 100-seat body brings a party proportionally as close to taking the majority as winning more than four races would in the 435-seat House of Representatives.

Senate races have also drawn substantial attention from every president since Carter because control of that chamber has been hotly contested since 1980, when Republicans won control, ending twenty-six years of a Democratic majority. While Carter might not have perceived much danger of losing control of the Senate, Reagan was heavily incentivized to work to hold control of the chamber in 1982, 1984, and 1986 when the Democrats reclaimed the majority there, and to try to retake control in 1988. The Senate remained in Democratic hands until the 1994 elections, and Republicans then held it until Senator Jim Jeffords of Vermont defected from the Republican Party in May 2001, shifting control of what had been a 50-50 Senate to the Democrats. Republicans retook the chamber in the 2002 elections and lost it in 2006. As of this writing in 2011, the Democrats hold control by a narrow margin. For each president in this period, the possibility of retaking the Senate or the threat of losing control was quite real, incentivizing him to lend support to his party's candidates.[10]

While presidents often devote relatively little time to raising money for House races, the Republican takeover of the House in 1994 that ended forty years of Democratic control presaged extensive second-term fundraising for House races by both Bill Clinton and George W. Bush. Before 1994, many regarded Democratic control of the lower chamber as a political fact of life. Republicans held the House for twelve years before Democrats retook control in 2006 and lost it again to the Republicans in 2010. While presidents may see less political payoff to raising money for House races than for Senate contests, the current era in which each party believes that it might take control of the House in the next election has made presidents of both parties much more aggressive about fundraising to build their party in the House.

Each president except Reagan exhibited a clear pattern in his first term—fundraising for other party members in the first two years in office gave way to a focus on the president's reelection campaign and the national committee in the third and fourth years of the administration. Because George W. Bush and Barack Obama both opted out of public funding for their reelection campaigns and the accompanying matching funds and spending limits, each spent more time raising funds for his own reelection and the national committee, and relatively less for fellow party members, resulting in much more pronounced patterns of party building followed by a focus on themselves. All three two-term presidents since the mid-1970s engaged in extensive party building in their second term, with Bill Clinton, a president who purportedly genuinely enjoyed his role as fundraiser-in-chief, setting staggering records for his unprecedented party-building fundraising. To better understand these dynamics, I turn now to the question of to what extent presidents' fundraising represents an effort to boost their own fortunes or those of their fellow party members.

WHO BENEFITS FROM PRESIDENTIAL FUNDRAISING?

To what extent do presidents fundraise to help their own reelection prospects, and to what extent do their efforts benefit their fellow party members? Figure 3.1 reveals that only 8 percent of all presidential fundraisers directly benefited the president's own reelection bid. The vast majority of presidential fundraisers—92 percent—have not been directly for themselves but for their national party and other co-partisans. George W. Bush attended the most fundraisers for his reelection bid—fifty-seven—which constituted 17 percent of all his fundraising, but he still devoted more than 80 percent of his fundraising efforts to others. Bush spent so much more time fundraising for himself than did the other presidents in this study because he was the first sitting president to opt out of the public financing system during the nomination season, which freed him from the voluntary spending limits that come with public matching funds and led him to devote much more time to raising unprecedented amounts of money for his reelection bid.

Obama, who will be the first incumbent president to not participate in the public funding system at both the nomination stage and the general election stage, should easily eclipse Bush's record. After announcing his candidacy for a second term, he headlined 31 fundraisers for his own reelection bid between April 14 and June 30, 2011. Through the first two and a half months of George W. Bush's reelection fundraising, he had taken part in only 16 fundraisers, indicating that Obama's fundraising pace was about twice his predecessor's at a comparable point in the campaign. All of Obama's reelection fundraisers have been joint events whose proceeds go to the Obama Victory Fund, an account whose proceeds benefit both the Obama-Biden reelection campaign and the Democratic National Committee.

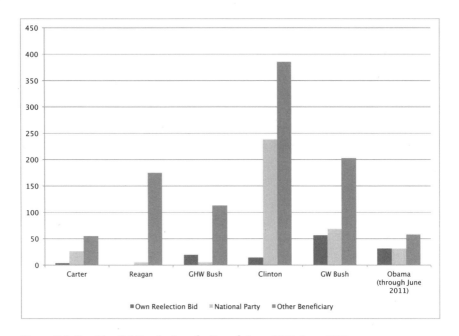

Figure 3.1: Presidential Fundraisers by Beneficiary, 1977–June 2011
Source: Data compiled by the author from the *Public Papers of the Presidents* and from Associated Press articles.

The first $5,000 in contributions from an individual at a given event goes to the campaign, with any additional amount benefitting the DNC.[11] In figure 3.1, these are counted as fundraisers for the president's own reelection bid and not as fundraisers for the national committee to avoid double-counting them. Two and a half years into his term, 63 of Obama's 121 fundraisers have been for his own reelection bid, the DNC, or both.

Money raised for the national committee in a president's first term often benefits a presidential campaign, through either the party's subsequent purchase of campaign ads or its get-out-the-vote efforts, but it is not known just how much money raised for the national party was used to benefit primarily the president himself, how much helped other candidates, and how much went toward efforts designed to boost the entire ticket. Tim Kaine, chair of the Democratic National Committee, made explicit the connection between fundraising for the national party and support for the president when speaking at the first fundraiser that Barack Obama attended as president in March 2009, more than two years before he started raising money for his own reelection bid. Kaine explained why the donors had chosen to contribute $30,400 per couple to attend the event by declaring, "You are here to support the Democratic National Committee, the political arm of the White House."[12] Both Bill Clinton and George W. Bush ramped up their fund-raising for their national committee in their reelection year, and all of Obama's reelection fundraisers to date have also benefited the Democratic National Committee. If we assume that all 161 first-term fundraisers for the national party held by these six presidents helped to boost the president's reelection bid, those combined with the 125 events that presidents held for themselves still only constitute 19 percent of all presidential fundraising since 1977, meaning that just over 4 in every 5 presidential fundraisers were for the exclusive benefit of a fellow party member—an indicator of substantial presidential party-building efforts.

Presidents raise funds for their fellow party members for many reasons. They aim to help to elect more co-partisans who will support their agenda in Congress or who will work to achieve party goals, including garnering maximum advantage from the redistricting process, in statehouses and state legislatures across the country. They also use their support to reward party members who have been loyal and to do favors for other candidates or officeholders who might someday feel obliged to return the favor. One study of George W. Bush's midterm campaign efforts in 2002 found that presidents can make the difference in close congressional elections, and that presidential campaign efforts can lead to more support from their beneficiaries in future votes in the House of Representatives.[13] Presidents also campaign in midterm elections because they will be seen as a referendum on the president whether or not he hits the stump. Politics is a team sport, and the president is the captain of his party's team.

Presidential fundraising can be quite helpful for a campaign. Research has shown that early fundraising on behalf of congressional candidates is particularly valuable to a successful campaign. This principle is also captured in the maxim expressed by the acronym that makes up the name of the interest group EMILY's List—"Early Money Is Like Yeast (it makes the dough rise)"—indicating that early fundraising leads to additional fundraising success that can make a candidacy viable.[14] Indeed, presidents often start raising money for their fellow party members early in their term in office. White House press secretary Robert Gibbs defended Barack Obama's early fundraising during a time of economic trouble, saying, "We haven't seen politics by either party stop in this period, though I think the president fully understands the situation the American people face. . . . It's also safe to assume that the president wants to see a strong party system in this country."[15]

To what extent does presidential fundraising demonstrate the commitment to building a strong party system? In the following sections, I examine the party-building efforts of each of the presidents who were elected via the plebiscitary nominating system and served under the campaign finance regime created by the Federal Election Campaign Act of 1974. I analyze the extent to which each president was a party builder or party predator, what their party-building priorities reveal about their political goals and their relationship with their party, and how well the perceived electoral threat and opportunity explain their party-building efforts.

Jimmy Carter took office at a time when Democrats were the dominant force in the Congress, as they had controlled both chambers since the 1954 elections, more than two decades earlier. When Carter assumed the presidency, Democrats controlled 292 House seats, compared with just 143 for the Republicans, and held 61 of the 100 seats in the Senate.[16] The Democratic coalition was broad, ranging from northeastern liberals to southern conservatives, and its hold on power seemed well entrenched.

A Strained Relationship with the Party

Jimmy Carter had only tenuous connections to the Democratic Party establishment during the 1976 campaign, which carried over into his term in office. As one Carter aide put it, "Those people didn't help us get elected—at least not in the primaries—so there naturally is going to be some alienation on both sides." Carter's independence from the traditional party apparatus was one of his political assets in the campaign, as he touted himself as a fresh face who would make an effective national leader.[17] In a postelection interview in 1976, Carter told journalist Jules Witcover that he thought that appearing with other Democratic candidates in 1976 had done damage to his image as an appealing outsider.[18] Carter still held this view six years later, when he was interviewed in the fall of 1982, two years after his electoral defeat at the hands of Ronald Reagan:

> When I was a candidate in '76, almost all the leaders of the Democratic Party from Bob Strauss on down were committed to other candidates. . . . So I got the nomination without the help or support of the Democratic National Committee members or executive officers. And I won the nomination on that basis by taking my case directly to the people and running to some degree as an outsider, not only from the Congress in Washington, but also from the Democratic National Committee. The biggest handicap I had politically speaking after the convention was to have to absorb the Democratic Party responsibilities. Instead of going into Ohio or Illinois or other states as a lonely candidate reaching out my hand to a voter and saying, "I need your help," I was immediately saddled with all the gubernatorial candidates, the congressional candidate, and the local

Table 3.1: Jimmy Carter's Fundraisers, by Beneficiary and Year
of Term

	Year 1	Year 2	Year 3	Year 4	Total	Percentage
National committee	2	3	2	19	26	30.6
State or local party	1	6	8	8	23	27.1
House campaign	0	3	3	3	9	10.6
Gubernatorial campaign	2	6	1	0	9	10.6
Senate campaign	0	8	0	0	8	9.4
President	0	0	0	4	4	4.7
Other	0	1	1	1	3	3.5
Multiple beneficiaries	0	2	0	0	2	2.4
Joint House-Senate event	0	0	0	1	1	1.2
Total	5	29	15	36	85	100.0

Source: Data compiled by the author from the Public Papers of the Presidents and from Associated Press articles.

candidates of the Democratic Party. I didn't particularly object to that, but it was a dramatic reversal in my image from a lonely peanut farmer looking for votes to an establishment figure who was wrapped up in the Democratic Party. I think it pulled us down a good bit in the polls because it was a reversal in my basic character as presented to the American people.[19]

Carter was a relatively inattentive party builder at the start of his term. Of the five fundraisers he took part in during 1977, two were for the Democratic National Committee, as shown in table 3.1, which details Carter's fundraising efforts by beneficiary and year of his term. He also raised money for the Democratic gubernatorial candidates in New Jersey and Virginia, and he headlined the state party's annual Jefferson-Jackson Day fundraising dinner in Iowa, the state in which his caucus victory the previous year had given him the momentum that would carry him to his party's nomination and the presidency.

Carter's involvement in party fundraising was minimal in spite of the dire financial situation his fellow Democrats faced, with the DNC $3.7 million in debt before it held its first presidential fundraiser with Carter in June 1977.[20] Additionally, the Carter campaign was still between $300,000 and $400,000 in debt at the close of 1977. In September 1977, the DNC needed to appeal to some of its most prominent supporters to guarantee an emergency bank loan of $195,000 just to fund the day-to-day operations of the national committee. Such presidential commitment is remarkably small in light of the subsequent efforts of Carter's successors. As one anonymous Democratic official put it at the time, "The President does not want to get involved . . . he just doesn't like fund-raising."[21]

This limited effort by Carter came in spite of his having appointed loyalists to the key positions at the DNC on January 22, 1977, a mere two days after being inaugurated.[22] Carter aides made clear that the president's limited involvement with the national party so early in his term was intentional, but they expected him to step up his coordinated party-building efforts.[23] Carter's limited fundraising early in his term did not spare him from Republican criticism. In May 1977, former president Gerald Ford, who himself had visited thirteen states since relinquishing the presidency to Carter in January, told the crowd at a Republican fundraiser, "I'm not running for anything, but old habits are hard to break. Besides, I figured if Jimmy Carter was still campaigning six months after the election, why shouldn't I?"[24]

Criticism of Carter came from within the party as well, but for different reasons. Complaints about Carter's relations with state and local Democratic Party leaders were aired publicly very early in his term. At the end of March, state party officials gathered in Washington and unanimously passed a resolution urging the White House and the Democratic National Committee to "insure that state parties participate fully and meaningfully" in decisions about nominations to political posts, fundraisers, and other political issues. The state party chairman from Maine, Harold C. Pachios, made the political stakes for the president quite clear when he urged the national party chairman to "go to the White House and tell the president he's going to need us to get re-elected in three years." Vice President Walter Mondale addressed the group and acknowledged its complaints, saying, "I know some of you have had your frustrations with the new administration . . . jobs you've wanted . . . projects . . . dams you want built . . . water that has not yet arrived."[25]

More than eight months later, similar criticisms surfaced again. In late 1977, *Newsweek* ran an article focused on the complaints by many Democrats about Carter's shortcomings as a party builder. According to one anonymous Democrat who formerly worked for the national committee, "The Democratic Party has waited eight years to have a President, and it's still waiting to be led." Complaints mostly focused on poor communication and lack of consultation between the White House and party leaders in Washington and across the country. One anonymous DNC member, speaking of the president, reported, "We only hear from him when he's in trouble." The article went on to catalog a list of complaints, most from anonymous sources, about a president who reached the White House without the support of the party machinery and, at least in their eyes, had not become adept at leading it once in the Oval Office.[26] The tense relationship between Carter and his party stemmed not from differences about policy but from dissatisfaction over the ways Carter handled the political elements of his job. One anonymous party strategist declared in December 1977, "There isn't any ideological animosity toward Carter. It is more a feeling of political incompetence, a failure by Carter to follow through on his own promises or to follow the traditional party approach to presidential politics. Whatever he's trying to do, and we're not too sure what that is, he isn't doing it very well."[27]

In December 1977, Joel McCleary, the treasurer for the DNC, asserted that this would change in 1978. "We have a commitment from the President for five fund-raisers. We're going to 'lean' the [DNC] operation, get the President and Vice President out of [Washington] traveling ... and put $1.7 million into the 1978 elections."[28] Carter's distance from fellow party members did decrease in 1978, when he actively and aggressively campaigned with many of them, including some who had criticized his policies. One reporter commented, "The president's calculated effort to identify himself with his party and its stalwarts was in marked contrast to his behavior in 1976, when he only occasionally acknowledged the existence of fellow Democrats running on the ticket he headed."[29]

As table 3.1 indicates, Carter more actively embraced his role of party leader in the midterm election year of 1978. Buoyed by rising approval ratings in the wake of the Camp David Mideast peace negotiations, Carter hit the campaign trail hard. But like any president, his help was more welcome in some places than others. Carter mostly avoided the West, where his support was weaker, and concentrated instead on competitive contests in the eastern states. He made full use of the trappings of the presidency, raising funds for his fellow party members and announcing millions of dollars in federal spending as he went. Contemporary analysts saw Carter's efforts as having two goals—to help elect members of Congress who would in turn help his legislative program, and to build support for himself in advance of his own reelection bid two years later.[30]

Carter was the guest of honor at eight fundraisers for Senate candidates that year, while he held only three fundraisers for candidates for the House of Representatives, including one for Speaker Tip O'Neill. Additionally, he headlined six fundraisers for gubernatorial candidates, as well as two more that jointly benefited both the Senate and gubernatorial candidates in those states. The president held five fundraisers for state parties and one for a local party to benefit the Democrats of Cook County, Illinois, which includes the Democratic stronghold of Chicago. He attended only three fundraisers in 1978 for the Democratic National Committee, two fewer than the five to which he had originally committed himself. Carter's second year in office would be the high-water mark of his relatively modest party-building efforts.

The president's party reliably loses seats in Congress in midterm election years. When the Democrats' majority fell to 277 House seats in 1978, Carter joined every president since the Civil War except Franklin Roosevelt in 1934 in watching his party's share of House seats shrink in a midterm election. Indeed, between 1934 and 2010, the president's party suffered average losses in midterm elections of 28

House seats and 3.6 Senate seats. In 1978, the Democrats' majority in the Senate shrank to 58 seats, leaving them with smaller but still sizable margins of control in both chambers of Congress heading into the second half of Jimmy Carter's first and only term as president.[31]

Carter's Limited Focus on His Reelection Bid

Carter engaged in very little party fundraising in the third year of his term, headlining only fifteen such events. Eight of these were for state parties, two were for individual House members, one was for the Democratic Congressional Campaign Committee, which helps to elect Democrats across the country to the House, and two were for the Democratic National Committee. Additionally, Carter raised money for one gubernatorial candidate, in the key primary state of New Hampshire, and for the mayor of Chicago. Carter's fundraising totals in his third year in office would have been higher had it not been for the taking of American hostages in Iran late that year. Engaging in partisan political activity can be particularly problematic for a president during a time of national crisis. In the weeks following the beginning of the hostage crisis on November 4, 1979, Carter canceled planned trips to Canada, Florida, Georgia, Washington, and Oregon, including several scheduled fundraisers, so that he could devote his efforts to the situation in Iran.[32]

The ongoing Iran hostage crisis led Carter to formally declare his candidacy for reelection with as little fanfare as possible on December 4, 1979. He began his speech in the East Room of the White House by discussing his focus on the situation in Iran, adding that the ballot deadlines in various primary states necessitated his announcing his candidacy. But, he declared, "My campaign travels must be, for a time, postponed. While the crisis continues, I must be present to define and to lead our response to an ever-changing situation of the greatest sensitivity and importance." Carter declined to attend a fundraising dinner that night at a nearby hotel because, in the words of his press secretary, he "simply felt his presence there would not be appropriate under the circumstances." He also canceled plans for an early campaign blitz of speeches and fundraising appearances in New York, New England, Chicago, Atlanta, and Austin, sending First Lady Rosalynn Carter, Vice President Walter Mondale, and other surrogates in his stead. The president's decision to minimize his political involvement did not stop his supporters from focusing on the upcoming election, as 2,800 dinners were held that night in various parts of the country to herald the beginning of the campaign.[33]

Two months later, Carter gave voice to his desire both to tend to the ongoing crisis and to focus exclusively on his role as a unifying national leader instead of taking part in political events:

What I have tried to forgo—and on some stretches of days what I have had to forgo—is the involvement of myself as a clearly identifiable, partisan campaigner, as a substitute for the President of our country. There have been times when I could not have left here had I wanted to, and there have been other times when I have felt that I needed to have a nonpartisan support for me as President. I think if I should change into a highly partisan campaigner, there would be a sense of belief among the American people that the intense interest in the American hostages, for instance, had been decreased.... I have left open the option of going from Washington when my presence here could be spared. But even then I would not want to go to a fundraising event for myself, or to participate in a strictly partisan event, until I consider the alleviation of these crises to be adequate.[34]

This pledge meant that Carter would forgo much of the party-building efforts his fellow Democrats expected from him, as well as the campaigning many thought necessary in the 1980 presidential nominating process to fend off a primary challenge from Senator Ted Kennedy of Massachusetts. Indeed, it would be another two and a half months before Carter would attend a political fundraiser and resume his party-building activities. When he addressed a Democratic Congressional Campaign Committee dinner in Washington, DC, on March 26, 1980, he did not discuss the coming elections and soon returned to his practice of avoiding partisan campaign activity in spite of pressure from some in his party to return to the campaign trail.[35]

Carter would yield on May 29, 1979, when he made his initial and final campaign trip of the 1980 nominating season, holding three rallies and two fundraisers to benefit the Carter-Mondale campaign in Ohio in advance of its key primary the following week. Addressing a crowd in Columbus after a period of six months in which he had refrained from political travel, he declared, "It's overwhelming to see this crowd here today. I've been waiting a long time for this moment."[36] As the hostage crisis stretched on and on, Carter further relaxed his self-imposed prohibition on electoral activities. As table 3.1 indicates, he headlined thirty-six fundraisers in 1980—four for his own reelection campaign, nineteen for the Democratic National Committee, and eight for state or local parties, whose electoral efforts would also help the president's prospects that fall. Additionally, he held three fundraisers for House candidates but did not attend any that year for Senate or gubernatorial candidates. While Carter's biggest fundraising beneficiary in 1980 was the DNC, those efforts would help both the national party and his reelection campaign. With his own date to face the voters approaching, Carter did little other fundraising for his fellow Democrats.

Carter's party-building activities mostly match Galvin's predation model. With the exception of modest party fundraising in 1978, Carter did relatively little to boost the fortunes of his party's candidates. In total, 57.7 percent of Carter's fund-raising efforts were devoted to the Democratic National Committee and to state and local parties. Both the timing of these events and the geography of the fund-raising for state and local parties suggest that Carter was trying to help his own reelection as much as, if not more than, help his fellow Democrats. Of the twenty-six fundraisers Carter headlined for the DNC, nineteen were in 1980, when a well-funded national party would help Carter's prospects in the fall. Of the twenty-three fundraisers Carter held for state and local parties, eighteen of them were in states in which Carter had won or lost the two-party vote in 1976 by under 8 percent, and of those, ten were in states that Carter had won or lost by 2.2 percent or less. Of the five fundraisers for state and local parties held in states that were not electorally competitive for Carter in the 1976 general election, one was in New Hampshire, a key state in the nominating process. Carter's fundraising for other Democrats often seemed to have an electoral benefit for the president himself as well.

Carter's behavior fits with the conventional wisdom among many political practitioners and observers that he was not a party man, and that his actions were typical of—and indeed helped to shape the expectation of—the weak ties between presidents and parties that we could expect to see in the era of the plebiscitary nominating system. A president who saw little threat to his party's majority status made relatively modest efforts to fundraise for his fellow party members. Carter himself summed up his party building well when he said in 1982, "My relationship with the Democratic Party was not particularly good and I could have done more had I made it a higher priority. It was not a burning commitment or interest of mine, and I think in the long run it was costly."[37]

RONALD REAGAN: FUNDRAISING FOR PARTY, NOT SELF

When Ronald Reagan defeated Jimmy Carter to win the presidency in 1980, he led a ticket that saw more congressional success than the party had experienced for decades. The Republicans retook control of the Senate for the first time since the 1954 elections, holding 53 of the chamber's 100 seats, and while the Democrats retained their majority in the House of Representatives, that majority shrunk to 242 seats.[38] A president's party usually gains seats in Congress in a presidential election year, averaging pickups of 15.5 House seats and 2.2 Senate seats in the twenty presidential elections between 1932 and 2008. The Republican gains in both chambers made 1980 a particularly good year for the party of the winning presidential candidate. Reagan was incentivized to protect his party's newly won Senate majority, and doing so would be one of his primary party-building focuses as president.

Table 3.2: Ronald Reagan's First-Term Fundraisers, by
Beneficiary and Year of Term

	Year 1	Year 2	Year 3	Year 4	Total	Percentage
State party	9	7	10	3	29	36.3
Senate campaign	0	12	10	2	24	30.0
Gubernatorial campaign	1	9	2	0	12	15.0
Joint House-Senate event	0	2	1	1	4	5.0
National committee	0	1	1	2	4	5.0
House campaign	0	2	1	0	3	3.8
Other	0	2	0	1	3	3.8
Multiple beneficiaries	0	1	0	0	1	1.3
President	0	0	0	0	0	0.0
Total	10	36	25	9	80	100.0

Source: Data compiled by the author from the *Public Papers of the Presidents* and from Associated
Press articles.

A Focus on the Senate and State Parties

Ronald Reagan was a more enthusiastic party builder than Jimmy Carter through
his first three years in office, though he held remarkably few fundraisers during his
reelection year of 1984. Reagan's 1981 fundraising efforts got off to a delayed start,
as explained in chapter 2, because of the assassination attempt in late March of that
year. In spite of the fact that he spent several months recovering from his wounds,
he still attended ten fundraisers that year, twice as many as a healthy Jimmy Carter
had headlined four years earlier. Nine of these were for the benefit of Republican
state parties—three in California and the other six in Illinois, Louisiana, New Jersey, New York, Texas, and Ohio. Reagan headlined an additional seven fundraisers
for state parties in 1982, making them the biggest beneficiary of his fundraising
efforts in his first two years in office. Throughout his first term, he consistently
boosted state Republican parties, holding more fundraisers for them than for any
other category of beneficiary in three of his four years, as table 3.2 shows.

   Reagan's aides designed a 1982 campaign strategy focused on Senate races. A
White House staffer explained, "Our top priority is to maintain the Senate because
that gives us at least one house [of Congress] where we can move forward with our
legislative program."[39] An internal White House memorandum from Richard S.
Beal in the Office of Planning and Evaluation to top Reagan aides Edwin Meese,
James Baker, and Michael Deaver laid out a proposed "1982 Presidential Targeting
Strategy" that anticipated that the historical trend of the president's party losing
congressional seats in the midterm elections would hold. Beal contended, "Based

on past results, it is almost certain that the GOP will lose a significant number of House and Senate seats. . . . It is possible to negate the normal mid-term election trend by a careful allocation of [the president's] resources and a pro-active strategy."[40] This strategy led to Reagan attending thirty-six fundraisers in 1982—seven more than Jimmy Carter did in 1978—twelve of which were for Senate campaigns.

While Reagan held the most fundraisers for Senate races in 1982, he spent very little time helping Republican candidates for the House of Representatives. The only time that year that he devoted a day to campaigning for just one House member was his trip to Peoria, Illinois, on October 19 to raise money for the leader of Republicans in the House of Representatives, Bob Michel, and to visit a nearby farm. In a high-profile race that was seen across the country as a referendum on the president's economic policies, a White House aide said, "It would be an important symbol if anything happened to Michel," who had been at the forefront of the push for Reagan's agenda in the House.[41] On October 26, 1982, Reagan made another of his few efforts for House candidates when he made a rare campaign trip to a state with no Senate race, and with no statewide race at all, for that matter. In North Carolina that day, Reagan headlined a fundraiser, spoke at a political rally at which he made the case for all the Republican House candidates in the state, and held a ceremony granting the Medal of Freedom to Kate Smith, a singer, for her work selling war bonds during World War II. It was Reagan's only political trip to the Deep South during the 1982 campaign season, despite his substantial popularity there—one news account noted that his speech at the rally was interrupted by applause more than forty times.[42]

One White House aide said that Reagan's 1982 efforts would take him to places where he had strong support and there were races close enough that the president's visit might put the candidate over the top.[43] Specifically, his advisers said in September that Reagan's primary focus would be on races in which Republicans on the ballot led or trailed their Democratic candidates by 1 percent or less.[44] The president concentrated on Senate campaigns in the West and Southwest, where his aides believed he could make the biggest difference. Said one White House official, "The president going to New York is not a major story. The president going to Montana is a major story. We want him to go into states where he will have impact."[45] Reagan by and large stayed away from Rust Belt states with high unemployment. As a spokesperson for the Democratic National Committee, Bob Neuman, put it, Reagan avoided states where his efforts could have hurt more than helped, "So he wound his way around the Rocky Mountains for days on end."[46]

Reagan worked to support his fellow Republicans in part because both his supporters and opponents acknowledged that the election results would be interpreted as a reflection of the president's political standing. In June 1982, the executive director of the Democratic National Committee, Gene Eidenberg, made the case that "we are likely to have a referendum on whether the policies associated with this administration are working." Beal, in his memorandum to Meese, Baker, and Deaver, concurred, arguing, "Regardless of the results of the 1982 election, President Reagan will be evaluated and judged on the basis of the outcome. Therefore, it is essential to anticipate and appreciate the possible outcomes, their consequences, their probability of occurrence, and what the President might do to affect the results."[47] White House political director Ed Rollins made a similar case publicly, saying, "The debate is very clear, the issues are very clear. There is no question that we are going to be held accountable for the fate of the economy."[48] The results of the midterm elections were indeed seen as a referendum on Reagan's record, and while the outcomes in Senate races were satisfactory from the president's perspective, those in the House were not. The Republicans increased their Senate majority to 55 seats, but saw the Democrats' majority in the House swell upward again, as they won 269 seats to the Republicans' 166.[49]

In Reagan's third year, he continued his pattern of headlining more fundraisers than had Jimmy Carter. Of his twenty-five money-raising events that year, ten were for Senate campaigns and ten were for Republican state parties. Additionally he raised funds for two gubernatorial races, headlined an annual joint House-Senate fundraising dinner, and attended one fundraiser for the Republican National Committee and one for a House member from Santa Barbara, California, near Reagan's ranch that served as his Western White House. Reagan's fundraising activities in his reelection year were quite limited. As explained in chapter 2, he did not appear at any fundraisers for the Reagan-Bush '84 campaign committee in large part because the fundraising efforts of the direct mail operation and those spearheaded by Vice President Bush were so successful that the campaign stopped soliciting funds in May 1984.[50] He attended only nine fundraisers in 1984—two for Senate campaigns, three for state parties, two for the RNC, one for a Republican women's group, and the annual joint House-Senate fundraising dinner. While his time was not consumed with his own reelection fundraising, he also did not invest much time in 1984 in raising money for his fellow party members.

Reagan's fundraising demonstrates that he was a party builder in his first three years in office. His two highest priorities were races for the U.S. Senate and state Republican parties. Unlike Carter, the timing and geography of his fundraising do not suggest direct self-interest as a motive for Reagan's fundraising. While Carter held the most fundraisers in his reelection year, Reagan held the fewest in the year when he would face the voters, instead devoting more time to helping his fellow Republicans financially in his first three years than had Carter. Unlike Carter's, Reagan's fundraisers for state parties were not predominantly in key electoral states for the next presidential contest. Of Reagan's twenty-nine first-term fundraisers for state parties, only thirteen were in states that Reagan had won or lost by under

10 percent in 1980. Reagan's focus on raising money for state parties matched his policy priorities—he was committed to helping the GOP at the state level, just as he spoke over and over again about the importance of returning more power in the area of public policy to the states. His focus on Senate races reflected his strong desire to avoid losses substantial enough to return that body to Democratic control.

Reagan's Second Term—Losing the Senate, Electing His Vice President

In 1984, Ronald Reagan was reelected in a landslide, as he carried every state except Minnesota, the home state of Democratic nominee Walter Mondale, as well as the District of Columbia. His sweeping success was accompanied by gains in the House, where the Republicans increased their numbers to 182 members to the Democrats' 253, as well as losses in the Senate, where the Republican majority shrunk to 53 seats.[51] With his own reelection no longer a question, Reagan devoted even more time in his second term to party-building efforts, as he labored in vain to preserve his party's Senate majority but succeeded in helping elect his vice president to the Oval Office.

Reagan resumed his party-building efforts in his second term, headlining twenty fundraisers in his fifth year in office, as depicted in table 3.3. His focus in 1985 and 1986 was again the Senate, as forty of the sixty-seven fundraisers he headlined in those two years were for Senate campaigns. In 1986, Republicans faced a challenging electoral landscape due in large part to their success six years earlier when they won control of the Senate for the first time since 1954. The large crop of newly elected Senate Republicans from 1980 would have to face the voters in their first reelection bid in 1986. The Republicans' success in 1980 provided many potential targets for the Democrats. Of the thirty-four Senate seats up that year, Republicans held twenty-two, a daunting number to defend.[52]

As Reagan raised funds for GOP candidates across the South in the summer of 1986, his explicit goal was party building. "This trip is part of our ongoing effort to build a strong GOP in the South—it's quite a dominant theme," explained Mitch Daniels, head of Reagan's White House Office of Political Affairs, who made the case that the president had both short- and long-term goals for the trip. "Obviously, we're fixed on the Senate races—nothing's more important—but in terms of the next five to 10 years, it could be that what is most important is what happens in the gubernatorial races." This July trip would consist of events in Texas, Florida, and South Carolina, and in each Reagan would headline a fundraiser to help his party build up the resources it would need to wage an effective campaign.[53]

Table 3.3: Ronald Reagan's Second-Term Fundraisers, by
Beneficiary and Year of Term

	Year 5	Year 6	Year 7	Year 8	Total	Percentage
Senate campaign	15	25	2	12	54	54.0
State party	3	9	2	11	25	25.0
Gubernatorial campaign	1	9	1	1	12	12.0
Joint House-Senate event	1	2	1	1	5	5.0
National committee	0	0	0	1	1	1.0
House campaign	0	1	0	1	2	2.0
Other	0	0	0	0	0	0.0
Multiple beneficiaries	0	1	0	0	1	1.0
President	0	0	0	0	0	0.0
Vice president	0	0	0	0	0	0.0
Total	20	47	6	27	100	100.0

Source: Data compiled by the author from the *Public Papers of the Presidents* and from Associated Press articles.

In addition to the forty fundraisers that Reagan headlined in 1985 and 1986 to help Senate candidates, an additional three were joint House-Senate fundraising events. Twelve were for state parties, ten were for candidates in governor's races, and one additional event was a joint fundraiser for the Senate and gubernatorial candidates in Florida. Reagan's final fundraiser in that election cycle was a gala to support the reelection campaigns of twenty-four endangered House members. Reagan asked voters to consider him when they cast their votes in 1986, saying that a Democratic Senate would make him "a six-year president." He contended that if people would "like to vote for me one last time," they should support Republican Senate candidates.[54] Though Reagan had clearly demonstrated his personal commitment to helping his party's candidates for office, his efforts fell short, as the Democrats retook control of the Senate that fall, by a margin of 55 seats to the GOP's 45, and expanded their margin in the House, winning 258 seats to the Republicans' 177.[55]

In Reagan's seventh year in office, he headlined only six fundraisers, the lowest total of his presidency. He also traveled less in 1987 than in any other year of his presidency except 1981, as he spent much of the year dealing with the fallout from the unraveling Iran-Contra scandal.[56] Of these six fundraisers, two were for Senate campaigns, two for state parties, one for a governor's race, and one was the annual joint House-Senate fundraising dinner. In Reagan's last year in office, however, he ramped back up his fundraising efforts, attending twenty-seven events. Of these, twelve were for Senate campaigns and eleven were for state parties. While Reagan did not headline a fundraiser that directly benefited the Bush-Quayle campaign, he was committed to helping his vice president win election to the presidency. He and Bush did jointly attend Republican Party fundraisers during the campaign, and many of the fundraisers Reagan headlined for state parties were in states that were important to Bush's reelection strategy. Newspaper articles called Reagan's commitment to help the GOP unprecedented for an outgoing president at the end of his second term. Bush's campaign manager, Lee Atwater, commented of Reagan, "He'll be a great surrogate," particularly throughout the Southwest and in California.[57] One newspaper account estimated that Reagan traveled 25,000 miles and headlined fundraisers that took in $10 million to help elect Bush. On the day before the election, he made his pitch by saying, "If I could ask you one last time, tomorrow, when mountains greet the dawn, will you go out there and win one for the Gipper?"[58] His efforts would help George H. W. Bush to become the first sitting vice president to be elected directly to the presidency since Martin Van Buren in 1836.[59]

With the exception of 1987, Reagan was a dedicated party builder throughout his second term. His 100 second-term fundraisers exceeded the 80 he headlined in his first term, and in three of the four years of his second term, his fundraising totals were greater than the number from the corresponding year in his first term. As in his first term, he headlined the most fundraisers in the midterm election year, not the presidential election year. His priorities within the party during his second term were similar to those in his first term, but with an even greater focus on Senate races. He worked to help elect Vice President Bush to succeed him, though his fundraising efforts for the cause were held for state parties and the national GOP. Over Reagan's eight years as president, he spent more than 73 percent of his fundraising efforts working on behalf of state parties and Senate candidates in an effort to hold the majority that Republicans had won in that chamber in 1980, and that they would surrender again to the Democrats in 1986. In stark contrast to Carter, whose biggest beneficiary was the Democratic National Committee, Reagan held only five fundraisers for the Republican National Committee in his eight years in office.

Reagan's patterns of party building belie the notion that presidents elected under the plebiscitary nominating system will be party predators who have weak ties to their parties. While Reagan was a Washington outsider who had challenged a sitting president of his own party for the Republican presidential nomination in 1976, when he arrived in Washington as president he showed much greater commitment than had Jimmy Carter to strengthening his party through his fundraising efforts. Much of his fundraising was driven by the very real threat of losing the Republicans' newly won control of the Senate. Reagan's patterns of fundraising are consistent with Galvin's story of Republicans as party builders dedicated to trying to win and maintain control of the Congress and strengthen the GOP at the state level.

GEORGE H. W. BUSH: THE STATES, THE SENATE, AND SELF

When George H. W. Bush assumed the presidency in 1989, he looked down Pennsylvania Avenue and saw a Congress controlled entirely by Democrats. While Bush had captured the White House, Democrats had expanded their margin in the House to 260 seats to the Republicans' 185, and they had maintained a 55–45 edge in the Senate.[60] As Bush sought to bring the Republicans back to power, he turned his focus to the states, as the impending 1990 census and subsequent reapportionment and redistricting of districts for the House of Representatives provided a substantial potential opportunity for the GOP.

Record-Breaking Party Building in Pursuit of Redistricting Gains

Like Reagan, George H. W. Bush's fundraising shows that he was a party builder, not a party predator. His 137 fundraisers exceeded Carter's 85, as well as Reagan's first-term total of 80 and his second-term total of 100, and Bush's 87 fundraisers over his first two years were greater than the totals from the first two years of a first term of each president in this study. As did Reagan, Bush devoted the most time to fundraising during his midterm election year, and, as table 3.4 indicates, like Reagan, two of his top priorities were state parties and Senate campaigns. But Bush dedicated the most time to governor's races, as he aimed to help the GOP have a greater say in the upcoming redistricting process. Overall, Bush had a relatively even spread among his three top priorities, devoting just over 20 percent each of his fundraisers to gubernatorial campaigns, to state parties, and to Senate races.

In 1989, Bush headlined eighteen party fundraisers, more than triple the five that Carter took part in during 1977 and almost double the 10 that Reagan attended in 1981. Six were for Senate campaigns, three for governor's races, three for state parties, and three for House campaigns. Another was the annual GOP joint House-Senate fundraising gala, and the final two were for two local races in New York, including one for mayoral candidate Rudy Giuliani. In 1990 Bush ramped up the pace even more, when his sixty-nine fundraisers more than doubled Carter's twenty-nine in his second year, and almost doubled Reagan's 1982 total of thirty-six. Bush's number of fundraisers would have been even higher had it not been for

Table 3.4: George H. W. Bush's Fundraisers, by Beneficiary and
Year of Term

	Year 1	Year 2	Year 3	Year 4	Total	Percentage
Gubernatorial campaign	3	28	2	0	33	24.1
State party	3	22	3	4	32	23.4
Senate campaign	6	10	7	5	28	20.4
President	0	0	4	15	19	13.9
House campaign	3	4	1	0	8	5.8
National committee	0	0	0	5	5	3.6
Joint House-Senate event	1	2	1	1	5	3.6
Other	2	1	0	2	5	3.6
Multiple beneficiaries	0	2	0	0	2	1.5
Total	18	69	18	32	137	100.0

Source: Data compiled by the author from the Public Papers of the Presidents and from Associated
Press articles.

the contentious budget debates in the fall of 1990 that led him to cancel at least
two fundraisers to focus on the negotiations in Washington. A spokesman for the
Republican National Committee made the case that the hotly contested budget
talks would not keep the president completely off the campaign trail. "I don't think
that was ever in doubt. It's the way the man is. He's available to do anything and
everything that makes sense [to help the GOP in the midterm elections]."[61]

The White House's aim for the president's campaigning in 1990 centered
around "plans to do more fundraising for other candidates than any president
in history." One aide discussed the president's schedule for the summer of 1990
and said that Bush would spend twenty-five days on the road for political events.
Explained a White House spokeswoman, "That's really 50 events, since we try to
do two every day." These plans were just the preliminary ones, as they did not include the president's even more aggressive campaign schedule for the two months
directly preceding the election. The spokeswoman said that the president's focus
would be Senate and governor's races, with relatively little time spent on House
campaigns.[62]

Fifty of Bush's record-setting sixty-nine fundraisers in the second year of
his term benefited governor's races (twenty-eight fundraisers) and state parties
(twenty-two), as he aimed to give the GOP a greater say in the upcoming redistricting process following the decennial census. The most important targets were
three states that were expected to gain substantial numbers of seats in the House
of Representatives through the reapportionment process—California, Florida, and
Texas. All three had Republican governors in 1990, and the president very much
wanted to keep the GOP in control of each statehouse in that fall's elections.[63]

The biggest prize was California, which was estimated to receive seven additional House seats. Democrats there controlled both chambers of the state legislature, but GOP senator Pete Wilson was making a gubernatorial bid to succeed the outgoing Republican governor. If Wilson lost, Democrats would be able to engineer a single-party gerrymander to maximize their advantage in the map of new congressional districts that would be in place for the next decade. Ed Rogers, who directed the White House Office of Political Affairs, said of California, "It is the mother lode of congressional seats," adding that electing Wilson "is the number one target" for the GOP.[64] In 1990, seven of the twenty-eight gubernatorial fundraisers Bush headlined were for Wilson, and four of the twenty-two events for state parties were for the benefit of the California GOP. In a speech at a May 1990 fundraiser in Dallas, Bush made the case that fundraising and campaigning were all the more important given the upcoming round of redistricting. He argued, "We have to win in 1990. If we don't, once again the opposition will gerrymander fair representation right out the window and into thin air."[65]

Unlike Reagan in 1986, Bush did not actively seek to make himself an issue in the 1990 campaigns. While Reagan had stumped in 1986 by making the case that if the Democrats took control of the Senate, it would make him "a six-year president" and that voters should support GOP candidates if they would "like to vote for me one last time," Bush made no such requests of the voters, instead talking about the candidates he supported and the policy positions they held.[66] One contributing factor was likely the unpopularity among Republican voters of the budget deal that Bush struck that fall with the Democratic Congress. The deficit reduction package included a mix of spending cuts and tax increases, which violated the memorable pledge Bush had made at the 1988 Republican National Convention, "Read my lips, no new taxes."[67] Bush's commitment to party building led him to campaign for those party members who supported him on big policy questions and those who did not. Two beneficiaries of his campaign help included a senator who deemed the budget deal a "turkey" and another Senate candidate who compared the tax increases to "a mugging." Bush downplayed these disagreements by contending that if there were more GOP members of Congress, they could avoid having to strike budget deals like this one.[68]

The 87 fundraisers that Bush headlined in 1989 and 1990 brought in an estimated $90 million for GOP campaigns, a remarkable total that demonstrated the commitment to party building of this former chair of the Republican National Committee.[69] In spite of Bush's record-breaking fundraising for his fellow Republicans, Democrats increased their majority in the Senate to 56 seats out of 100, and their total in the House swelled to 267 seats.[70] Democrats also won the governor's races in two of the states most important to Bush, Florida and Texas. But the president helped his single highest priority to achieve victory, as Pete Wilson was elected to be California's governor, ensuring that the GOP would have an important seat at the table drawing the Golden State's new congressional district lines after the upcoming reapportionment of congressional seats.[71]

The Reelection Bid Becomes the Primary Focus

Bush's total of eighteen fundraisers in 1991 would likely have been higher had it not been for the Persian Gulf War and the economic downturn that year. In 1990, Bush had defended his continuing political activity while tensions escalated in the Middle East. He addressed the question head-on when he spoke at a GOP fundraiser in Rhode Island on August 20, 1990. He shared with the crowd that a reporter on the flight up from Washington had asked him, "Well, don't you feel a little funny going to a political event at this time?" Bush explained his response, saying:

> And I knew exactly why the question was asked, and I certainly respect it. But life goes on, and we have an election coming up in the fall. And I think it's important that I conduct my duties of the presidency in the best way I possibly can. But you can't exclude the fact that there's a lot of things happening. And a lot of it gets right back to the kind of elected officials that we're going to have in the future. And so, I didn't think about changing this event.[72]

During a September 1990 political trip to the West Coast, Bush had told Republicans at a fundraiser for gubernatorial candidate Pete Wilson, "We will not allow our political life to be held hostage to a crisis. . . . We will vigorously campaign right up to the November election. For those of us at home, we can serve our country by being the best candidates, the best citizens and, yes, the best Republicans and Democrats we can be."[73] But in early 1991, with troops in harm's way, Bush did not attend any fundraisers; his first one that year would be in late May. Dave Carney, who headed Bush's White House Office of Political Affairs, later explained, "There's just something unseemly about raising money for partisan purposes when you're engaged in an act of war or an economic recovery."[74]

Bush, who had devoted himself to party building in a record-setting fashion during his first two years in office, did so to a far lesser degree as his own reelection bid intensified. The president began fundraising for his own reelection campaign in late 1991, as four of his eighteen fundraisers that year benefited the Bush-Quayle reelection committee. His efforts helped his campaign take in more than $10 million that year.[75] Of the thirty-two fundraisers Bush took part in during 1992, fifteen were for his reelection committee and another five were for the Republican National Committee. Interestingly, Bush, a former RNC chair, did not headline a single fundraiser for the national committee until his last year in office. One reason that Bush did so little party building in 1992 is that his own reelection fundraising progressed much more slowly than anticipated. His campaign had aimed to follow the lead of Reagan, whose campaign had quickly raised the maximum allowed under law to those participating in the public funding program. When Bush took part in his first reelection fundraiser on October 31, 1991, his aides talked of an early flurry of activity to raise $30 million, commenting, "We want to be able to get out of the field before the others get in."[76] Bush's plummeting popularity and the surprisingly strong challenge he received from Pat Buchanan complicated this plan. As a result, Bush was still personally participating in Bush-Quayle fundraising events through the end of May 1992.

Of Bush's fifty fundraisers in his last two years in office, almost half were devoted to his own campaign (nineteen) or the national party (five), whose efforts would help the Bush-Quayle ticket. Senate campaigns were Bush's next biggest focus in 1991 and 1992, as the president headlined twelve events to help candidates for the upper chamber of the national legislature. Additionally, Bush held seven fundraisers for state parties, headlined two joint House-Senate fundraising galas, and attended two for governor's races, one for a House member, and two closed press events for unspecified GOP beneficiaries.

In Bush's first two years in office, he exceeded both Carter's and Reagan's party-building efforts, as he attended more fundraisers in the midterm election year of 1990 than in his other three years in office combined. Like Reagan, his second year was his most active fundraising year, and like Carter, his focus during his last two years was primarily his own reelection. As Reagan did, Bush held far more fundraisers for state parties than for the Republican National Committee, for which he raised money only in 1992. His three biggest beneficiaries were governor's races, state parties, and Senate campaigns. Of Bush's thirty-two fundraisers for state parties, sixteen were in states that he had won or lost by less than 8 percent in 1988. Three more were in the key nominating states of Iowa and New Hampshire, and an additional two were in the perennial battleground state of Ohio, so his efforts for the state GOP in these states would likely help him in his own reelection campaign as well.

In his first two years, Bush was a record-setting party builder, as his aides touted the most extensive presidential midterm fundraising campaign in history. But as his own reelection bid consumed much of his attention, his efforts for his fellow Republicans waned. His work to help win governor's races and to aid state parties would bear fruit, as the gains Republicans made in the redistricting process following the 1990 census would set them up for historic gains in the House of Representatives in 1994, two years after Bush was defeated at the polls by the then governor of Arkansas, Bill Clinton.

BILL CLINTON: AN UNPRECEDENTED PARTY BUILDER

When Bill Clinton took office, he, like every Democratic president who had served since John F. Kennedy in the early 1960s, enjoyed united party government in Washington. Democrats controlled the House by a wide 258 to 176 margin, and the Senate with 57 of 100 seats.[77]

With majorities this large, few imagined that just two years into Clinton's term, the political landscape in Washington would change in a way that it had not for four decades.

A First-Term Focus on Party, Then Self

Bill Clinton dedicated himself substantially to helping his fellow Democrats in the first two years of his term at a pace that exceeded that of both Carter and Reagan, though his sixty-three fundraisers in 1993 and 1994 were shy of George H. W. Bush's record of eighty-seven in his first two years. Clinton's focus on Senate races, which benefited from twenty-six of his sixty-three fundraisers in 1993 and 1994, was greater than that of Carter, Reagan, or Bush in their first two years, and his twelve events for the Democratic National Committee far exceeded the totals for each of his three predecessors in their first two years. As table 3.5 indicates, Clinton held only five fundraisers for state parties, signaling the beginning of a shift from supporting state parties to the national party committee that would characterize Clinton and his successors. Clinton, the former governor, held nine fundraisers for Democratic gubernatorial candidates, about on a par with former governors Carter and Reagan, but well shy of Bush's thirty-one fundraisers for governors in 1989 and 1990 on the eve of the redistricting process.

Clinton's efforts were not rewarded at the ballot box in 1994. Like every president before him since Franklin Roosevelt in 1934, his party lost House seats in the midterm elections. But unlike any Democratic president since Harry Truman, he lost control of both chambers of Congress. Republicans won 230 seats in the House, marking the first time they had held a majority there since the 1954 elections. They took the Senate, too, holding 52 seats after Election Day 1994 and gaining another 2 by March 1995, as two Democrats switched parties. After forty long years in the wilderness since they had last held majorities in both chambers of Congress during the first two years of the Eisenhower administration, the Republican victories shook Washington like an earthquake.[78]

In 1995 and 1996, Clinton turned much of his attention to fundraising that would benefit his reelection bid directly or indirectly. He began to hold events for the Clinton-Gore campaign earlier than Bush had done for his reelection cam-

Table 3.5: Bill Clinton's First-Term Fundraisers, by Beneficiary
and Year of Term

	Year 1	Year 2	Year 3	Year 4	Total	Percentage
National committee	5	7	2	49	63	37.7
Senate campaign	5	19	2	8	34	20.4
State party	0	5	5	5	15	9.0
President	0	0	13	1	14	8.4
House campaign	1	3	0	8	12	7.2
Gubernatorial campaign	1	8	1	2	12	7.2
Other	2	4	1	2	9	5.4
Multiple beneficiaries	1	0	0	5	6	3.6
Joint House-Senate event	1	1	0	0	2	1.2
Vice president	0	0	0	0	0	0.0
Total	16	47	24	80	167	100.0

Source: Data compiled by the author from the *Public Papers of the Presidents* and from Associated Press articles.

paign committee four years before, and he held thirteen of his fourteen reelection fundraisers in 1995, while most of Bush's reelection fundraising took place in the fourth year of his term. Like Carter, Clinton spent the most time fundraising in his reelection year, when he particularly ramped up his DNC fundraising. His total of forty-nine events for the national committee in 1992 exceeded the total reelection year fundraising of each of his three predecessors. Clinton and the Democrats took unprecedented advantage of the soft money loophole, which allowed national parties to evade contribution limits and instead raise money in unlimited quantities that could be used for party-building activities such as get-out-the-vote drives and issue-based television advertisements. These efforts would help both the Clinton-Gore campaign and down-ticket Democratic candidates. Clinton also held ten fundraisers for Senate races, another ten for state parties, eight for House races, and three for governor's campaigns in 1995 and 1996. While Clinton certainly was not ignoring his fellow party members, he rarely made appeals on the basis of their shared party name. In his lengthy 1996 convention speech, he referred to the Democrats regaining power in Congress just once. At campaign appearances with fellow Democrats, he avoided mentioning their common party label. Even as Clinton raised money for his fellow party members, he was attempting to remain above the partisan fray.[79]

Like some of his predecessors, Clinton was strategic about his state party fundraising efforts. Of the fifteen state party fundraisers he headlined in his first term, eleven were in states in which he had won or lost the two-party vote by under 10 percent in 1992, a list that included the two key nominating states of Iowa and New Hampshire. California, which was essential to Clinton's 1996 reelection strategy, was one of the other four states. When Clinton raised funds for state parties in his first term, he predominantly did so in states in which he had his own electoral interest.

Clinton's first-term fundraising was notable for another reason—the large proportion of fundraisers he held that were not mentioned in the *Public Papers of the Presidents,* many of which were closed to the press. In Bill Clinton's first term, 63 of 167 fundraisers did not appear in the *Public Papers*—a full 38 percent, much higher than Carter's 1 percent, Reagan's 3 and 6 percent, and George H. W. Bush's 12 percent. Journalists at the time reasoned that Clinton did not want to be seen in a tuxedo at high-dollar fundraisers filled with lobbyists. A White House aide explained that it was common practice for presidents not to allow press into fundraisers held in private homes and promised more access in the future.[80] Clinton's second term provided a marked contrast, however, as only 3 percent of his fundraisers did not appear in the *Public Papers.* The shift was largely a result of media pressure for transparency following allegations of fundraising improprieties during his 1996 reelection bid, which are discussed in chapter 6.

Had Bill Clinton served only one term, he would have gone down in history as a president who dedicated substantial time to electing fellow Democrats in his first two years, and then set records for time spent raising money for his own reelection and the national party in his next two. In many ways, his first-term fundraising pattern was similar to that of George H. W. Bush, but with slightly less party building in his first two years and a greater focus on party fundraising in his third and fourth year when it would benefit his own reelection bid. This latter use of the national party appears to fit Galvin's party predator model, as Clinton helped the national committee raise record sums but did so when it would help him to secure a second term in the White House. But Clinton was indeed reelected, and in his second term he would go on to set a staggering pace of unprecedented party-building fundraising.

Party-Building Fundraising Like No President Before or Since

When Bill Clinton became the first Democrat since Franklin Roosevelt to be elected to a second full term as president, he saw his party gain ground in the House, as the number of Republican-held seats dropped to 228, and lose ground in the Senate, where Republicans claimed 55 seats following the 1996 elections.[81] Having secured his reelection, he, like Ronald Reagan, held even more fundraisers than in his first term in an effort to help his fellow party members. But that is about where the similarities end, as Clinton would headline an unprecedented 471 second-term fundraisers, as compared to Carter's 85 over four years, Reagan's 180 over eight years, George H. W. Bush's 137 over four years, and Clinton's 167 in his first term.

The single largest beneficiary of Clinton's record-setting fundraising was the Democratic National Committee, for which Clinton attended 175 second-term fundraisers, followed by 108 for Senate campaigns and 89 for House races—a sharp departure from the practices of past presidents who had not devoted much time or effort to fundraising for House members. Clinton's efforts for governors (31 events) and state parties (23 events) pale in relative comparison to his other fundraising priorities, even though these numbers are in the ballpark of and in some cases exceed the number of fundraisers Carter and Reagan devoted to each type of beneficiary per term; it is only as a proportion of Clinton's overall fundraising efforts that these commitments appear relatively small. Overall, Clinton's focus was overwhelmingly national, as events to benefit the national party and races for the national legislature accounted for almost 80 percent of his record-setting fundraising.

Clinton's unprecedented program of second-term party building can be attributed to several factors: his efforts to help retire the substantial debt of the Democratic National Committee left over from the 1996 election season; a drive to win back control of the House and Senate from the Republicans; his goal of electing Vice President Al Gore to succeed him in the Oval Office; and the unprecedented run by First Lady Hillary Clinton for a U.S. Senate seat in New York. Additionally, Clinton devoted record-setting amounts of time to party fundraising because, in spite of his efforts, the GOP raised more money than did the Democrats. For example, while the Democratic National Committee received $37 million in contributions between April and June 2000, the Republican National Committee took in $36 million in just June of that year alone.[82] White House press secretary Joe Lockhart explained, "Republicans always out-raise Democrats, always have more resources. The president believes it's important that Democrats be as competitive as they can. The president has been willing to take the time to go out and energize Democrats around the country, including those who have the resources to help the party fund the elections."[83]

Clinton's love of politicking played a role in his prodigious fundraising efforts as well. At a fundraiser in August 1998, he expressed a desire to run for a third term if he could. "If it weren't for the 22nd Amendment, I'd give the American people another chance to elect or defeat me because I believe in what we're doing," he declared. Many observers cited Clinton's enjoyment of fundraising. Stephen Hess, a former aide to President Dwight D. Eisenhower and a presidential scholar, said of Clinton's fundraising, "He is absolutely phenomenal and unique. He is simply very good at it. He's a man of compulsions. This is one of them. No other president enjoyed it as much as he did." An official from the public interest group Common

Table 3.6: Bill Clinton's Second-Term Fundraisers, by
Beneficiary and Year of Term

	Year 5	Year 6	Year 7	Year 8	Total	Percentage
National committee	48	40	41	46	175	37.2
Senate campaign	14	20	13	61	108	22.9
House campaign	5	18	11	55	89	18.9
Gubernatorial campaign	5	13	3	10	31	6.6
State or local party	3	5	4	11	23	4.9
Multiple beneficiaries	0	13	2	4	19	4.0
Other	2	2	3	6	13	2.8
President	0	0	0	0	0	0.0
Joint House-Senate event	0	0	8	1	9	1.9
Vice president	0	0	4	0	4	0.8
Total	77	111	89	194	471	100.0

Source: Data compiled by the author from the *Public Papers of the Presidents* and from Associated Press articles.

Cause concurred, saying, "The remarkable thing about Bill Clinton is that he seems to enjoy fundraising, he seems to sort of relish in it. He is just a master of the art."[84]

As table 3.6 illustrates, in 1997 and 1998 Clinton held 188 fundraisers, 88 of which were for the Democratic National Committee. Contrast those numbers with those of Jimmy Carter, who had made news when he committed to 5 fundraisers for the DNC in 1978 and then ended up holding only 3 such events. Neither Carter, Reagan, nor Bush devoted much effort to national committee fundraising throughout their term in office. Carter ramped up his efforts for the DNC in his reelection year, as Clinton did in his first term, while Reagan and Bush together headlined 10 RNC fundraisers over their collective twelve years in office. In early 1997, Clinton explained his commitment to retiring the $14.4 million in debt that the DNC had on its books in the wake of the 1996 elections, saying, "I have been doing a lot and I will do more. . . . we're just going to have to work double hard now to pay the money back and we'll do that."[85]

Clinton headlined 34 fundraisers for Senate races and 23 for House races in the first two years of his second term, in addition to 13 Unity '98 events, which benefited jointly the Democratic National Committee, the Democratic Senatorial Campaign Committee, and the Democratic Congressional Campaign Committee. His 111 events in 1998 came during the Monica Lewinsky scandal, which would eventually lead to Clinton's impeachment in December 1998 and acquittal by the Senate in early 1999. Clinton raised money at such an unprecedented pace in part because his policy priorities would be more likely to pass if Democrats retook control of Congress. His additional incentive, of course, was that a Democratic Congress would be far less likely to pursue impeachment proceedings against him. One anonymous Democrat, referring to the party's leader in the House, Dick Gephardt, who would be in line to become Speaker of the House if the Democrats took control, summed up these dynamics, saying, "Speaker Gephardt would change the complexion on Capitol Hill."[86]

Clinton's efforts in 1998 did not win back control of Congress for the Democrats, but he did help to buck the historical trend of the president's party losing seats in midterm elections. There was no gain or loss of seats in the Senate; in the House, the Democrats actually gained seats, cutting the Republican majority to 223 members, just 5 above the magic number of 218 needed to control the chamber. This marked the first time the president's party had picked up seats in the House in a midterm election since 1934.[87] Many analysts attributed the Democrats' success to the voters' reaction to Republican efforts to impeach Clinton. While this may be true, it is certain that Clinton's prodigious efforts in 1998, in which he headlined a record number of fundraisers, helped provide Democratic candidates with the financial resources they needed to run competitive campaigns.

Clinton's 188 fundraisers in 1997 and 1998 exceeded the single-term totals of Carter and George H. W. Bush, as well as the two-term number of fundraisers headlined by Reagan. But even Clinton's own record-setting fundraising activity in the first two years of his second term paled next to that during his final two years in office, when he headlined 283 fundraisers—an average of more than 2.5 fundraisers every week. Again, the Democratic National Committee was the chief beneficiary with 87 events, followed by 74 for Senate campaigns and 66 for House campaigns, a much more substantial commitment to House races than Clinton's predecessors had made. In contrast, Carter, Reagan, and Bush collectively head-lined just 21 fundraisers that were exclusively for House campaigns over a period of sixteen years. Clinton's dedication to raising money for House races over a two-year period was more than triple the total commitment of his three predecessors in the Oval Office over a sixteen-year period. The biggest individual beneficiary of Clinton's efforts was his wife's campaign for the U.S. Senate, for which he headlined 37 fundraisers. While Clinton participated in only 4 events exclusively for the Gore campaign, his 87 events for the national committee certainly helped provide many resources for the Gore-Lieberman ticket.

Unlike George H. W. Bush in 1990, Clinton did not devote much attention to governor's races and state parties on the eve of another round of reapportionment and redistricting. A decade earlier, George H. W. Bush had held thirty-one fund-raisers for governor's races and twenty-five for state parties in 1989 and 1990, while Clinton only held thirteen and eight, respectively, in 1999 and 2000. This is sur-prising, given the importance of governor's races and state legislative campaigns to shaping the balance of power in the House of Representatives for the coming decade, but it is not to say that Clinton and the national Democrats did not devote resources to redistricting. Indeed, the national party shared some of its fundraising bounty with state parties. The shift away from direct presidential fundraising for state parties is important. While Carter, Reagan, and George H. W. Bush all made fundraising efforts for state parties one of their higher priorities, Clinton, George W. Bush, and Obama did not. Instead, these latter presidents spent more time raising funds for national party committees, which served partly as a funnel through which much money would flow to other parts of the party.

The nationalization of party fundraising did not always meet the needs of those at the state level. When Clinton traveled to New York City in September 1998 on the night before the Democratic primary that would select the party's challenger to incumbent Senator Alfonse D'Amato, he did not go to help local Democratic candidates there. Instead, he headlined a national party fundraiser at an exclusive performance of the popular play *The Lion King* that would raise an estimated $3.5 million. The chairman of the DNC said that $300,000 from the event would benefit the state party, but New York Democrats complained, worried that party donors would be reluctant to give to the party's newly minted nominee so soon after contributing amounts ranging from $350 to $100,000 to attend the national party fundraiser. The state party chairwoman, Judith Hope, commented, "It's not helpful. It's a source of frustration. The timing here is particularly unfortunate." Said another party member, "Everyone calls New York the ATM state. You come and make your withdrawals, and you leave."[88]

In 2000, Clinton campaigned very little with Gore, though if the choice had been his, he would have done much more for his vice president. Said Gore that year, "We're not going to campaign together, because I'm determined to campaign as my own man and present my own vision." Clinton made clear why Gore felt the need to stand on his own in a radio interview with Tom Joyner, who said to the president, "It would be nice if we could get four more years from you." Clinton's response, that by voting for Vice President Gore, "you can get the next best thing," infuriated the Gore team. The vice president's campaign kept Clinton largely off the stump, but the president did devote himself to party fundraising, yielding by one estimate $105 million for his party's campaigns in the 2000 elections. Clinton's efforts for the DNC were designed in part to make sure that the party had substantial resources to counter attacks by the Bush campaign in the summer of 2000. Because Bush had opted out of public funding, he would not be bound by the nominating season spending caps that would constrain Gore. Clinton did his best to make sure that the DNC could fight as a proxy on behalf of Gore if need be.[89]

After a first term in which his party-building efforts in his first two years gave way to a focus on his own reelection bid, Clinton's willingness to commit his time to party-building fundraising efforts in his second term was unprecedented. As he was the first Democratic president to have lost control of Congress since Harry

Truman, Clinton's fundraising efforts were a response to the threat that a Republican Congress posed to his legislative agenda. While his biggest priorities were the DNC and Senate campaigns, he devoted more effort to House races than had any of his predecessors. Even the segments of the party to which he devoted relatively little effort, such as governor's races and state parties, still benefited in absolute terms at levels similar to those of some of Clinton's predecessors, since he did so much fundraising. Clinton served as president at a time when parties exploited unregulated soft money raised by the national committees to its full potential, and Clinton's fundraising certainly benefited the party, himself, and other Democratic candidates. His efforts represented a nationalization of party fundraising, a trend that his successors would continue.

GEORGE W. BUSH: RECORD FUNDRAISING FOR HIMSELF AND NATIONAL REPUBLICANS

George W. Bush was sworn in as president in January 2001 following a thirty-six-day recount in Florida. The narrow victory he scored there gave him an Electoral College majority and made him only the fourth person to assume the presidency after having lost the popular vote, following in the footsteps of John Quincy Adams in 1824, Rutherford B. Hayes in 1876, and Benjamin Harrison in 1888. The close presidential election was accompanied by slender margins of control on Capitol Hill. Republicans still held the House by a narrow margin, with 221 seats to the Democrats' 212. The Senate was an even split, with 50 seats for the Democrats and 50 seats for the Republicans, who controlled the chamber due to Vice President Dick Cheney's tie-breaking vote in his role as president of the Senate. Thus, Republicans held the White House, Senate, and House for the first time since 1954. In May that year, however, Senator Jim Jeffords of Vermont left the Republican Party and became an independent who caucused with the Democrats, giving them an effective 51-49 majority and control of the chamber.[90] The narrow margins meant that both parties saw the 2002 elections as an opportunity to take or retain control of each chamber, and George W. Bush would play a central role in the Republican efforts to do so.

An Aggressive Midterm Effort and Unprecedented Reelection Fundraising

George W. Bush's first-term fundraising revealed him to be yet another ambitious party builder. While his efforts did not compare with those of Clinton's second

Table 3.7: George W. Bush's First-Term Fundraisers, by
Beneficiary and Year of Term

	Year 1	Year 2	Year 3	Year 4	Total	Percentage
President	0	0	41	16	57	32.9
National committee	1	1	2	27	31	17.9
Senate campaign	3	19	1	4	27	15.6
Gubernatorial campaign	0	23	2	2	27	15.6
House campaign	0	12	0	1	13	7.5
State party	0	8	0	0	8	4.6
Multiple beneficiaries	1	5	0	0	6	3.5
Joint House-Senate event	1	2	0	1	4	2.3
Total	6	70	46	51	173	100.0

Source: Data compiled by the author from the *Public Papers of the Presidents* and from Associated Press articles.

term, Bush's 173 first-term fundraisers exceeded Clinton's first-term total of 167, continuing the upward trend in first-term presidential fundraising. As table 3.7 illustrates, Bush's first-year total of six fundraisers was low, as he did not take part in any fundraising in the fall of that year after the terrorist attacks of September 11, 2001. But his seventy events in 2002 were the largest first-term midterm election year total yet. Like Reagan and George H. W. Bush, the younger President Bush spent the most time fundraising in his second year in office, though he started his reelection fundraising earlier than his predecessors, so most of his efforts there were completed in his third year, leaving him free to fundraise for others in his fourth year.

Bush's top priorities in his first two years were governor's races, for which he held twenty-three fundraisers, and Senate campaigns, which benefited from twenty-two such presidential events, as well as three joint House-Senate galas. On a fundraising trip to Texas in 2002 in support of GOP Senate candidate John Cornyn, Bush declared, "The Senate races are very important to me. I want the Republicans to take control of the Senate."[91] Having enjoyed unified party control on Capitol Hill for a fleeting four months before Jeffords's defection, Bush very much wanted to help his party retake the majority in the Senate and maintain control of the House. His twelve fundraisers just for House members in his first two years in office were more than any other president since Carter had held over a similar period in a first term, though they were far fewer than Clinton's second-term efforts in House races.

Bush's eight fundraisers for state parties—the only ones he would hold in his first term—were relatively few compared with those of his Republican predecessors. Four of these were held in Florida, which Bush had won by the narrowest of margins in 2000, and where his brother, Jeb, was seeking reelection as governor. The other four came in Alaska, Connecticut, Mississippi, and Texas, all states in which Bush had won or lost the two-party vote by at least 17 percent. Bush's patterns of state party fundraising did not follow those of some of his predecessors, whose efforts largely took place in states key to their electoral fortunes. Bush's relative neglect of state GOP organizations followed Clinton's trend, as he also spent relatively little time raising funds for state parties.

The president put his prestige on the line by fundraising and campaigning aggressively in the 2002 midterm elections. As had been the case for his predecessors, the midterm outcomes would be seen as a referendum on his leadership as president, and with his approval sky-high following the terrorist attacks of September 11, 2001, he was well positioned for his efforts to pay off. Republicans gained ground in the House, increasing their majority to 229 seats, marking only the second time that a president's party had gained House seats in midterm elections since the Great Depression. The GOP also retook control of the upper chamber, picking up two seats to give them a 51-seat majority. One news account estimated that Bush's midterm fundraising efforts yielded $180 million for his fellow Republicans, including $8 million for his brother Jeb's winning campaign for a second term as governor of Florida.[92]

Like Carter, George H. W. Bush, and Clinton before him, Bush turned his fundraising focus to his own reelection campaign as his date with the voters approached. As table 3.7 indicates, fifty-seven of Bush's ninety-seven fundraisers in 2003 and 2004 were for the Bush-Cheney reelection committee—much more than for any president before him, as he was the first to reject public funding in the nominating process and thus spent much more time raising money that far exceeded the spending caps that limited the campaign activities of candidates who accept public funds. Bush held an additional twenty-nine fundraisers for the RNC in his third and fourth years in office, with twenty-seven of those coming in his reelection year. Like each other president in this study except Reagan, Bush did little fundraising for the national committee in his first years in office and then ramped up his efforts when they would also help his reelection bid.

Bush's fundraising efforts for his own reelection came at the expense of his party-building efforts. Bush attended only eleven fundraisers in 2003 and 2004 that were not for either his own reelection or the RNC, including five for Senate races, four for gubernatorial campaigns, one for a House race, and another joint House-Senate fundraiser. After devoting record time to campaigning for his fellow Republicans in 2002, Bush did relatively little to help them financially in 2003 and 2004 aside from his efforts for the RNC. After being a party builder in 2002, his efforts, like Clinton's before him, seemed more predatory in 2003 and 2004, as he focused on winning a second term in the White House.

Working to Hold the House, Senate, and White House

When Bush was reelected in 2004, Republicans held on to control of both chambers of Congress. Their number of House seats increased slightly to 232, and their majority in the Senate grew to a more comfortable 55 seats.[93] Bush then turned his attention to retaining the gains Republicans had made. While Bush's 155 second-term fundraisers represented a substantial commitment that was greater than any four-year total for Carter, Reagan, or George H. W. Bush, he became the only two-term president in this study to hold fewer fundraisers in his second term than his first. As table 3.8 illustrates, his party-building focus in his second term shifted to House campaigns, the RNC, and Senate campaigns as he worked to hold the Republican majorities in Congress and help position his party for the 2008 elections. Like Clinton, Bush did not focus much on state parties, holding only 8 fundraisers for them over his second four-year term, which was a departure from the practices of his Republican predecessors. Instead, also like Clinton, Bush consistently raised money for the national committee throughout his second term, which represented the continuing nationalization of presidential fundraising efforts.

In 2005 and 2006, Bush held 27 fundraisers for House races, in addition to two joint House-Senate galas, dedicating even more time to House races than any of his predecessors in the first two years of a term. He held eighteen fundraisers for Senate races, fifteen for the Republican National Committee, and nine that jointly benefited the state party and a prominent candidate in that state. One account estimated that Bush's fundraising efforts yielded $193 million for his fellow party members.[94] Despite his prodigious efforts, Republicans lost both chambers of Congress to the Democrats on Election Day in 2006. In the House, the GOP surrendered the majority it had held for twelve years, as the Democrats won 233 seats. And in the Senate, the Democrats picked up 6 seats, counting two independents who caucused with them, giving them an effective 51-49 majority.[95] For his final two years as president, Bush would face a Democratic Congress.

Bush continued his aggressive party-building efforts in his last two years in office, when he held 73 fundraisers, with 22 benefiting the RNC, 17 for House candidates, 15 for Senate candidates, and 2 joint House-Senate galas. He held six events for multiple beneficiaries, four of which jointly benefited the presidential campaign of Senator John McCain and the RNC. Bush held six fundraisers for state parties and five for governor's races. His totals would have been even higher had he not canceled several fundraisers in the midst of the financial crisis in the fall of 2008.[96] McCain, like George H. W. Bush in 1988 and Al Gore in 2000, had to decide how closely to associate himself with a sitting president of his own party, but in McCain's case, the president he was seeking to replace was quite unpopular. When Bush welcomed John McCain to the White House in March 2008 as the presump-

Table 3.8: George W. Bush's Second-Term Fundraisers, by
Beneficiary and Year of Term

	Year 5	Year 6	Year 7	Year 8	Total	Percentage
House campaign	2	25	2	15	44	28.4
National committee	4	11	9	13	37	23.9
Senate campaign	6	12	10	5	33	21.3
Multiple beneficiaries	0	9	1	5	15	9.7
Gubernatorial campaign	1	7	2	3	13	8.4
State party	0	2	2	4	8	5.2
Joint House-Senate event	1	1	1	1	4	2.6
Other	0	1	0	0	1	0.6
Total	14	68	27	46	155	100.0

Source: Data compiled by the author from the *Public Papers of the Presidents* and from Associated Press articles.

tive Republican nominee, he was asked about whether his low approval ratings would be a drag on the ticket. Bush expressed his desire to do whatever he could to help McCain, saying, "If my showing up and endorsing him helps him, or if I'm against him and it helps him, either way, I want him to win."[97]

In contrast to Bush's first term, when his soaring popularity made him an asset on the campaign trail, many of his second-term fundraisers were closed to the press and did not appear in the *Public Papers of the Presidents*. Bush held relatively few closed fundraisers in his first term (16 percent), but a majority (61 percent) of his second-term fundraisers was held away from public scrutiny. With Bush, political unpopularity accounts for his raising cash behind closed doors in his second term; despite his lowered approval ratings, he was still the Republican Party's preeminent fundraiser, even if his efforts were conducted away from the public's view. Many of Bush's 2008 fundraisers were closed to the press. In the words of White House spokesperson Dana Perino, "Yes, there have been a couple of closed press fundraisers. There have been many. But remember he's not on the ballot. Senator John McCain aspires to be the leader of this party and we intend to make sure that the light can fully shine on him, as it should, as he heads into the last 90 days before the election."[98]

Bush remained a powerful fundraiser, even with his approval ratings below 30 percent in the closing days of his presidency. One August 2008 account estimated that he had brought in a total of $968 million for himself and his fellow Republicans in his eight years as president.[99] Bush's record as a party builder was similar to Clinton's in a number of ways. In their first terms, both presidents raised funds aggressively for their fellow party members in the midterm elections, though Bush did so more than Clinton. And both turned more predatory in their third and fourth years, holding relatively few fundraisers for their fellow party members and instead focusing their efforts on their own reelection campaign and the national committee, which was dedicated in large part to helping reelect the president. In their second terms, both presidents worked to hold or retake both chambers of Congress, though Bush's fundraising efforts, which were substantial in comparison to those of any other president, were dwarfed by those of Clinton. In an era in which both parties believed they could retake control of Congress in the next election, both presidents were devoted party builders.

BARACK OBAMA: A RECORD NATIONAL FOCUS

When Barack Obama was elected president in 2008, it was the second consecutive election in which the Democratic Party had made substantial gains across the country, and the cumulative results of both elections left the Democrats with commanding majorities on Capitol Hill. In the House, they won 257 seats, more than any party had held there since the Democrats had lost power in 1994. And in the Senate, they held 59 of the chamber's 100 seats, which included two independents who caucused with their party. Their total would rise to a filibuster-proof 60 seats when veteran Republican senator Arlen Specter switched to the Democratic Party in April 2009.[100] Despite these apparently comfortable margins of control, Obama was an aggressive party builder for the Democrats, as he set a fundraising pace in his first two and a half years in office that surpassed those of his presidential predecessors.

As table 3.9 shows, Obama's twenty-four fundraisers in 2009 represented a greater first-year commitment to party building than that of any of his five predecessors in the Oval Office. Obama headlined sixty fundraisers in 2010, fewer than both Presidents Bush in the second year of their first terms but more than Carter, Reagan, or Clinton in their second year. His total of eighty-four fundraisers in his first two years as president exceeded the totals for all of his immediate predecessors except George H. W. Bush's eighty-seven in 1989 and 1990.

In his first two years in office, Obama held almost two-thirds of his fundraisers for two beneficiaries—the Democratic National Committee and Senate campaigns—with his attention divided approximately equally between the two. Of Obama's eighty-four fundraisers in 2009 and 2010, twenty-nine were for the DNC and twenty-seven were for Senate campaigns, making him the first president in this era to focus so much on national committee fundraising in his first two years in office. While Clinton and George W. Bush fundraised heavily for the national committee, each waited until his reelection year to ramp up national committee fundraising and then did so consistently throughout his second term. Obama did

Table 3.9: Barack Obama's Fundraisers through June 2011, by Beneficiary and Year of Term

	Year 1	Year 2	Year 3 (Jan.–June)	Total	Percentage
National committee	10	19	3	32	26.4
Obama Victory Fund	0	0	31	31	25.6
Senate campaign	4	23	2	29	24.0
House campaign	2	7	1	10	8.3
Gubernatorial campaign	5	4	0	9	7.4
Multiple beneficiaries	0	3	0	4	3.3
Joint House-Senate event	3	2	0	4	3.3
Other	0	1	0	1	0.8
State party	0	1	0	1	0.8
Vice president	0	0	0	0	0.0
Total	24	60	37	121	100.0

Source: Data compiled by the author from the *Public Papers of the Presidents* and from Associated Press articles.

not wait, holding more fundraisers for the DNC in his first two years than the twenty national committee events that his five immediate predecessors held collectively in their first two years in office.

Obama headlined nine fundraisers for governor's races and another nine for House campaigns, five joint House-Senate fundraisers, and three events with joint beneficiaries, all of which were for both Senator Barbara Boxer of California and the DNC. Obama held only one fundraiser for a state party, in Florida in 2010, which was a perennial battleground state that the president had carried narrowly in 2008. Obama's lack of focus on state parties stands in stark contrast to George H. W. Bush's 22 fundraisers for state parties twenty years earlier in 1990, in the last midterm election preceding a round of redistricting. This is yet another indicator of the nationalization of party campaign financing. While Carter, Reagan, and George H. W. Bush all committed substantial time to fundraising for state parties, the three most recent presidents did not. Instead, they devoted record efforts to raising money for their fellow party members at the national level.

While some of that money raised for the national party was subsequently directed to the states, Democrats in Texas in 2010 echoed the earlier complaints of New York Democrats when Obama traveled to Austin and Dallas for a pair of fundraisers for the DNC and the Democratic Senatorial Campaign Committee. While the state party had been promised $250,000 as its share of the fundraising receipts, some Texas Democrats said that it was not enough. "If they'd invest this money in Texas, we'd be a blue [Democratic] state," said one local Democrat. "They [national party leaders] come down here and drag the sack and spend the money on themselves." According to the Center for Responsive Politics, in 2007 and 2008,

the DNC raised $6.5 million from contributors in the Lone Star State and trans-
ferred only $204,000 to the state Democratic Party. Said one Texan donor to the
party, "Unfortunately, that leaves no money here to get the other side of the story
out. I've been working with some of the national Democratic groups to get money
back into the state."[101] The nationalization of presidential fundraising has left some
states feeling that they have received the short end of the stick.

An Earlier Focus on Reelection Fundraising

Despite Obama's extensive fundraising efforts in his first two years in office, the
Democrats lost 63 seats in the House in 2010 as Republicans reclaimed the majority there after four years out of power. In the Senate, the Democratic caucus shrunk,
but the Democrats retained control, as they still held 53 seats in the chamber.[102] In
Obama's third year, his focus shifted primarily to his own reelection campaign. He
attended six fundraisers in March for the benefit of fellow party members—three
for the DNC, two for Senate races, and one to benefit campaigns for the House.
But after announcing in April 2011 that he would seek another term as president,
all thirty-one fundraisers that he held up until the end of June 2011 were for the
Obama Victory Fund, a joint account of the Obama-Biden reelection campaign
and the Democratic National Committee. The first $5,000 in contributions from
an individual attending these events goes to the campaign, with any additional
amount benefiting the DNC.[103] While some of these are low-dollar events, many
of them feature contributors who have given $35,800, which includes $5,000 for
the Obama reelection campaign, the maximum allowed by law, as individuals can
give $2,500 for the nominating process and another $2,500 for the general election.
Additionally, the limit on annual contributions to the national party is $30,800,
so the Obama Victory Fund's biggest donors max out their contributions to the
Obama campaign for the entire reelection cycle and to the national committee for
the year. As of June 30, 2011, the Obama Victory Fund had taken in $86 million in
its first three months of existence, including more than $47 million for the Obama
campaign and more than $38 million for the Democratic National Committee.[104]

Obama began his reelection fundraising earlier than his predecessors, and he
has started with a stronger push. George W. Bush and Bill Clinton headlined their
first reelection fundraisers on June 17 and June 23 of their third year in office, respectively, and George H. W. Bush held his first such event on October 31 of his
third year. Reagan did not headline any reelection fundraisers for his own campaign, and Carter waited to hold the first such event until May 29 of his reelection
year. Obama's thirty-one reelection fundraisers through June 30 already exceed
the four, zero, nineteen, and fourteen headlined by Carter, Reagan, George H. W.

Bush, and Clinton for their entire own reelection campaign, respectively. George W. Bush set records when he attended fifty-seven fundraisers for his own reelection campaign committee in 2003 and 2004; Obama will likely eclipse that total in 2011 alone. Obama's early start and increased dedication to fundraising reflect the time involved in raising large totals of money in the small increments regulated by federal contribution limits. Because Obama has made it clear that he will be the first sitting president not to take public funding for the general election, which has relieved past presidents of the need to spend their own time raising funds in the final months of the campaign, the number of fundraisers he will attend for his own reelection could easily surpass the combined totals of his five immediate predecessors in the White House as he heads what could be the first billion-dollar presidential campaign effort.

Through June of his third year in office, Barack Obama's 121 fundraisers were more than any of his five immediate predecessors had held at the same point in their term. By the end of June of their third year in office, Carter had headlined 44 fundraisers, Reagan 63, George H. W. Bush 90, Clinton 74, and George W. Bush 84. Despite these larger numbers, Obama appears to be on track to follow the pattern of Clinton and George W. Bush—substantial party-building fundraising in his first two years, followed by a principal focus on his own reelection campaign and the national committee in his third and fourth years. It remains to be seen if he will engage in substantial party-building efforts as his reelection bid gains steam, and whether he will follow the patterns of Clinton and George W. Bush as an aggressive second-term party builder if he is elected to another four years in the White House.

CONCLUSIONS

Who benefits from the permanent campaign? As presidents have devoted more and more of their time to political fundraising, they have done so both for themselves and for their fellow party members, and the extent to which they have done so has increased over time. Of the presidents first elected via the plebiscitary nominating system and who have served during the campaign finance regime created by the Federal Campaign Finance Act of 1974, all but Carter have been aggressive party builders, though there have been important variations in the ways in which they strove to support their fellow partisans. The overwhelming majority of presidential fundraising has been not for the president's own reelection campaign but for the national committee and other beneficiaries. While presidents' own electoral fortunes may benefit directly from a well-resourced national committee, they will gain only indirectly from their efforts to elect more senators, House members, governors, and others of their same party. While Reagan focused more on his party than on himself in his first term, George H. W. Bush, Clinton, and Obama all devoted much time to raising funds for their fellow party members in their first or only midterm election year and then shifted their efforts primarily to their own re-election committee and the national party in their third and fourth years in office. All three two-term presidents devoted substantial time and effort to party building in their second four years in office. The beneficiaries of presidential fundraising have varied by president, revealing where presidents place their political chips and how they see their role as party-builder-in-chief.

Polsby and Kernell argued the presidents produced by the plebiscitary nominating system since the 1970s would be outsiders with weak ties to their party, and Milkis contended that the growth of executive power has made parties weaker and less relevant. The evidence presented here demonstrates that when it comes to presidential fundraising, with the exception of Carter, every president has demonstrated a significant commitment to helping provide financial resources for their fellow party members who are running for office. These findings largely line up with those of Galvin, who argued that Republican presidents would seek to build their parties in an effort to win congressional majorities and strengthen their party across the country, while Democrats before Clinton's second term would do so to a much lesser extent. While Clinton fundraised aggressively for his fellow Democrats in 1994, their loss of both chambers of Congress that year led him to embark upon an unprecedented party-building effort in his second term, and both George W. Bush and Obama, seeing control of Congress within reach or about to slip from their grasp, have campaigned ambitiously for their fellow party members throughout most of their terms in an era in which no political party can count on long-term majority status.

As the costs of congressional and gubernatorial races have risen dramatically, presidents are asked to help raise funds in the small increments prescribed by federal contribution limits for their fellow party members. Soft money in the 1990s and 2000s led to even more presidential fundraising for party committees, but its ban in 2002 did not lead to a slowdown in this activity. If anything, presidents pressured to raise just as much if not more money were incentivized to devote more time to fundraising, as money had to be gathered in smaller, regulated increments. The greater amounts of time presidents have spent raising money for their fellow party members are in part due to the intersection of rising campaign costs, relatively small contribution limits, and a competitive electoral environment.

Table 3.10 highlights the relative fundraising priorities during each presidential term and makes clear several of the key dynamics discussed throughout this chapter. First, party-building fundraising has become nationalized. While state and at times local parties were a consistent fundraising priority for Carter, Reagan, and

Table 3.10: Fundraising Priorities by President, 1977–June 2011 (percent)*

Beneficiary	Carter	Reagan (First Term)	Reagan (Second Term)	GHW Bush	Clinton (First Term)	Clinton (Second Term)	GW Bush (First Term)	GW Bush (Second Term)	Obama (through June 2011)	Total
National committee	31	5	1	4	38	37	18	24	26	25
Senate campaign	9	30	54	20	20	23	16	21	24	23
House campaign	11	4	2	6	7	19	8	28	8	13
State/local party	27	36	25	23	9	5	5	5	1	11
Gubernatorial campaign	11	15	12	24	7	7	16	8	7	11
President	5	0	0	14	8	0	33	0	0	6
Multiple beneficiaries	2	1	1	1	4	4	3	10	2	4
Senate-House (joint)	1	5	5	4	1	2	2	3	4	3
Other	4	4	0	4	5	3	0	1	1	2
President–national committee (joint)	0	0	0	0	0	0	0	0	26	2
Vice president	0	0	0	0	0	1	0	0	0	0
Total	100	100	100	100	100	100	100	100	100	100

*Note: Highlighted values indicate each president's top fundraising beneficiaries in a given term.

Source: Data compiled by the author from the Public Papers of the Presidents and from Associated Press articles.

George H. W. Bush, the three most recent presidents, Clinton, George W. Bush, and Obama, have focused very little on state parties, instead working to aid the Democratic and Republican National Committees. Even in years preceding the decennial reapportionment and redistricting processes, Clinton and Obama did not devote themselves to state parties and gubernatorial races, as George H. W. Bush did substantially in 1990. The rise of national party fundraising is certainly related to the prevalence of soft money in the 1990s and early 2000s, which allowed presidents to raise funds without the restraints of contribution limits, but this national focus has continued beyond the soft money ban enacted by the Bipartisan Campaign Reform Act of 2002. It is important to note that not all funds raised for the national committees stay with the national committees, as they regularly transfer funds to state parties and individual campaigns. But even if other parts of the party benefit indirectly from the funds that presidents raise, it is significant that so much money from presidential fundraising now flows through the national party organization.

The most consistent beneficiary of presidential fundraising efforts has been Senate campaigns, which have been among the top three beneficiaries for every president since Carter. In contrast, most presidents have devoted little time to House races, with the only exceptions being Clinton and George W. Bush in their second terms. With so few Senate seats, each race is important to the battle for control of the chamber, where the fate of much of the president's agenda will be decided, and as the majority party there has changed six times since 1980, presidents of both parties have seen a Senate majority as winnable in most years. While presidents often devote much less time to raising money for House races, the two presidents who did so in their second terms, Bill Clinton and George W. Bush, made these efforts after Republicans ended 40 years of Democratic control of the chamber in 1994. This would be the first of three changes in the majority party there over the ensuing sixteen years. An era in which each party believes that it might retake or retain the majority in the House in the next election has heralded increased presidential fundraising commitment to races for seats in that body.

The choice of both George W. Bush and Obama to opt out of the public financing system at the nominating level in 2004 and at both the nominating and general election stages in 2012 has gone hand in hand with relatively less party building. For Carter, Reagan, George H. W. Bush, and Clinton, all of whom participated in the public funding program at both the nominating and general election stages, their fundraising for their own campaigns never topped 14 percent of their first-term fundraising. The spending caps associated with the public system held down the amount of money presidents raised, and it appears that presidents in turn devoted more time to helping their fellow party members. When George W. Bush opted out of public nominating funding, he then devoted 33 percent of his first-term fundraising to his own reelection campaign and an additional 18 percent to the RNC, most of which took place in 2004, meaning that he spent less time proportionally fundraising for just his fellow party members than any prior president in the FECA era. Through June 2011, Obama has followed a similar path, with 26 percent of his fundraisers for the Obama Victory Fund and an additional 26 percent for just the DNC. While both Bush and Obama fundraised aggressively for their fellow party members for the midterm elections of their first terms, their increased fundraising for themselves thereafter led them to devote less time proportionally to their fellow Republicans and Democrats.

The decline for some beneficiaries has been proportional, not absolute. The 16 percent of fundraisers for Senate races in George W. Bush's first term marked the first time since Carter's term that a president had devoted less than 20 percent of his fundraisers to the Senate. But in absolute terms, Bush held twenty-seven first-term fundraisers to benefit senators, lower than Clinton's first-term total of thirty-four but about on a par with George H. W. Bush's twenty-eight and more than Reagan's first-term total of twenty-four. While Bush's increased fundraising for himself in his first term made Senate races less of a relative priority, he still supported them with a substantial number of fundraisers. But Obama's focus has been so heavily on the national committee, the Obama Victory Fund, and Senate races that even in absolute terms he has paid relatively little attention to supporting other categories of Democrats.

The results of so much presidential fundraising for himself and his fellow party members can be both positive and detrimental. Presidents with stronger ties to their parties might be able to govern more effectively and enact more of their agenda, moving us closer to the responsible party model long touted by a number of political scientists. But the increasing devotion of a president's scarcest resource, his time, to the money chase necessarily leaves him with less time to spend on other pressing matters. Additionally, a president who invests so much effort in raising money and acting as party leader can find it more difficult to reach out to the other party. One example of this took place in South Dakota in April 2002. George W. Bush held an official event there with the state's two Democratic senators, majority leader Tom Daschle and Tim Johnson, and the state's lone House member, Republican John Thune. After the official event, Bush headlined a fundraiser for Thune, bringing in $350,000 for his campaign to defeat Johnson's reelection bid to the Senate and help to do away with the Democrats' 51-49 margin of control in the chamber and thus relieve Daschle of his duties as majority leader.[105] Such an event surely complicates a president's ability to work with legislators of the other party whom he is trying to defeat at the ballot box.

When Senator Evan Bayh, Democrat of Indiana, retired from the Senate, he wrote a column that was published in the *New York Times* that looked back to when his father had served in the Senate:

In my father's time there was a saying: "A senator legislates for four years and campaigns for two." Because of the incessant need to raise campaign cash, we now have perpetual campaigns. If fund-raising is constantly on members' minds, it's difficult for policy compromise to trump political calculation. Our most strident partisans must learn to occasionally sacrifice short-term tactical political advantage for the sake of the nation. Otherwise, Congress will remain stuck in an endless cycle of recrimination and revenge. The minority seeks to frustrate the majority, and when the majority is displaced it returns the favor. Power is constantly sought through the use of means which render its effective use, once acquired, impossible.[106]

Presidential fundraising efforts might help to build the president's party, but the costs to governing could be substantial, as I discuss more in chapter 6. In the next chapter, I examine the geography of the permanent campaign. Systematic analysis of strategic presidential travel indicates that the targeting of key Electoral College and presidential nominating states throughout a president's term in office is on the rise.

4. Strategic Travel and the Permanent Campaign

The last few months, I have been looking for invitations to speak. On a strictly nonpolitical basis, of course. I even visited one state that does not have an early primary next year. The darned scheduler resigned before I could fire him.

Jimmy Carter, speaking at a Democratic Party fundraiser, May 9, 1979

You know, they say that because of the 24-hour news cycle, we're all in a permanent campaign. And when you're in a permanent campaign, it's hard to take the time to go to someplace you have no chance of winning—Nebraska—or someplace you have no chance of losing—the [Health and Human Services] Building.

Bill Clinton, speaking at the Department of Health and Human Services, December 20, 2000

As Bill Clinton and George W. Bush drew close to the end of their respective eight years as president, each was confronted with a choice. Both men had traveled to forty-nine of the fifty states that they had led as president, and they had to decide whether to visit the fiftieth and final state in their waning days in office. Clinton had yet to set foot in Nebraska; Bush, in Vermont. Clinton did choose to make his first and only presidential trip to Nebraska on December 8, 2000, when he gave a morning speech on foreign policy at the University of Nebraska at Kearney, then flew to Offutt Air Force Base in Bellevue, where he spoke to the community before attending a fundraiser for the Nebraska Democratic Party in nearby Omaha. While a journey to Vermont by Bush would have allowed him, in the words of his former press secretary, Ari Fleischer, "to check the box to say he was in all 50 states," Bush did not make the trip. For both Clinton and Bush, their relative neglect of these two states was interpreted to be the result of clear political considerations. Each was a sparsely populated state with few Electoral College votes that had given the president little support in his two bids for the White House. Why, reasoned journalistic accounts at the time, would either president expend the effort to go to such a place?[1]

Press accounts are often quick to attribute electoral motivations to many presidential trips, as was evident in 2011 when Barack Obama became the first president to visit Puerto Rico since Gerald Ford, and the first in fifty years to travel to the island for the purpose of meeting with Puerto Ricans; Ford visited Puerto Rico to attend an international summit, and Lyndon Johnson visited a military base there, but Obama's trip was the first since John F. Kennedy's in 1961 in which the president's visit was centered around the people of Puerto Rico themselves. An Associated Press article describing the trip captured the flavor of much of the coverage of the visit:

> Cheering crowds in the steamy tropical heat are expected Tuesday when President Barack Obama makes a rare presidential visit to Puerto Rico. But the nearly 4 million U.S. citizens who live on the island and can't vote in the general election aren't really the point. Organizers are hoping this trip, the first in decades by a president to the U.S. Caribbean territory, will generate good will on the mainland, particularly in Florida, where the fast-growing Hispanic population will be essential to Obama's re-election effort in 2012.[2]

This theme was echoed in media outlet after media outlet. The headline of an article in the *Miami Herald* declared, "Obama Visit to Puerto Rico: It's All about Florida." *Politico's* headline read, "Barack Obama Goes in Quest of Hispanic Votes." A headline in the *New York Times* asserted, "In Visit to Puerto Rico, Obama Has Eye on Mainland."[3] The consistent message was that Obama's trip was driven by electoral motivations.

Viewing presidential actions through the lens of the permanent campaign leads one to ascribe cynical, election-related motivations to much of what presidents do. From this point of view, Obama's trip to Puerto Rico, Clinton's neglect of Nebraska, and Bush's absence from Vermont were not incidental decisions but rather the result of strategic political choices. This chapter aims to analyze systematically presidential travel in order to understand presidential priorities. If the notion of the permanent campaign explains presidential behavior well, then presidents' travel, especially in their first term in office, would be expected to favor key states in ways that reflect the institutional incentives of the Electoral College and the rules of the nomination process in order to maximize their chances of reelection.

THE IMPORTANCE OF PRESIDENTIAL TRAVEL

As noted earlier, a president's time is his scarcest resource. When a president chooses to travel around the country he leads in order to meet the people he represents, his decision to go to a specific place and not others can reveal a great deal about his strategic priorities. Presidents travel for many reasons: to advance their own reelection interests; to raise funds; to support their fellow party members; to exert pressure on recalcitrant legislators; to promote their policy agenda or achievements in a setting outside the nation's capital; to attend ceremonial events; to respond to natural disasters or other crises; to influence public opinion; or simply to get out of Washington. What they do and where they do it can illuminate the priorities of a presidency. This point was well illustrated in George W. Bush's memoir, when he cited his numerous visits to the Gulf Coast in the wake of Hurricane Katrina as testament to his commitment to rebuild the devastated region.[4]

A tremendous amount of effort goes into preparing for a presidential journey. An advance team lays the groundwork for each presidential trip, coordinating details that range from security to public relations. At least three helicopters—one bearing the president, and two providing security and serving as decoys—usually ferry the president from the White House to Andrews Air Force Base, where he boards Air Force One. A large entourage accompanies the president, including support planes carrying personnel and military and communications equipment, and cargo planes bearing armored vehicles, the president's limousine, and at times his helicopter, Marine One. On occasion, in the case of travel to dangerous overseas destinations, a decoy plane decorated to look like Air Force One may make the journey as well. In short, moving the president and what has been called his mobile White House around the country and the world requires no small investment of time, money, and political effort.[5]

Presidents have forged some of the most enduring images of their administration while traveling around the country or across the world. One need look no further than Abraham Lincoln dedicating a cemetery to fallen Union soldiers in Gettysburg, Pennsylvania, in November 1863, or John F. Kennedy in Berlin almost a hundred years later declaring his solidarity with the people of that embattled city, or George W. Bush speaking to rescue workers through a megaphone in New York City following the attacks of September 11, 2001, to see clearly the importance of travel in shaping the public's perception of a president. Many presidents have been at their best when speaking directly to the people and drawing on the energy of the crowds they addressed in moments that would become emblematic of their leadership.

Presidents have often seen travel as one of their best tools for reaching out to the American people. Ronald Reagan, whose presidency inspired Samuel Kernell's analysis of presidents going public, made the case on the morning after the 1986 midterm elections in which the Republicans lost control of the Senate, which they had held for the first six years of Reagan's administration. The president wrote in his diary that day about a postelection meeting with "our team. Message was telecast. I called for going to bat to get the rest of our program by taking our case to the people."[6] Former Clinton adviser George Stephanopoulos recounted, "Clinton's favorite remedy for personal and political malaise was to hit the road." In reference to Clinton's campaign efforts for the 1994 midterm elections, Stephanopoulos wrote that "advising Clinton to stay off the campaign trail in October was like asking him not to breathe."[7]

Scholars have found that presidents have good reason to want to take their message directly to the people. While presidents often have a combative relationship with the Washington press corps, local media frequently provide more favorable coverage when a president comes to town.[8] Political practitioners also see the media benefits to a presidential visit. Charles Black, a former head of the Republican National Committee, said, "When a president goes into a state, he can dominate the local news for at least 24, sometimes 36 or 48 hours. You can't go too many times, as long as you have a message and something to say."[9] Sig Rogich, a White House aide to George H. W. Bush, went so far as to write a memorandum to the president on January 24, 1990, in which he made the case about the benefits of local media coverage of presidential travel:

> Some will point to the fact that every trip we take should have a national media hook. I disagree. And I wanted you to note the amount of good exposure we are getting in case the subject comes up. This same coverage has been true in Chicago, Houston, Atlanta, Miami, Nashville, Cincinnati, etc. . . . all within the top 100 National ADI (market size). It is subtle, but effective travel strategy, and it is giving us maximum, positive exposure without national media nit-picking. When you think about it, we begin to receive good coverage when the trip is announced, during the days leading up to the visit, the day of the visit and the day after—all generally positive. Conversely, most national stories are debated with counterpoints by the opposition, as well as the commentators. Just thought you would be interested in what I perceive to be an important ingredient in our favorable ratings.

President Bush handwrote his response on the memorandum: "Sig—I agree with you!! Thanks!! GB."[10]

The argument that Rogich makes and Bush seconds coincides neatly with the research of political scientists Jeffrey Cohen and Richard Powell, who studied the effects of presidential visits on public opinion within the visited states. They found that a trip by the president to a state does lead to an increase in the president's approval rating in the state, but that these dynamics occur only in nonelection years in large states, which they categorize as states with more than 5 million people.[11] Five of the six cities mentioned by Rogich—all except Nashville—meet the criteria, demonstrating the convergence of practical political wisdom and political science research.

Presidential visits do indeed generate much local excitement. Some Californians slept outside on the night before Barack Obama's first presidential visit to the state in order to get tickets to a town hall meeting with the president in Costa Mesa the next day.[12] A trip by Obama in September 2009 to Troy, New York, a small city near Albany, prompted a front-page story that began, "Bruce Springsteen and the Dalai Lama drew huge audiences in the Capital Region, but President Barack Obama's speech Monday is by far the most coveted ticket of the year, mostly because there are so few of them." Unlike the California town hall event, no tickets were given away to the public, and local officials worked the phones in an effort to get tickets for themselves and their constituents. The guest list, however, was controlled by White House aides, who invited a select group of students, business leaders, and elected officials. When Obama traveled to upstate New York, media coverage focused on the rare nature of such a presidential visit. One article discussed the visits by seven presidents to the region over the prior 143 years—Andrew Johnson, Grover Cleveland, William Howard Taft, Franklin Roosevelt, Harry Truman, Bill Clinton, and George W. Bush.[13] Another local newspaper captured much of the local focus with the headline "Presidential Visits Rare, Especially by Republicans."[14] This type of emphasis is typical—residents of locales across the country care greatly about presidential attention, are sensitive to their relative lack of it, and celebrate the rare times when presidents do come to visit.

Presidential travel matters on several levels. It is tremendously important to presidents and to their aides who determine how best to allocate the scarce resource that is the president's time. Enormous efforts are required to put together the logistical and security arrangements necessary for any presidential journey. And the visits make memorable impressions on the local populace, often resulting in extensive positive press coverage of the president, the relatively unfiltered dissemination of his message, and an increase in the president's job approval ratings. Because of these dynamics, presidential travel matters for what it can tell us about a president's priorities.

PRESIDENTIAL TRAVEL AND THE PERMANENT CAMPAIGN

If one accepts the permanent campaign's premise that electoral considerations drive decisions throughout a president's term in office, then certain expectations follow about how presidents will allocate their time. The logic of the permanent campaign implies that the strategic targeting of key electoral states should be evident in decisions about where and how often a president travels throughout his term in office. More competitive states should receive more presidential attention than states that vote reliably for one party or the other, as these are the states whose electoral outcome is most in doubt. Competitive states that are also populous should be the most likely to receive attention from the president. Specifically, presidents should be expected to pay particular attention to sizable states that they marginally won or lost in the previous election. Additionally, presidents should devote disproportionate attention to the largest states that offer the greatest electoral payoffs due to the unit rule used by forty-eight of the fifty states, under which a state allocates all its Electoral College votes to the winner of the statewide vote. Nebraska and Maine are the only states that do not employ the unit rule; both allocate two Electoral College votes to the statewide winner, and one Electoral College vote to the winner of each congressional district. These same institutional incentives should consistently disadvantage certain classes of states that are unlikely to be an important part of presidential coalitions. Small states should tend to get less attention from presidents than large states, as they offer little electoral reward; small states that consistently vote for the party that does not hold the presidency should be effectively left out of a president's constituency and should thus receive little to no presidential attention.

If the permanent campaign exists, then we should see substantial temporal, as well as geographic, variation. The logic of the permanent campaign suggests both change and continuity within presidential terms. While reelection years involve more presidential attention to the states than do other years of a president's term, if electoral concerns permeate a president's term, one would expect to see targeting of key electoral states throughout a president's term in office. Presidents should behave differently during their first term than in their second, when reelection is no longer a priority.

The past several decades have witnessed a professionalization of campaigning, that, along with expanded powers of the presidency, should lead to more recent presidents and their staffs becoming more efficient in targeting their efforts and resources at electorally key states. Finally, while all presidents respond to similar institutional incentives, we will see substantial variation by presidency, according to each individual's degree of pursuit of reelection. These hypothesized dynamics are those that would result if a permanent campaign for the presidency did indeed exist. While these assumptions might not seem radical to the contemporary political ear, they represent a departure from conventional wisdom on the subject.

Until recently, many scholars who study what presidents do and say have not focused on presidential speeches outside of Washington, DC. Instead, their emphasis has been on so-called major presidential addresses. In one prominent example, Lynn Ragsdale, writing in her epically useful volume, *Vital Statistics on the Presidency,* introduces data on public presidential appearances by writing, "Presidents also make appearances at locations outside of Washington, D.C. . . . . These U.S. appearances are largely ceremonial. Presidents travel to a particular community to commemorate a local event, meet civic groups and local leaders, or survey damage caused by natural disasters."[15] While a presidential speech to autoworkers in Ohio might pale in importance when compared with an inaugural or State of the Union address, discounting these presidential efforts as merely ceremonial does not lend them their proper significance.

While a number of studies have looked at how the incentives of the Electoral College structure the allocation of campaign resources,[16] few have examined the extent to which they relate to the activities of sitting presidents. Roderick Hart's comprehensive study of presidential speechmaking and travel between 1945 and 1985 is the definitive source on the subject for the forty years following World War II. His examination of the geography of presidential rhetoric led to one simple and clear conclusion—that in the aggregate, population is the single most important factor related to where presidents speak. While examining a forty-year period at the aggregate level certainly masks some important variation, as he put it, "No matter where one looks—at region, at population, at party affiliation, or at a combination of these variables—it is clear that voter density drives presidential speechmaking."[17] Said simply, presidents tend to go where the people are. Additionally, Hart found that the geographic focus of election year travel is substantially different from that during the rest of a president's term. While presidents in the aggregate appear to go where the people are, in election years, they follow the incentives of the Electoral College and dramatically decrease their visits to states that are electorally safe for one party or the other, while devoting substantially more attention to states that Hart calls "neutral"—that is, those that in common parlance are swing states or battleground states.[18]

Both of these key findings—that population is the key driver of presidential travel in the aggregate, and that in election years presidents shift their focus to competitive states—are important and logical. They are also at odds with the logic of the permanent campaign. If the lines between campaigning and governing are now much less distinct than they once were, presidents should focus on key electoral states throughout their terms in office, not just as Election Day nears. Hart's analysis was certainly accurate for the period that he studied. Have these dynamics changed in recent years? Recent studies of the ways presidential travel relates to Electoral College incentives by this author and by Emily Charnock, James McCann, and Kathryn Dunn Tenpas suggest that the answer is yes.[19] This study aims to dive more deeply into these questions by focusing in depth on the period from 1977 through 2011, beginning with the last two presidents Hart studied, and continuing through the subsequent four, in order to examine how presidents elected via the plebiscitary nominating system govern once in office.

Studies of the strategic allocation of presidential travel are relatively rare in large part because of the challenges associated with putting together the necessary data. In order to analyze these dynamics, I created a database of presidential travel by examining the *Public Papers of the Presidents* to track both the days a president spends and the number of events he holds in each state. Because a large number of public presidential events occur in the Washington, DC metropolitan area as part of the president's regular activities, events in Maryland and Virginia are not included in the following discussion. A presidential event held at Andrews Air Force Base in Maryland or at the Pentagon in Virginia is not a representative example of a president traveling to the states. Unfortunately, this also removes from the analysis presidential events held in places such as Baltimore, Maryland, and Norfolk, Virginia. While this is regrettable, excluding these states seemed preferable to either including them in their entirety, which would encompass a great deal of presidential activity in the suburbs of the nation's capital, or including presidential events in Maryland and Virginia only if they took place outside of the Washington Beltway, which would result in data for only part of these states that would be difficult to compare to other states. The 4,526 presidential events outside of Washington, DC, Maryland, and Virginia over a thirty-five-year period provide a rich trove of evidence to address the question of the extent to which presidential travel patterns correspond to electoral incentives.

THE ROLE OF FUNDRAISING IN PRESIDENTIAL TRAVEL

The two previous chapters focused on presidential fundraising, which is a key element of presidential travel. As table 4.1 reveals, the vast majority of presidential fundraising events take place outside of Washington, DC, Maryland, and Virginia. Of the 1,488 fundraisers over this thirty-five-year period in the fifty states and the District of Columbia, 288 took place in the nation's capital, and an additional 41 were held in its two neighboring states, with 24 of these 41 events in the Maryland and Virginia suburbs that ring Washington, DC. The majority of these DC-area fundraisers took place during the presidency of Bill Clinton, who headlined a staggering 163 fundraisers in the District of Columbia, Maryland, and Virginia in his second term—a higher total than Carter, Reagan, or George H. W. Bush held across the entire the country in any of their terms in office. DC-area events are an important indicator of the president's commitment to raise funds for himself and his party, but they do not require the investment of time necessary to attend fundraisers farther afield from the White House. An additional 1,159 fundraisers, which represent 77.9 percent of all presidential fundraisers since 1977, were held in the other forty-eight states of the Union. This chapter will focus on the role that these 1,159 fundraisers play in the larger picture of strategic presidential travel.

Levels of presidential fundraising travel and overall presidential travel have both risen substantially over the almost thirty-five years from Jimmy Carter's inauguration in 1977 through the end of June 2011, Barack Obama's third year in

Table 4.1: Presidential Fundraisers in and Outside of the
Washington, DC, Area, 1977–June 2011

President	DC	Maryland	Virginia	Other 48 States	Total
Carter	9	1	2	73	85
Reagan (first term)	12	0	1	67	80
Reagan (second term)	15	2	2	81	100
GHW Bush	11	1	2	123	137
Clinton (first term)	25	0	6	136	167
Clinton (second term)	153	5	5	308	471
GW Bush (first term)	21	2	1	149	173
GW Bush (second term)	25	2	7	121	155
Obama (through June 2011)	17	1	1	101	120
Total	288	14	27	1,159	1,488

Note: Barack Obama also held one fundraiser in Puerto Rico on June 14, 2011, which is excluded from the counts here because it did not take place in one of the fifty states or the District of Columbia.
Source: Data compiled by the author from the *Public Papers of the Presidents* and from Associated Press articles.

office, as figure 4.1 indicates. The rise in total events is relatively steady over time, especially during first terms in office, with the important exception of Ronald Reagan, who registered the lowest levels of public events outside of the nation's capital of the six presidents studied. This is most likely due, at least in part, to his relatively advanced age when he assumed the presidency and his lengthy recovery from the attempt on his life in 1981. The overall trend is one of increasing presidential travel, with George W. Bush holding almost twice as many first-term events across the country as Jimmy Carter did twenty-five years earlier. While each two-term president in this study has held fewer events in his second term than in his first, even George W. Bush's lower second-term total far exceeds the numbers for Carter or for Reagan in either of his terms. Given the surge in presidential travel in a reelection year, Obama will likely continue the trend of rising first-term travel.

The role of fundraising in presidential travel is a significant one. Figure 4.1 details the numbers of fundraisers, related events, and events not related to fundraisers attended by each president outside of the Washington, DC, area. An event related to a fundraiser is one that took place within thirty miles of a fundraiser on the same, previous, or next day, since presidents often pair a fundraiser with another public event that is not a fundraiser, and it is difficult to determine whether the fundraiser or the other event was the driving force behind the visit. Pairing a fundraising event with an official presidential event means that taxpayers will bear more of the costs of the trip, according to a formula laid out by law that allocates the expenses of presidential travel according to its political or official purposes.

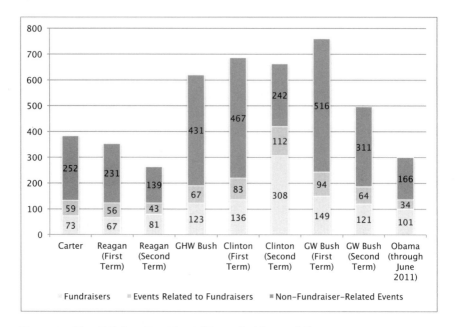

Figure 4.1: Non-DC-Area Presidential Events by Type and Term, 1977–June 2011
Source: Data compiled by the author from the *Public Papers of the Presidents* and from Associated Press articles.

Presidential staff often field questions about whether the fundraiser or the official event was planned first; if the fundraiser came first, reporters frequently try to ascertain, with little success, whether the official event was added as an afterthought so that the public would bear more and the campaign would bear less of the expense of the trip.

Presidents have held 4,526 events outside of Washington, DC, Maryland, and Virginia between 1977 and June 2011, of which 1,159, or 26 percent, have been fundraisers. More than one in every four presidential events outside of the DC area has been for the purpose of financing political endeavors. An additional 612 events, or 14 percent of the total, have been events related to fundraisers, which means that almost 40 percent of all presidential events outside of the DC area were either fundraisers or events that took place on the same trip as a fundraiser. The high-water mark of this practice came in Clinton's second term, when 63 percent of all his events across the country were fundraisers and related events. The lowest percentage belongs to George H. W. Bush, whose 31 percent of events that were fundraisers and related events still represents a substantial investment of time, with more than 3 of every 10 events being or related to political fundraising events. Second-term fundraising efforts for Reagan, Clinton, and George W. Bush all reflect an increased percentage of travel devoted to fundraising. Interestingly, while the number of first-term fundraisers has risen substantially, their percentage of total events remained remarkably constant from Jimmy Carter's 19 percent through George W. Bush's 20 percent. However, Barack Obama's 34 percent of events as fundraisers represents a substantial increase in commitment to first-term fundraising relative to his predecessors.

To shed light upon the electoral dynamics of the states in which presidents raise funds, table 4.2 breaks down presidential fundraising activity by margin of electoral victory or defeat in the previous election. It demonstrates that presidents fundraise predominantly where they are popular, as 80 percent of fundraisers were held in states that the president carried in the prior election. And of the 20 percent of fundraisers attended in states the president lost in the prior election, almost half of them took place in states that the president lost by 5 percent or less. In six of the nine presidential terms examined in this study, the most fundraisers took place in states won by more than 15 percent. Not surprisingly, presidents tend to find financial support in states where they found electoral support, and they spend little time seeking funds in places where they met electoral defeat.

These data are in large part a function of how many states a president won in the prior election. Ninety-four percent and 100 percent of Reagan's first- and second-term fundraisers, respectively, took place in states that he had carried in the previous election. Because he carried forty-three out of the forty-eight states in this study in his first election and forty-seven of these forty-eight states in his reelection bid, there simply were not many states he lost in which he could fundraise. But analysis by margin of victory shows that Reagan held 31 percent of his first-term fundraisers and 83 percent of his second-term fundraisers in states that he won by 15 percent or more, supporting the notion that greater financial support is found where presidents earned greater success at the ballot box. The numbers are much more illustrative for the other presidents. Jimmy Carter carried only 22 of these 48 states, George H. W. Bush carried 38, Bill Clinton carried 31 in 1992 and then 30 in 1996, George W. Bush won 29 in 2000 and 30 in 2004, and Barack Obama carried 26 of these 48 states in 2008. Even though Carter won just 22 states, he still held 60 percent of his fundraisers in states that he carried.

The geography of presidential fundraising does not follow the incentives of the Electoral College, which would lead presidents to spend the most time in the swing states that had been narrowly won or lost in the previous election. Instead, presidents spend the most time raising money in states where they are popular. Different factors drive where presidents raise money. First, presidents plan events in places where there is enough financial support to merit the investment of their time. Second, when raising money for fellow party members, presidents often travel to their co-partisan's state. These trips sometimes coincide with their own

Table 4.2: Fundraisers in States Won or Lost in Last Election, by President and Margin of Two-Party Victory or Defeat, 1977–June 2011

President by Term	States Won in Prior Election					States Lost in Prior Election					Total
	0.00%–5%	5.01%–10%	10.01%–15%	15.01% or More	Subtotal (States Won)	0.00%–5%	5.01%–10%	10.01%–15%	15.01% or More	Subtotal (States Lost)	
Carter	18	10	10	6	44	20	6	3	0	29	73
	25%	14%	14%	8%	60%	27%	8%	4%	0%	40%	100%
Reagan (first term)	15	13	14	21	63	4	0	0	0	4	67
	22%	19%	21%	31%	94%	6%	0%	0%	0%	6%	100%
Reagan (second term)	0	7	7	67	81	0	0	0	0	0	81
	0%	9%	9%	83%	100%	0%	0%	0%	0%	0%	100%
GHW Bush	31	10	26	29	96	14	6	7	0	27	123
	25%	8%	21%	24%	78%	11%	5%	6%	0%	22%	100%
Clinton (first term)	12	21	14	69	116	19	1	0	0	20	136
	9%	15%	10%	51%	85%	14%	1%	0%	0%	15%	100%
Clinton (second term)	10	40	100	119	269	12	26	0	1	39	308
	3%	13%	32%	39%	87%	4%	8%	0%	0%	13%	100%
GW Bush (first term)	32	14	11	28	85	23	9	18	14	64	149
	21%	9%	7%	19%	57%	15%	6%	12%	9%	43%	100%
GW Bush (second term)	20	21	11	30	82	16	4	15	4	39	121
	17%	17%	9%	25%	68%	13%	3%	12%	3%	32%	100%
Obama	16	2	13	61	92	4	1	4	0	9	101
	16%	2%	13%	60%	91%	4%	1%	4%	0%	9%	100%
Total	154	138	206	430	928	112	53	47	19	231	1,159
	13%	12%	18%	37%	80%	10%	5%	4%	2%	20%	100%

Source: Data compiled by the author from the *Public Papers of the Presidents*, Associated Press articles, and Dave Leip's Atlas of U.S. Elections, http://uselectionatlas.org/ (accessed May 21, 2011).

electoral map, but often they do not. In 2009 and 2010, Barack Obama headlined three fundraisers in Las Vegas in support of Senate majority leader Harry Reid's reelection bid. While it was an added bonus for the president that Nevada is a battleground state and early caucus state that Obama carried in 2008 and wants to win again in 2012, that was not the driving factor behind his visit. Obama also was the star attraction at three fundraisers in Illinois to benefit Senate candidate Alexi Giannoulias. Obama's home state of Illinois is about as safe an electoral bet for the president's reelection bid as a state can be, but that did not deter the president from investing substantial time to raise funds in an effort to keep his old Senate seat in his party's hands. Presidents go where they can raise funds to help themselves and their party members, and doing so most frequently takes them to states in which they are popular.

Indeed, many motivations for presidential travel do not necessarily align with Electoral College incentives. George W. Bush and Barack Obama each spent substantial time on the Gulf Coast to respond to Hurricane Katrina and the Gulf of Mexico oil spill, respectively, not to boost their own electoral fortunes in those states. Presidents who aim to pressure recalcitrant legislators often travel to their home states to do so, and those states might have little to do with the president's electoral geography. Presidents travel for a myriad of reasons, many of which can be expected to work against, not with, the president's electoral interests. In spite of this tendency to spend time in states that are not key to the president's hopes of reelection, do the incentives of the Electoral College manifest themselves in a president's travel patterns in the aggregate? I turn to this question now.

THE GEOGRAPHY OF PRESIDENTIAL TRAVEL

To understand the relationship between aggregate patterns of presidential travel and the dynamics of the Electoral College while taking into account other factors, I employ regression analysis. Because the dependent variable, the number of presidential public events held in each state in each year, is a count of an event, which only takes on positive, integer values and is not normally distributed, regression analysis using ordinary least squares would yield inefficient, inconsistent, and biased estimates. Instead I use maximum likelihood techniques to estimate a negative binomial regression model, a type of regression analysis for count data with a variance that is greater than the mean.[20] Because the data are longitudinal, with repeated observations of states over time, I use a fixed effects negative binomial model.[21] This model takes into account that there likely is unobserved heterogeneity among the states in the study—that is, that they vary in ways that are not measured by the variables in the model. The fixed effects estimator calculates

Table 4.3: Assessing the Relationships between Presidential
Events and Electoral Size and Competitiveness, 1977–June 2011

	Presidential Events
Electoral College votes	.028***
	(.006)
Margin of victory or defeat in a state in the prior election	–.959*
	(.488)
Electoral College votes × margin	.079***
	(.024)
First term	.166*
	(.056)
Year of term	.194***
	(.024)
Miles from Washington, DC	–.0002**
	(.0001)
Constant	–.583

Note: Fixed effects negative binomial models; * p<.05; ** p<.01; *** p<.001.

Source: Data compiled by the author from the *Public Papers of the Presidents*; Associated Press articles; Dave Leip's Atlas of U.S. Elections, http://uselectionatlas.org/ (accessed May 21, 2011); and Frequent Flyer Services, http://www.webflyer.com/travel/milemarker (accessed March 10, 2006).

coefficients by looking at variation within each state but not across states, so unobserved heterogeneity among states does not affect the model's estimates. Table 4.3 presents the results of the negative binomial model.

The model indicates that greater numbers of Electoral College votes, closer margins of victory or defeat in the prior presidential election, and the interaction of the two are all statistically significant predictors of greater numbers of presidential events in a state, as the logic of the permanent campaign would predict. Because lower values of the margin of victory and defeat indicate more competitive elections, that coefficient's negative sign indicates that closer elections predict greater numbers of presidential public events in a state. The interaction term aims to take into account the fact that while presidents target states with many Electoral College votes and states that are more competitive, the states that offer the most potential reward are those that are both rich in Electoral College votes and competitive—in recent elections, Florida, Ohio, and Pennsylvania come readily to mind as the most prominent examples.

These findings are statistically significant controlling for whether the observation is during the president's first term, in which year of the term the observation falls, and the number of miles between Washington, DC, and the state in which the event takes place.[22] Each of these control variables is statistically significant as well, with directions of effects that are logical. Presidents are predicted to hold more events in their first term, in a later year of their term, and in states that are closer to Washington, DC. These findings indicate that, in spite of the many factors pulling presidents in many different directions, the incentives of the Electoral College are reflected in patterns of presidential travel, even when controlling for other important factors. Presidents hold more events in large states and in competitive states, and the interaction between state size and competitiveness also predicts greater numbers of presidential events. This model captures the important fact that, in the aggregate, presidents tend to spend more time in more populous states, competitive states, and states that both have more Electoral College votes and are more competitive—that is, battleground states with substantial numbers of Electoral College votes.

This regression analysis is useful in establishing these general relationships, but to understand more clearly the dynamics of presidential travel and electoral incentives, we must examine in greater depth the ways in which electoral size and competitiveness relate to patterns of presidential attention to the states. To do so, we turn next to the geographic distribution of presidential travel. Which states do presidents visit most and least, and which states are disproportionately favored and neglected? We begin with the states that presidents choose not to visit in a given term.

Where Presidents Don't Go

If studying where presidents go can reveal something about what they do care about, then examining the states that rarely if ever play host to a presidential visit is illuminating as well. Presidents claim to be unifying national leaders, but the rules of our electoral system incentivize presidential candidates and reelection-focused presidents to pay attention to certain states more than others. One prominent example of a politician who did not sufficiently heed the incentives of our electoral system is Richard Nixon during the 1960 presidential campaign. When Nixon accepted his party's nomination for the presidency at the Republican National Convention that year, he made a pledge:

> I've also been asked by my friends in the press on either side here: "Mr. Vice President, where are you going to concentrate? What states are you going to visit?" This is my answer: In this campaign we are going to take no states for granted, and we aren't going to concede any states to the opposition. I announce to you tonight, and I pledge to you, that I, personally, will carry this campaign into every one of the fifty states of this nation between now and November the eighth.[23]

Nixon made good on his promise, but doing so may have cost him the election. On the final weekend of the campaign, he made the long trip to Alaska, the only state he had not yet visited, to appeal for votes in that sparsely populated state's first presidential election following its admission to the Union the previous year. He ended up carrying Alaska's three Electoral College votes, but while he was there, Democratic nominee John F. Kennedy campaigned in vote-rich Illinois, New Jersey, and New York and throughout New England. When Nixon lost a very close race to Kennedy, his focus on appealing to all the states instead of those that would matter most in the election was widely viewed as a substantial mistake.[24] A more strategic candidate would not have campaigned as Nixon did, and, in the view of the permanent campaign, a state like Alaska is likely to get little attention throughout a presidents' term in office as well.

What sorts of states do presidents not visit? Table 4.4 provides the states that received no presidential visits in a given term from 1977 through June 2011. Most of the states that presidents chose not to visit were sparsely populated and electorally noncompetitive and had voted for the Republican presidential nominee in the previous election. Overall, presidents had won these neglected states in the previous election twenty-five times and lost them twenty-eight times. Forty-three of these states, however, had voted for the Republican presidential candidate in the previous election, while only 10 had supported the Democrat. Their average number of Electoral College votes was 4.5, ranging from twenty-two states with the minimum three Electoral College votes to a maximum of Massachusetts' twelve Electoral College votes, which received no visits from George W. Bush during his second term after he lost the two-party vote there to home-state candidate John Kerry by 25.5 percent in the 2004 election. These neglected states are not electoral battlegrounds. On average, the president who chose not to visit them had won or lost the two-party vote in these states by 19.9 percent in the most recent election, and thirty-three of these fifty-three states had been won or lost by more than 15 percent in the previous presidential election.

Proportionally, Democrats neglected more states than did Republicans, as the three Democratic presidents who were in office for 14.5 years of this study failed to visit a total of twenty-four states across their collective three and a half terms. Of these twenty-four states, twenty-one had been carried by Republicans, including all of Carter's neglected states, all of Clinton's first-term neglected states, and all of Obama's neglected states to date with the exception of tiny Vermont, which, despite a long history of Republican support, has become a consistent supporter of Democratic presidential candidates in recent years. Republicans, on the other hand, had largely met electoral success in their neglected states, winning twenty-two out of the twenty-nine states that did not receive a visit in a given presidential term over their twenty years in the White House. This suggests that both Republicans and Democrats tend to neglect similar states, which tend to be small states where Republicans do well in presidential elections. George H. W. Bush was the only president in this study to visit all fifty states in a single term, a function of his dedication to visit all the states that he led as president. Bush, of course, was not reelected, suggesting to cynical observers that a tighter focus on key electoral states might have better served his own self-interest.

There is substantial overlap in neglected states across presidencies. Vermont, the loneliest presidential state, hosted no presidential visits in seven of the nine presidential terms since 1977. As discussed earlier, George W. Bush did not set foot here as president. The Green Mountain State gave him his lowest vote totals in both 2000, when he lost it by 10 percentage points, and 2004, when he lost it by 20 points. Vermonters' disapproval of Bush was not expressed only on Election Day. By the end of 2008, thirty towns and cities in Vermont had adopted resolutions urging Bush's impeachment. "In March [2008], Brattleboro voters approved a resolution (unenforceable, town officials say) calling for Bush and Vice President Cheney to be arrested if they ever show up in town."[25] Given these dynamics, Bush's decision to stay away is not surprising.

Vermont was not always so hostile to Republican presidents. In fact, speaking at a GOP breakfast fundraiser in Burlington, Vermont, in October 1990, George H. W. Bush discussed his strong attachment to the state. "It's easy to have a very special feeling for this place. It's not just, I guess, the beauty of the Green Mountains. Maybe it's the fact that Vermont, as I was reminded by Messrs. Jeffords and Smith, has voted for more Republican Presidential candidates than any other State in the history of this country. Why wouldn't a Republican President love Vermont?"[26] Almost two decades later, his son could have offered him a persuasive answer to that question.

Sparsely populated North Dakota and South Dakota were the next most neglected states, with each playing host to no presidential visits in four of the nine presidential terms over the past three and a half decades. An additional six states—Idaho, Maine, Montana, Rhode Island, Utah, and Wyoming—were each not visited during three presidential terms. These eight most-neglected states averaged a mere 3.6 Electoral College votes. Given that all states are allocated at least three Electoral College votes, these neglected states are some of the most thinly populated in the country.

The most recent presidents display an even greater tendency for their neglected states to be noncompetitive. Of the eight states in table 4.4 that were won or lost by less than 5 percent in the last election, six of them were on Carter's and Reagan's lists, while the other two took place during Clinton's and George W. Bush's second terms, meaning that none of the last four presidents failed to travel during his first term in office to a state that he had won or lost by under 5 percent in the previous election. Distance from Washington, DC, appears to be a factor too, as many of

Table 4.4: States Presidents Did Not Visit, by Term,
1977–June 2011

President by Term	State	Electoral College Votes	Won or Lost by President in Last Election	Margin of Victory or Defeat: Two- Party Vote (%)	Party Supported in Last Election
Carter	AZ	6	Lost	17.2	Republican
	MT	4	Lost	7.6	Republican
	ND	3	Lost	6.0	Republican
	NV	3	Lost	4.5	Republican
	SD	4	Lost	1.5	Republican
	VT	3	Lost	11.5	Republican
Reagan	DE	3	Won	2.5	Republican
(first term)	ID	4	Won	45.0	Republican
	ME	4	Won	3.8	Republican
	ND	3	Won	42.0	Republican
	NH	4	Won	34.1	Republican
	RI	4	Lost	12.3	Democrat
	SD	3	Won	31.3	Republican
	VT	3	Won	7.2	Republican
Reagan	AK	3	Won	38.1	Republican
(second term)	DE	3	Won	19.9	Republican
	ME	4	Won	22.1	Republican
	MN	10	Lost	0.2	Democrat
	MS	7	Won	24.6	Republican
	MT	4	Won	22.6	Republican
	NM	5	Won	20.7	Republican
	OR	7	Won	12.2	Republican
	RI	4	Won	3.7	Republican
	UT	5	Won	50.2	Republican
	VT	3	Won	17.3	Republican
	WV	6	Won	10.5	Republican
	WY	3	Won	42.8	Republican
GHW Bush	None; Bush visited all 50 states				
Clinton	MS	7	Lost	9.9	Republican
(first term)	ND	3	Lost	15.7	Republican
	NE	5	Lost	22.6	Republican
	UT	5	Lost	27.5	Republican
Clinton	ME	4	Won	25.3	Democrat
(second term)	MT	3	Lost	3.4	Republican
	VT	3	Won	26.4	Democrat
	WY	3	Lost	15.0	Republican

Table 4.4, *continued*

President by Term	State	Electoral College Votes	Won or Lost by President in Last Election	Margin of Victory or Defeat: Two-Party Vote (%)	Party Supported in Last Election
GW Bush	ID	4	Won	41.7	Republican
(first term)	RI	4	Lost	31.3	Democrat
	VT	3	Lost	10.9	Democrat
GW Bush	MA	12	Lost	25.5	Democrat
(second term)	OR	7	Lost	4.2	Democrat
	SD	3	Won	21.8	Republican
	VT	3	Lost	20.6	Democrat
	WY	3	Won	40.6	Republican
Obama	AR	6	Lost	20.3	Republican
(through June 2011)	ID	4	Lost	26.0	Republican
	KS	6	Lost	15.2	Republican
	ND	3	Lost	8.9	Republican
	NE	5	Lost	15.2	Republican
	OK	7	Lost	31.3	Republican
	SC	8.3	Lost	9.1	Republican
	SD	3	Lost	8.6	Republican
	UT	5.3	Lost	29.1	Republican
	VT	3	Won	37.8	Democrat

Note: Electoral College votes that are not whole numbers are the average of two different values during a presidential term; the change resulted from the reapportionment process following a decennial census.

Source: Data compiled by the author from the *Public Papers of the Presidents;* from Associated Press articles; and from Dave Leip's Atlas of U.S. Elections, http://uselectionatlas.org/ (accessed May 21, 2011).

the states on this list are in the West, including Alaska, though small states in the Northeast and Midwest make appearances in the table as well. The states that presidents visit least tend to be small, noncompetitive, Republican-leaning, and often well removed geographically from Washington, DC. There is a good deal of overlap in the states that presidents of both parties rarely visit. It is clear that presidents of both parties largely ignore small, uncompetitive states. Which states do presidents visit most, and which states are disproportionately visited and ignored?

The Most Disproportionately Favored and Neglected States

Presidents tend to spend the most time in the most populated states. Figure 4.2 depicts the total number of days that presidents held events in each of the forty-

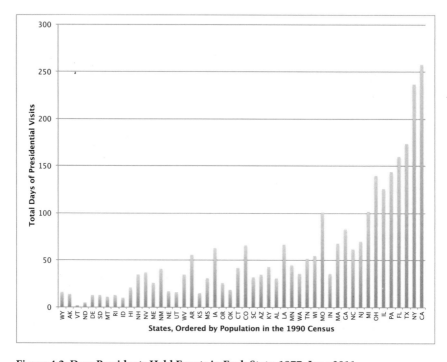

Figure 4.2: Days Presidents Held Events in Each State, 1977–June 2011
Source: Data compiled by the author from the *Public Papers of the Presidents*, from Associated Press articles, and from the U.S. Census (1990).

eight states in this study from 1977 through mid-2011. The states are listed from left to right in order of their population in the 1990 census, which is the census that fell closest to the midpoint of the period examined. The clear trend is a relationship between the number of days in a state and its population, and thus its electoral size. Simply put, populous states tend to get more attention from the president. The least-visited state is Vermont, the third-least-populated state, which hosted presidential visits on just 2 days over thirty-five years, while California, the most populous state in the Union, is the most visited, hosting presidents on 258 days. Presidents travel more often to states where greater numbers of people live, which is a perfectly reasonable tendency. While the general trend of visiting states where more people live is clear, there is substantial variation across states with relatively similar populations.

The story of presidential attention, however, goes beyond population and electoral size. Which states are most disproportionately favored and neglected? To address this question, we turn to the extent to which presidential visits exceed or fall short of the number that would be predicted by a state's population. To pro-

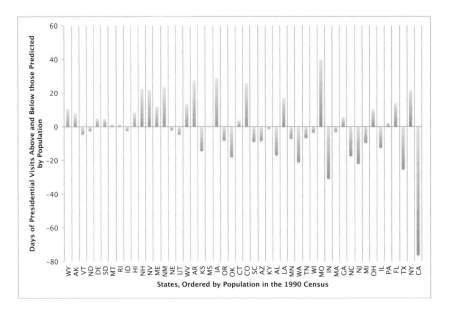

Figure 4.3: Disproportionate Attention: Presidential Visits Above and Below those
Predicted by Population, 1977–June 2011
Source: Data compiled by the author from the *Public Papers of the Presidents,* from Associated
Press articles, and from the U.S. Census (1990).

duce the data displayed in figure 4.3, I calculated how many of the 2,800 days of
presidential visits over this thirty-five-year period each state would have received
had they been allocated according to population and then subtracted that number
from the total number of days of events the state actually hosted. This approach allows us to see which states received more and less attention than their population
alone would predict and then address the questions of which states truly seem to
benefit from the Electoral College in terms of presidential attention and whether
presidential activity in election years resembles or differs sharply from the rest of
a president's term.

The states in figure 4.3 are, like those in figure 4.2, ordered by their population
in the 1990 census, but the data present a very different picture. While figure 4.2
showed a clear relationship between presidential visits and population, and thus
electoral size, these proportional data reveal that the story of presidential attention
is much more complex. Those states with positive values in figure 4.3 are those
that have been disproportionately favored by days of presidential visits relative to
population from 1977 through June 2011. Those with negative values have hosted
presidents less often than their population would predict.

The most disproportionately favored state is Missouri, which since 1977 has hosted forty visits more than its population would have predicted. Perhaps not co-incidentally, it is a perennial presidential battleground state and bellwether. When John McCain narrowly beat Obama there in 2008, it was only the second time since 1900 that the state was not carried by the winning presidential candidate.[27] The seven next most disproportionately favored states all received between 21 and 29 more presidential visits than expected based on population—Iowa (29), Arkansas (28), Colorado (26), New Mexico (23), New Hampshire (23), Nevada (22), and New York (22). Of these states, Iowa and New Hampshire, whose early caucus and primary, respectively, make them critical to success in the presidential nominating process and which have recently been competitive general election states as well, jump out. One need do no more than contrast New Hampshire with the least proportionally favored state, Vermont, its slightly less populous neighbor and inverted geographic twin, to suggest that electoral dynamics have propelled New Hampshire to the forefront of presidents' political consciousness.

Presidents of both parties spend much time in New York to speak at the United Nations, attend fundraisers, and more. Three other states on this list, Colorado, New Mexico, and Nevada, have recently been hotly contested in presidential elections. Other states receiving more visits than predicted include three additional presidential home states—Arkansas for Clinton, Georgia for Carter, and Maine, which was one of two home states for George H. W. Bush. The three populous battleground states of Florida, Ohio, and Pennsylvania, which have been central to the outcome of recent presidential elections, received fourteen, ten, and two visits more than expected, respectively, and were won or lost, on average, by 8.5 percent, 5.6 percent, and 6.4 percent in the six presidential elections preceding the first terms in this study. Wyoming, Alaska, Delaware, and Hawaii, which have three or four Electoral College votes apiece, hosted between thirteen and twenty-one days of presidential visits over thirty-five years and received between five and eleven more days of visits than expected. These states did not receive much absolute presidential attention, but their small population meant that any substantial attention they received would be disproportionate, since their population alone would predict very few presidential visits.

Examining the most disproportionately neglected states reveals additional dynamics of presidential priorities. While California hosted more days of presidential visits than any other state outside of the DC area, it still held events on seventy-six fewer days than its population alone would predict. Texas is similarly situated; while it hosted presidents on more days than any state except California and New York, if visits had been proportional to population, it would have hosted presidents on an additional twenty-six days. The second most disproportionately neglected state is Indiana, which, before becoming a presidential battleground state in 2008 that Barack Obama carried by the narrowest of margins, had not been won by a Democratic presidential candidate since Lyndon Johnson's victory there in 1964. Noncompetitive Indiana hosted thirty-one fewer events than predicted by population. The other states to host more than 10 fewer events than expected were New Jersey (22 fewer), Washington (21), Oklahoma (18), North Carolina (18), Alabama (17), Kansas (14), and Illinois (13). It is clear that while population plays a major role in the geography of presidential attention, there is a great deal of variation that population alone does not explain.

Figure 4.3 reveals interesting patterns in the aggregate. To understand better how these dynamics play out for each president since 1977, I calculated disproportional visits to states within the first term of each presidency, since that is when we would expect the targeting of key electoral states to occur. Table 4.5 provides a summary of the electoral dynamics of the states that received at least one day of presidential visits more than would be predicted by the state's population. The data are divided into the first three years of a presidential term and the reelection year to indicate better the extent to which key electoral states were favored at different points in a president's term. For each president, the table displays the number of states that received at least one more day of presidential attention than predicted by population, the number and percentage of these states that were battleground states, the number of times that the key nominating states of Iowa and New Hampshire were disproportionately visited, and the average number of Electoral College votes and margin of victory or defeat in the last election.

The data on battleground states were generously shared by Darshan Goux, who has extensively studied the evolving concept of the battleground state and its strategic role in presidential campaign strategy. These data for Carter and Reagan result from Goux's extensive archival research at presidential libraries, and the data for George H. W. Bush, Clinton, and George W. Bush are drawn from the research of Daron Shaw, who has both studied and helped to craft presidential battleground state strategy.[28] Battleground states for Obama's reelection campaign were determined by the author based on the results of the 2008 election and a campaign strategy video released by the Obama-Biden reelection organization in late 2011.[29]

The table shows that for all presidents except Reagan, at least 70 percent of these disproportionately visited states in election years were battlegrounds, and that the more recent presidents have accorded battleground states with disproportionately more attention earlier in their term as well. While only 27 and 29 percent of the states that Carter and Reagan, respectively, disproportionately visited in their first three years were battleground states, the percentages rose to 50, 41, 62, and 52 percent, respectively, for George H. W. Bush, Clinton, George W. Bush, and Obama, indicating that recent presidents, especially George W. Bush, focused disproportionately on key electoral states throughout their terms in office.

Table 4.5: States Visited More Than One Day More Than Predicted by Population in Specific Years, First Terms 1977–June 2011

President	Years	Number of States	Number of Battleground States	Percentage of Overvisited States That Were Battlegrounds	Average Margin of Victory or Defeat (%)	Average Electoral College Votes	Iowa or New Hampshire
Carter	First three years	15	4	27	14	9	1
	Reelection year	12	10	83	4	20	0
Reagan	First three years	14	4	29	24	16	1
	Reelection year	17	9	53	11	14	1
GHW Bush	First three years	10	5	50	14	17	2
	Reelection year	25	18	72	14	14	1
Clinton	First three years	17	7	41	13	9	1
	Reelection year	24	17	71	9	13	2
GW Bush	First three years	21	13	62	6	8	3
	Reelection year	18	13	72	4	11	2
Obama	First two-and-a-half years	25	13	52	16	15	1

Source: Data compiled by the author from the Public Papers of the Presidents; from Associated Press articles; from the U.S. census (1990); from Darshan Goux, "The Battleground State: Conceptualizing Geographic Contestation in American Presidential Elections, 1960–2004" (PhD diss., University of California, Berkeley, 2010); from Daron R. Shaw, "The Methods behind the Madness: Presidential Electoral College Strategies, 1988–1996," Journal of Politics 61, no. 4 (1999): 893–913; from Daron R. Shaw, The Race to 270: The Electoral College and the Campaign Strategies of 2000 and 2004 (Chicago: University of Chicago Press, 2006); and from Dave Leip's Atlas of U.S. Elections, http://uselectionatlas.org/ (accessed May 21, 2011).

The electoral size and margin of victory or defeat in the previous presidential election also indicate presidential targeting. Carter's actions reflect the traditional expectation about increased targeting during election years—in 1980 the states in which he spent disproportionate time were much more populous and electorally competitive than in his first three years in office. Reagan's pattern is similar, though he focused more on slightly smaller states in his reelection year, while spending much more time in the more competitive states as he made his case for a second term. Both George H. W. Bush and Bill Clinton's disproportionate travel focused slightly more on the more competitive states in 1992 and 1996 than earlier in their terms, but the differences are relatively small. The standout here, however, is George W. Bush, who focused on the most competitive states throughout his first term. He had won or lost the states he disproportionately visited in his first three years by 6 percent on average, and in his reelection year he focused even more on states he had narrowly won or lost by an average of 4 percent. George W. Bush did not wait until the election year to focus disproportionately on key electoral states; he did so throughout his term in office.

While battleground status and electoral size and competitiveness reflect the general election incentives of the Electoral College, presidents with an eye on the nominating process will pay particular attention to the key states of Iowa and New Hampshire, and every president since Carter spent disproportionate time in one or both early nominating states in the first three years of their term, when their efforts were likely geared toward preempting any potential challenge to their renomination. Carter, whose success in the 1976 Iowa caucuses was critical to propelling him to the Democratic nomination, spent over three days more in Iowa in 1979 than its population would have predicted. Reagan, who in 1980 had lost the Iowa caucuses to George H. W. Bush, spent just over one day more in Iowa in 1982 than population would have predicted. Similarly, George H. W. Bush disproportionately visited New Hampshire in 1989 and Iowa in 1990, and Bill Clinton spent a disproportionate amount of time in Iowa in 1995. George W. Bush spent disproportionate time in Iowa in 2001 and 2002 and in New Hampshire in 2002; Obama, who, like Carter, owes his presidency in large part to his success in the Iowa caucuses, spent disproportionate time there in 2010. The consistent pattern is one of presidents across this thirty-five-year period visiting these key nominating states more than their population would predict in their first three years in office.

Table 4.6 displays another indicator of disproportionate presidential attention by detailing the percentage of first-term presidential events held in states that the president's reelection campaign would classify as battleground states. The highlighted years in the table are those in which the percentage of days the president spent in battleground states exceeded the percentage of the population living in those states. The patterns displayed reflect several important findings. First, our

Table 4.6: Percentage of Days in Battleground States, by
President and Year of First Term, Compared with the Percentage
of the U.S. Population in Those States, 1977–June 2011

President	Year of First Term 1	2	3	4	Percentage of U.S. Population* in These States
Carter	48	54	53	84	73
Reagan	63	47	50	56	48
GHW Bush	56	51	60	73	55
Clinton	68	69	61	74	74
GW Bush	42	46	42	73	32
Obama (through June 2011)	48	50	47		36

*Note: This refers to the population of the forty-eight states in this study. Highlighted values are those for which the percentage of visits is greater than the percentage of the population in those states.

Source: Data compiled by the author from the *Public Papers of the Presidents;* from Associated Press articles; from the U.S. census (1970, 1980, 1990, 2000, 2010); from Darshan Goux, "The Battleground State: Conceptualizing Geographic Contestation in American Presidential Elections, 1960–2004" (PhD diss., University of California, Berkeley, 2010); from Daron R. Shaw, "The Methods behind the Madness: Presidential Electoral College Strategies, 1988–1996," *Journal of Politics* 61, no. 4 (1999): 893–913; and from Daron R. Shaw, *The Race to 270: The Electoral College and the Campaign Strategies of 2000 and 2004* (Chicago: University of Chicago Press, 2006).

two most recent presidents are the only ones who disproportionately targeted battleground states in every year of their first term as president. Though only 32 percent of the U.S. population lived in George W. Bush's battleground states, he spent 42, 46, 42, and 73 percent of his days of travel in these states in each of the four years of his first term. Similarly, while only 36 percent of the U.S. population lives in Obama's battleground states, he spent 49, 50, and 47 percent of his days of travel in those states in his first two and a half years as president. While Clinton spent a lower percentage of his travel in battleground states than their populations would have justified during his first three years, his totals for each year are close to the percentage of the population in those states. Reagan and George H. W. Bush both disproportionately targeted battleground states in every year but their second, when the electoral geography of their fellow Republicans drove much of their travel, but even in these years they spent almost as much time in battleground states as predicted by population. Only Jimmy Carter did not disproportionately target battleground states throughout his term in office. But the travel of four of his five successors all reflected disproportionate attention to battleground states throughout much or all of their first term as president.

Table 4.7: First-Year Travel to Battleground States,
1977–June 2011

President	Number of Battleground States	Number of These States Visited in First Year of Term	Percentage
Carter	18	8	44
Reagan	17	7	41
GHW Bush	24	18	75
Clinton	27	21	78
GW Bush	15	11	73
Obama	15	15	100

Source: Data compiled by the author from the *Public Papers of the Presidents;* from Associated Press articles; from Darshan Goux, "The Battleground State: Conceptualizing Geographic Contestation in American Presidential Elections, 1960–2004" (PhD diss., University of California, Berkeley, 2010); from Daron R. Shaw, "The Methods behind the Madness: Presidential Electoral College Strategies, 1988–1996," *Journal of Politics* 61, no. 4 (1999): 893–913; and from Daron R. Shaw, *The Race to 270: The Electoral College and the Campaign Strategies of 2000 and 2004* (Chicago: University of Chicago Press, 2006).

One final way to look at the extent to which specific presidents targeted key electoral states not only in election years but throughout their terms in office is to examine the extent to which they visited them early in their tenure as president. Table 4.7 reveals a clear trend of recent presidents traveling to greater percentages of battleground states in their first year in office. The percentages jump from 44 for Carter and 41 for Reagan to 75, 78, 73, and 100 for George H. W. Bush, Clinton, George W. Bush, and Obama, respectively. In recent years, presidents are all the more likely to touch down in key electoral states early in their terms.

Obama's early travel provides an illustrative example. On February 9, he made his first trip out of the DC area as president, traveling to Elkhart, Indiana, which he had narrowly carried the previous November, becoming the first Democrat to do so since 1964. The next day, he flew to Florida, a perennial battleground state that he had carried by less than 3 percent of the vote. On February 12, he traveled home to Illinois for two events, and less than a week later he journeyed to Colorado, a battleground state that he had carried, the first time a Democrat had done so since 1992. From there he headed to Arizona, a state he lost by less than 10 percent to favorite son John McCain. Later that month, on February 27, he traveled to North Carolina, which he had won by under 1 percent, becoming the first Democrat to carry the state since 1976. His travels in March would take him to Ohio, Pennsylvania, and California, and in April he would go to Iowa and Missouri. In May he returned to Arizona, Indiana, and California and made his first presidential trips to New Mexico, Nevada, and New York. In just over four months in office, Obama traveled to fourteen states outside of the DC area. Of these, only three were safe Democratic states—Illinois, California, and New York. Eight were states that he had won or lost by less than 10 percent, including some of the most competitive states from the 2008 election. The final three—Pennsylvania, New Mexico, and Nevada—were states that Obama carried by more than 10 percent but were considered battleground states during the 2008 campaign and likely will be again in 2012. Clearly, the White House made a point of the president traveling to key electoral states early in his term in office.

WHY THE RISE IN TARGETED TRAVEL?

Presidents are strategic actors who respond to the institutional incentives of their political environment. Goal-oriented presidents aim to win reelection to secure their legacy and enact their policy priorities. The evidence presented in this chapter demonstrates that their efforts to win reelection are not confined to their fourth year in office. Instead, the incentives of the nominating process and the Electoral College are reflected in patterns of presidential travel throughout their terms in office. Regression analysis shows that in the aggregate, from 1977 through June 2011, states with greater numbers of Electoral College votes, smaller margins of victory or defeat in the previous election, and the interaction of these two factors—that is, larger states with more competitive elections—have been more likely to receive greater numbers of visits by the president, even when controlling for other relevant factors. Even though presidents have spent one in every four events outside of the Washington, DC, area at fundraisers over the past three and a half decades, and these events were overwhelmingly in states where the president was popular, in the aggregate, presidents still spend more time in the more competitive states.

The states that presidents of both parties do not visit have much in common. They are overwhelmingly sparsely populated, noncompetitive states that were carried by Republicans in the previous election. While presidents do spend more time in the most populous states, population does not account for important variation in presidential attention, as certain states are disproportionately favored. Battleground states have received disproportionate attention throughout most presidents' first terms in office over the past thirty-five years, and they have been so most markedly for our most recent presidents, especially George W. Bush. Presidents have increasingly visited greater percentages of battleground states in their first year in office, showing that electoral targeting starts soon after a president enters the Oval Office.

Both Iowa and New Hampshire, the key nominating states that are central to any president's successful renomination, have been disproportionately visited by president after president since 1977. In May 1979, Carter himself acknowledged his propensity to focus his travel on such key electoral states. Speaking at a fundraiser to benefit the Democratic Congressional Campaign Committee, he joked, "The last few months, I have been looking for invitations to speak. On a strictly nonpolitical basis, of course. I even visited one state that does not have an early primary next year. The darned scheduler resigned before I could fire him."[30] Presidents aim to lock in support in the early nominating states to reduce the possibility of an intraparty challenge. When Bill Clinton convened a conference at Iowa State University in April 1995 to discuss issues facing rural America, one of his top aides acknowledged the clear political undertones of holding an event like this in Iowa. Harold Ickes, head of the White House Office of Political Affairs, explained, "We're gearing up as if there will be a primary opponent. My view, though, is there won't be."[31]

Like Carter, Clinton also joked about the common perception that presidents focus disproportionately on key electoral states just weeks after his first and only trip to Nebraska in the final weeks of his term. While addressing employees of the Department of Health and Human Services (HHS), a department whose aims are seen as in line with many of the policy preferences of the Democratic Party, Clinton said:

> You know, they say that because of the 24-hour news cycle, we're all in a permanent campaign. And when you're in a permanent campaign, it's hard to take the time to go to someplace you have no chance of winning—Nebraska—or someplace you have no chance of losing—the HHS Building. Right? So I might say, just parenthetically, I had a wonderful time in Kearney, Nebraska, and in Omaha, and you would be amazed at all the letters I've gotten. I have already received more letters than I thought there were Democrats in the State of Nebraska. It was quite wonderful.[32]

Recent presidents have been criticized for spending much of their time in key electoral states. One Obama administration aide offered this response to justify such efforts:

> The president has routinely traveled outside of the Washington area and visited a diverse range of communities because we've found that the president's agenda for strengthening the economy and creating jobs, for example, is most resonant and persuasive when it's presented in the context of the communities who are dealing with these challenges firsthand. It's no surprise that this president, like previous

presidents, most frequently visits those areas where there is a high concentration of voters who are most likely to be persuaded—so-called swing voters.[33]

This explanation is notable for two reasons. First, it was given in late 2009. Less than a year into Obama's term as president, his aide describes the people the president is trying to reach not as citizens or constituents but as voters, even though they would not get the chance to vote for or against the president again for almost three more years. Second, the aide argues that the president goes to places with many swing voters. But there are swing voters in every state—even in Vermont, Utah, and Texas. Focusing on swing states is another matter entirely, however, and it is one that the aide does not squarely address.

White House press secretary Robert Gibbs acknowledged, "It's hard [to look] at a map and not see red, purple and blue states. But as the president said famously, people aren't looking for red, blue or purple solutions, only those that will improve their daily lives." Gibbs went on to explain that the destination of Obama's first trip outside the DC area as president, which took him to Elkhart, Indiana, in early February 2009, was not tied to the fact that Obama had narrowly carried the state in 2008, becoming the first Democrat since 1964 to do so. Instead, Gibbs said that the White House had looked to hold an event in the community with the highest unemployment rates. It just happened to find that community in a key electoral state.[34]

Ari Fleischer, a former press secretary to George W. Bush, was more forthright when he addressed the same issue years after his boss had left the White House. "A smart White House is a savvy mix of policy and politics, and in our democracy there's nothing wrong with it," said Fleischer. "If you're all substance and no politics, you lose support on Capitol Hill. If you're all politics and no substance, you lose support among the people. If people don't like it, they can move from a safe state to a swing state and see their president more."[35]

Why do we see an increasing prevalence of targeted presidential travel favoring key electoral states throughout a president's term in office? One likely reason is that recent presidents know that the possibility of being defeated in a reelection bid is quite real. Before Jimmy Carter beat Gerald Ford in 1976, a sitting president had not been defeated at the polls for forty-four years, since Herbert Hoover lost to Franklin Roosevelt in 1932. Between 1976 and 1992, however, three of the four presidents who submitted their fate to the voters lost, as Ford, Carter, and George H. W. Bush all were beaten by challengers from the other party. In the week before the 1992 election, as Bush was waging an uphill battle to be reelected, he told television host Larry King in an interview, "For a long time I decided I wouldn't get in the arena. . . . Some thought it was a little late. I've had some criticism of that

STRATEGIC TRAVEL AND THE PERMANENT CAMPAIGN   119

from my own party."[36] His successors have heeded this lesson and have tended to electoral concerns throughout their terms in office.

Of the three presidents since 1976 who have been reelected, only Reagan won in a landslide. While Bill Clinton earned a second term with a comfortable Electoral College vote margin, he won only 49.2 percent of the popular vote, meaning that more Americans voted for someone other than Bill Clinton than for the president. George W. Bush won a popular majority in 2004, but his slim Electoral College majority rested on his victory in Ohio, which he carried by just under 120,000 votes.[37] As John Kerry said to Tim Russert in January 2005, "If you take half the people at an Ohio State football game on Saturday afternoon and they were to have voted the other way, you and I would be having a discussion about my State of the Union speech."[38] Additionally, Ford, Carter, and George H. W. Bush all faced significant intraparty challenges to their renomination prior to their losing efforts in the general election. In short, presidents are well aware that they might lose and are determined to do what they can to ensure that they do not.

The targeting of key electoral states is also the consequence of the type of president produced in recent years by the rules structuring presidential nominating and general election campaigns, as presidents and their aides continue to employ once in office the same strategies that secured them the White House in the first place. As Nelson Polsby and Samuel Kernell have argued, presidents now attain their office by taking their case to the people instead of by courting party leaders.[39] And they go to the people during the campaign in a manner structured by the strategic incentives of the nominating calendar and the Electoral College system. Once in office, they continue to do so.

It is understandable that presidents might return to campaign mode throughout their term in the White House. Doing so brings them back to what worked well enough to land them in the highest office in the land. On one May 1978 campaign swing, Carter's aides wanted him to sleep at the houses of supporters instead of at hotels, as he had in the 1976 campaign. He attended a fundraiser and spoke at a large outdoor rally, in an effort, in the words of one of his aides, "to get back to our winning game."[40] Later that month, Carter returned to the anti-Washington rhetoric that had helped him to reach the White House. "After a year and a half, I am still frustrated by the federal bureaucracy. There is in Washington an iron triangle of bureaucracy, congressional committees and well-organized special interests who can mobilize strong opposition to the reforms we need." The president of the United States, the ultimate Washington insider, was campaigning for the midterm elections as if he were still the outsider he had been as a former governor of Georgia first running for the White House.[41] Focusing presidential attention on key electoral states is a natural outgrowth of these tendencies.

Karl Rove, a chief political adviser to George W. Bush both on the campaign trail and during his presidency who was often accused of bringing a campaign's mentality into the White House, leveled the same charge at the Obama administration in an op-ed column in the *Wall Street Journal*. Rove wrote:

> Team Obama is suffering from Extended Campaign Syndrome. In an election, campaign staffers are often just trying to survive until the next week or the next primary. They cut corners because they are fatigued or under pressure. They can be purposely combative and even portray critics as enemies. Carrying this mindset into the White House can get you into trouble, a lesson the Obama administration is now learning the hard way.... Life inside the White House is far different from life inside a presidential campaign. The spotlight is brighter and scrutiny greater.... What worked in the Obama campaign will often backfire on the Obama presidency. But old habits are hard to leave on the trail.[42]

Rove was discussing how a campaign treats the opposition, but his general point about campaign practices continuing into an administration's tenure in the White House are applicable to the targeting of key electoral states as well. Political observers expect to see key electoral states receive disproportionate attention from candidates during the closing months of a presidential campaign. A candidate who devoted too much attention to electorally safe states at the expense of battleground states would be pilloried for political malpractice. But sitting presidents also devote disproportionate time to key electoral states throughout their terms in office. They do not travel exclusively to these states; indeed, they travel widely for a variety of reasons. But a number of measures indicate that the incentives of our electoral system manifest themselves in the patterns of attention paid by U.S. presidents. No electoral system is neutral. Any system sets up rules of the game that provide incentives that structure candidate behavior. A president concerned about the prospect of renomination and reelection might respond to these incentives throughout his term in office; the evidence here indicates that presidents do.

In a 2010 interview with Diane Sawyer, Barack Obama was asked, "Ever in the middle of all that's coming did you think maybe one term is enough?" Obama responded:

> You know, I would say that when I—the one thing I'm clear about is that I'd rather be a really good one-term president than a mediocre two-term president. And I—and I believe that. You know, there's a tendency in Washington to think that our job description of elected officials is to get reelected. That's not our job description. Our job description is to solve problems and to help people. And, you know, that's not just the view of the elected officials themselves. That's also the filter through which the media reads things.[43]

The media's focus on electoral motivations can help to fuel the perception that presidents care more about key electoral states than the other states they lead, and this could be damaging to a president's image as a unifying national leader. Presidents do care about the representative nature of their jobs, and they want to be the president of all the people. Obama's point that the media tend to focus on the political elements of any presidential action is a valid one. But given the objective empirical evidence presented here, there are good grounds for the media focus on the political nature of presidential travel, for when presidential travel is looked at objectively over a period of several decades, clear patterns reflecting electoral incentives emerge. If some states are treated as neglected backwaters and they also happen to offer no electoral reward, while those states with electoral payoff receive disproportionate attention, the president could be seen more as a calculating electioneer than a national leader, which could pose political difficulties for him.

In the next chapter, I turn to how these strategic decisions are made. Who decides when and where the president will travel and fundraise? To address these questions, I examine the changing roles of presidential staff and the institutionalization of the permanent campaign within the White House itself.

5. The Evolving Role of White House Staff in Electoral Decision-Making

When then-senator Barack Obama was running for president in June 2007, he offered a sharp rebuke to the administration of George W. Bush in Manchester, New Hampshire, accusing it of mixing politics and policy:

> This has been the most politicized White House in history and the American people have suffered as a result. Now, presidents obviously want to surround themselves with those people who share their views and their beliefs. There's nothing wrong with that per se, but the days of firing eight qualified U.S. attorneys because of their politics is over. The days of using the White House as another arm of the Republican National Committee are over.[1]

This sort of criticism of the Bush White House did not come only from the Democratic side of the partisan divide. Obama's Republican opponent in the election, Senator John McCain, made clear that he would run the White House differently than had both George W. Bush and Bill Clinton, when he declared in June 2008, "There is a time to campaign, and a time to govern. If I'm elected President, the era of the permanent campaign of the last sixteen years will end."[2] Later that year, McCain became more explicit about just how he aimed to end the permanent campaign when, during a *60 Minutes* interview in September, he promised, "I would move the political office out of the White House and into the Republican National Committee. I think we've got to have a White House that is without politics."[3]

Whether it is either possible or desirable in a democratic society to have a White House that is without politics is a debatable premise. Nevertheless, McCain was pointing to the White House Office of Political Affairs as a key factor in the blurring of the lines between campaigning and governing at 1600 Pennsylvania Avenue. In June 1978, Jimmy Carter became the first president to officially designate an aide to handle political issues when he named Timothy Kraft to be assistant to the president for political affairs and personnel. This action was in part a response to the criticisms discussed in chapter 3 of Carter's poor interactions with the Congress and with fellow Democrats across the country. When Ronald Reagan was inaugurated in 1981, the White House Office of Political Affairs was officially created. It has existed, with brief interruptions when it was dismantled during certain but not all reelection years, ever since.[4]

We have seen that presidents devote more and more time to their role as fundraiser-in-chief, that they do so in support of their own electoral fortunes and those of their fellow party members, and that patterns of strategic presidential travel increasingly demonstrate the targeting of key electoral states throughout a president's term in office. This chapter examines the source, rather than the manifestations, of the decisions that shape the permanent campaign by focusing on who is involved with making decisions about electoral considerations. To study changing dynamics within the White House itself, I draw upon archival research at presidential libraries and the commentary of presidential aides. First, I demonstrate that White House aides now often make decisions about electoral concerns that were once made by the Democratic and Republican National Committees. I then contend that these changes and evolving norms have increasingly blurred the lines between campaigning and governing. Because the political roles of the White House staff have been institutionalized, each incoming president arrives at a White House where the path of least resistance is one that perpetuates the permanent campaign.

It is worth reiterating at this point that the political decisions focused on in this book are ones with a clear electoral element. While efforts to advance the president's legislative agenda, boost his public approval, and a number of other undertakings are inherently political, the questions of interest here are those related to the electoral efforts of the president and his party. This chapter begins by focusing on the dynamics of White House staffing and decision-making in the Truman and Reagan administrations, and then briefly surveys these dynamics for each of the presidents elected via the plebiscitary nominating system. Why look farther back in time beyond the thirty-five years examined in most of this book? While the presidency has always been a political office, the ways in which those dynamics play out have changed dramatically in the post–World War II era. The structure and nature of the White House staff, the role of the national party committee, and the norms governing partisan presidential conduct have all evolved substantially since the time of Harry Truman's presidency. These changes have shaped the manner in which a presidential administration deals with the inherent tension between campaigning and governing.

In the Truman administration, the White House staff was small, and the Democratic National Committee handled most overtly partisan political work. Norms about the limited involvement of the White House in such political matters were fairly firmly in place. The presidency of Ronald Reagan, the first in which the White House Office of Political Affairs existed, provides an illustrative counterpoint to that of Truman. In the intervening years, the White House staff grew substantially, and many political functions formerly performed by the national party organization were incorporated into the White House. These contrasting dynamics provide an understanding of how the presidency has evolved and frames a discussion of these dynamics in other recent administrations.

THE ROLE OF WHITE HOUSE STAFF AND THE NATIONAL
COMMITTEE IN THE TRUMAN ADMINISTRATION

The size of and roles played by the White House staff in Truman's time were tremendously different from those of our most recent presidents. Most political considerations were handled not by presidential aides on the government's payroll who worked in the White House but rather by the Democratic National Committee (DNC). Speaking in 2006, Truman aide George Elsey explained that administration's reliance on the DNC for political functions:

> The White House staff didn't have an in-depth political staff that could do this. That's what the committee was for. Nowadays there are the Karl Roves. There are huge numbers of politically oriented, politically minded people. And this is not true just of [the George W. Bush] administration, it's been true in at least several—most of the recent ones that devote all of their time and their attention to the politics, just plain partisan politics of the situation. There was nobody in the White House staff to do that in those days. The White House was too limited. Nowadays there are huge congressional liaison organizations, that's been building up through the years at the White House. We didn't have congressional liaison. Harry Truman was the congressional liaison. Harry Truman met every Monday morning with congressional leaders. There was no speech writing staff per se. Because [Truman's special counsel Clark] Clifford and his successor, [Charles] Murphy, and those of us who worked with Clifford and Murphy were jacks-of-all-trades. We handled all kinds of things in addition to just speeches. ... The difference between the White House then and the White House today is incalculable. You can't even conceive of how limited and how narrow and how small it was.[5]

Elsey's assertions are supported by data on the size of the White House staff. While exact numbers of White House staff are difficult to come by, various scholars have concluded that the White House staff grew by about a factor of ten from Truman's time to Reagan's.[6]

With such relatively limited White House staff, the Truman administration relied extensively on the Democratic National Committee. That relationship was coordinated by Truman himself and his appointments secretary, Matthew Connelly, who described his duties thus:

Officially, I was appointments secretary, I handled all the appointments for the President. In addition, I had to act as a sort of contact man for the politicians from all over the states. Every politician who came into Washington could not get in to see [Truman], it would be impossible, so that job fell on me with the result they could go home and say, "Well, no I didn't see the President, but I talked to his secretary and he's going to get me some help," because it saves face for them in their home state, or have dinner with them or go to a cocktail party for a state delegation and that was all left to me just to keep politics a little bit smooth. I handled all the politics in the White House except for Truman and at his own level and their level, he would handle it. And we maintained a liaison with the national committee, to see about political things—working together is part of the game.[7]

Elsey, who in addition to his duties in the White House drafted most of Truman's whistle-stop speeches during the 1948 presidential campaign, corroborated Connelly's account and emphasized the extent to which most other members of the White House staff had little interaction with the national committee:

Matt was pretty closemouthed and it's understandable and proper that he should have been. He was the link between the President and the various, or the successive chairmen of the national committee and he simply didn't open up and gossip to others on the White House staff on matters of concern to the President in his political role. Now, you may find this hard to understand. How could we be involved in a presidential campaign, for example, without staff members, such as myself, without dealing with Connelly all the time? Well, I'll try to explain it this way. Connelly would deal with the committee on patronage matters, on where, and when, and how, the President should put in an appearance to be of maximum effectiveness to others on the Democratic ticket, the junior members of the staff, such as myself, were in effect, told after such decisions had been made. Matt would work with the President and the committee on an itinerary for a presidential swing. We would be given the itinerary after those decisions had been made, and our job then was to produce the kinds of speeches and the kinds of statements that would be effective, under the circumstances. So, that is how it happens that I can be as ignorant as I am on the details and the day-by-day manner in which Matt Connelly worked with the President on political matters.[8]

While this coordination with the national committee took place throughout Truman's almost eight years in office, it was particularly evident during the 1948 presidential campaign. In the fall of 1947, Elsey, Clark Clifford, Charlie Murphy, and Charlie Ross determined that the White House would need more support during the campaign of the upcoming year. Elsey reports, "The obvious answer was to build up a team in the headquarters of the Democratic National Committee."

The result was the creation of the DNC's Research Division, which was located in a separate building from committee headquarters. Its staff was devoted to "preparing material for use by the President's associates in drafting speeches and digging up the information he would need during the course of the campaign." This division would fulfill much of the role of the legal campaign organizations created in later years, such as the Committee for the Reelection of the President in 1972 and Reagan-Bush '84.[9]

Elsey and Connelly describe a White House staff that by and large was not deeply involved in partisan politics but instead relied heavily on the Democratic National Committee. The papers of Truman and his aides available at the Truman Library lend support to their depiction of the dynamics in the Truman administration. Table 5.1 provides information on who authored and received certain memos related to overtly political plans in the Truman White House. These memos were gathered by the author at the Harry S. Truman Library and Museum with the aid of archivists there who provided guidance about which staff members were most likely to have played a role in electoral planning. In archival research, one can never be sure of what one has not found. The memos detailed in table 5.1 are a sample, not the entire universe, of those related to political planning in the Truman White House. Given the consistency of the dynamics they present and the accounts of Truman's aides, we can be fairly certain that the picture they paint of political decision-making is an accurate one. That picture is one in which most electoral planning was handled by the Democratic National Committee, not White House aides on the government's payroll. These dynamics present a stark contrast to our most recent presidential administrations.

Very few of these memos originated in the White House. Instead, most came from the Democratic National Committee's Research Division, which was headed by William Batt Jr. Interestingly, most went not to Connelly but to Clark Clifford, who was special counsel to the president and was in charge of the White House speech-writing team for the 1948 campaign. Several of the memos are unsigned. Clifford indicated that such memos were usually "an assembly job. And that's why you can't find any one individual that says, 'Yes, I wrote the memo.'" The "assembly job" involved a team effort by White House staff, usually with the input of staff of the Democratic National Committee as well.[10]

The documents cover a wide range of political topics. The first one chronologically is a letter from DNC chairman Robert Hannegan to one of Truman's White House aides, suggesting that the president not meet with shipbuilding magnate Henry Kaiser when he visits California that year because Kaiser had turned down a personal request from Hannegan to help the Roosevelt-Truman ticket in 1944. Most are memos from DNC Research Division chairman William Batt Jr., covering topics as diverse as the DNC's role in planning presidential trips, the presi-

Table 5.1: Truman Administration Political Planning Memos

Date	From (Person)	From (Office/Position)	To (Person)	To (Office/Position)	Title/Subject
6/6/45	Robert Hannegan	DNC chair	Edward McKim	Chief administrative assistant to the president	Political Advice for Truman's West Coast Trip
11/19/47	Clark Clifford	Special counsel to the president	Harry Truman	The president	Clifford-Rowe Memorandum— 1948 Political Strategy
1947	Unsigned	N/A	No recipient listed	N/A	Unsigned Political Strategy Memos in Clark Clifford's Files
4/5/48	Unsigned	N/A	No recipient listed	N/A	DNC Research Division Functions
4/20/48	William Batt Jr.	DNC Research Division	Gael Sullivan, Clark Clifford	DNC executive director, special counsel to the president	The Negro Vote
5/2/48	William Batt Jr.	DNC Research Division	Clark Clifford	Special counsel to the president	Effects on Campaign of Calling a Special Session of Congress
7/22/48	William Batt Jr.	DNC Research Division	Clark Clifford	Special counsel to the president	How the President Can Reach the People
8/6/48	William Batt Jr.	DNC Research Division	Clark Clifford	Special counsel to the president	Participation of Mrs. Franklin D. Roosevelt in the Signing of the Bill Authorizing the Loan for the United Nations Building
8/11/48	William Batt Jr.	DNC Research Division	Clark Clifford	Special counsel to the president	Notes on the Presidents' Campaign
8/17/48	William Batt Jr.	DNC Research Division	Clark Clifford	Special counsel to the president	Presidential Speeches at Veterans' Meetings
8/17/48	Clark Clifford	Special counsel to the president	Harry Truman	The president	The 1948 Campaign
9/13/48	William Batt Jr.	DNC Research Division	Charles Murphy	Administrative assistant to the president	President's Speech in Los Angeles
1948	George Elsey, William Batt Jr.	Assistant to the special counsel to the president, DNC Research Division	No recipient listed	N/A	Campaign Strategy Memo
3/6/50	David Bell	Special assistant to the president	Charles Murphy	Special counsel to the president	President's Trip West in May

Source: Data compiled by the author from the Harry S. Truman Library.

dent's ability to get his message through to the people, a strategy for courting the "Negro vote" in the upcoming campaign, the desirability of appealing to veterans' groups, the public relations benefits of inviting Eleanor Roosevelt to a bill-signing ceremony, and the impact on the campaign of calling a special session of Congress that summer.

Three that were authored by White House staff reflect the input of outsiders at the DNC and elsewhere. The famed memorandum of November 1947 that laid out much of what would become Truman's winning strategy for the 1948 presidential election nominally came from special counsel Clifford but was written in large part by former FDR aide James Rowe, who was working for a law firm at the time, and thus would come to be known as the Clifford-Rowe memorandum. An undated memo in 1948 setting forth campaign strategy has no author officially listed, but in the corner of the first page a handwritten note reveals that it was "Prepared by GME [Truman aide George M. Elsey]; Parallels memo of [DNC Research Division chairman] Wm. L. Batt." A subsequent memo from Clifford dated August 17, 1948, uses much of the same language, illustrating both how the "assembly job" memos were put together and the role of the DNC in shaping even the political advice given to the president that appeared to come directly from White House staff.

The national committee was central not just to the formulation of political strategy but also to deciding the particulars of how Truman's travel could reap the most political benefits. When Truman was invited to the West Coast in 1948 to receive an honorary degree from the University of California, Berkeley, and again in 1950 to dedicate the Grand Coulee Dam, Truman laid out the main purpose of the trip; then, in the words of George Elsey, he "let the Democratic National Committee make whatever use it could of his desire to go out there. Well, like Berkeley. He'd be happy to go. And let's let the Committee figure out how we can get some brownie points out of the exercise. . . . The initiative for this, that, and the other would have been coming from the Committee."[11]

The final memo listed in table 5.1 is an exception to the general trend of political advice originating from outside the White House. On March 6, 1950, David Bell, whose title at the time was special assistant to the president, sent a memo to Charles Murphy, who had taken over for Clifford as special counsel to the president, in which he recommended that the president's proposed trip to Oregon to dedicate the Grand Coulee Dam take place after the May 19 Democratic primary there so that he could "be of direct assistance to the successful Democratic candidates." He also suggested that the president make speeches en route in both Wisconsin and Idaho to aid Democratic political prospects, and that he avoid California due to a contested Democratic primary for the U.S. Senate seat. Additionally, he advised that given the choice of traveling to Portland, Oregon, or Seattle, Washington, the president would find it more politically advantageous to visit the former. In a follow-up memo from Bell to Murphy on March 8, he delved into further detail about the political advantages of the president making stops in certain places on the trip and urged that the Democratic National Committee get started preparing material for the president's speeches, as it had done in the 1948 campaign.[12]

Years later, Matthew Connelly provided additional evidence of the political nature of the trip, attesting:

> That dam was probably the most rededicated dam that we have had in this country, and it was used as an instrument to get the President known in that territory so the people of that territory would have an idea of what the President was like. And actually it was political motivation because the dam sure didn't need another rededication. It was an instrument as an excuse for that trip to keep it on a non-political basis.[13]

Elsey called this memo a sign of the evolution of the White House staff within the Truman administration. "We learned some things in 1948 and we capitalized on them. And tried to do a little better job in 1950 than we had done earlier. And the staff, you see, was larger by this time ... [and included] more people who had a political orientation and political concerns than had been true at the beginning of the Truman Administration." Elsey attributed the shift in part to special counsel Murphy. "Charlie Murphy had spent years on the Hill. Clifford had had no experience on Capitol Hill at all. So Murphy would be much more attuned to thinking about senators, congressmen, and the significance of senatorial and congressional and gubernatorial races than anybody from the White House corps."[14] Murphy, in an oral history interview, concurred, attesting that when he arrived at the White House, "I naturally tended toward becoming interested in legislative matters as that had been my background."[15] It is worth emphasizing, however, that this instance of a White House aide advocating a political trip seems to be an exception rather than the norm in the Truman administration. Additionally, even as the memo provides evidence of an increased White House sensitivity to such concerns later in Truman's presidency, Bell still called on the DNC to help with the preparation of materials for the political parts of the president's trip, demonstrating the extensive relationship with and continued reliance upon the national committee.

The evidence found at the Truman Library indicates that most partisan political planning originated not in the White House but in the Democratic National Committee, which is consistent with the accounts of Truman administration aides. While the White House was certainly not apolitical, Truman administration documents, interviews, and oral histories lend support to the notion that the White House staff in that administration largely outsourced most such electoral strategizing to the Democratic National Committee, both because it was expedient and, as I shall now discuss, because it was deemed proper.

Prevailing Norms

Truman and his aides were concerned with questions of propriety when it came to the lines between campaigning and governing. When Truman's assistants decided in 1947 that the White House staff would need more support as the 1948 campaign heated up, they did not look to add more politically minded people to the White House staff. According to White House aide Elsey, the Truman team "concluded that it would be a big mistake to try and build up a 'stable,' if you will, of speech-writers in the White House or, for that matter, any place on the government payroll. *The latter would not have been proper at all* [emphasis added]."[16] Instead, their recommendations led to the establishment of the DNC's Research Division, which was dedicated to providing material for the president's campaign efforts.

Truman, like other presidents, went to great lengths to manage the tension between his roles as a unifying national figure and a divisive political leader. The Clifford-Rowe memorandum of November 19, 1947, which set forth a strategy for Truman to deal with these contradictory demands as he planned for the presidential election of 1948, reveals some of the norms prevalent at the time. Special counsel Clifford and former FDR aide Rowe wrote:

> Since he is President, he cannot be politically active until well after the July
> Convention. The people are inconsistent and capricious but there is no argument
> that they feel deeply on this—: He must be President of all the people and not
> merely the leader of a party, until the very last minute. Therefore, he must act
> as a President almost up to Election Day. Lincoln set the pattern by remaining
> "judiciously aloof" (to use his own phrase) in Illinois while his henchmen carried
> on the political war for him. Dewey, Taft, Stassen and Wallace are free as birds to
> attack him but once he stoops to answer them on their level, he has done himself
> severe damage. Only Wilson broke this rule of being President of the people—in
> 1918 by asking for a Democratic Congress—and the people punished him for it by
> returning a Republican one.
>
> So a President who is also a candidate must resort to subterfuge—for he
> cannot sit silent. He must be in the limelight. He must do the kind of thing
> suggested above to stay in the limelight and he must also resort to the kind of trip
> which Roosevelt made famous in the 1940 campaign—the "inspection tour." No
> matter how much the opposition and the press pointed out the political overtones
> of those trips, the people paid little attention because what they saw was the Head
> of State performing his duties.[17]

Much of this advice sounds a bit quaint to the modern ear, and yet it is still quite relevant. Presidents no longer remain "judiciously aloof" but instead campaign vigorously for themselves and their co-partisans. But the notion of subter-

fuge is one that resonates. When recent presidents' travels for official and supposedly nonpolitical purposes happen to take them to battleground states, and when
the events they hold there have the look and feel of campaign rallies, there is far
less subtlety in the subterfuge than was practiced in the time of Truman.

One example of the subterfuge that Truman engaged in was the June 1948 trip
to Berkeley, California, to accept an honorary degree. George Elsey said that the
president's goal was to "appeal directly to the American people. On the third of
June, the President started on a 9,000-mile cross-country tour to the West Coast.
The trip was advertised as being non-political, but anything the President does in
a political year is very closely watched."[18] According to Elsey, Charles Murphy recounted that "the President referred to it many times since then as his non-political
campaign trip."[19] Interestingly, in a November 18, 1948, memo from White House
aide Stephen Spingarn to Clifford titled "Summaries of the President's Campaign
Speeches," the first speeches of the campaign listed are on June 4 at the start of the
trip west to Berkeley, indicating that the White House viewed the June trip as the
unofficial opening of the 1948 campaign.[20] The subterfuge was necessary both to
maintain the illusion that the president was not actively campaigning before the
traditional start of the election season on Labor Day and so that the trip could be
paid for with public funds.[21] It is worth noting, however, that this subterfuge took
place in an election year and not earlier in Truman's term.

Truman himself resisted some actions that might be perceived as too political.
In early 1951, as Truman's public support was declining against the backdrop of an
unpopular war in Korea and a slumping economy at home, George Elsey wrote
an internal White House memorandum advocating that Truman hold events at
military bases to improve his image and promote his programs. Elsey reasoned
that such events would allow Truman to make the case to the American people,
"in his own words, rather than filtered through the Washington press corps," about
why the Korean War was worth fighting. After reluctantly making one such trip to
Aberdeen, Maryland, Truman refused to do any similar events, declaring them to
be "gimmickry." Truman thought that the trips were too blatantly political. Elsey,
alert to these concerns himself, recounted:

> I felt that much of the criticism of Truman's war could be overcome if he'd
> simply get out and get out to the country again. And that was why I was
> proposing to keep it from seeming too overtly political, to visit defense
> installations. FDR, after all, had done that. He made a western swing to visit the
> military camps in 1942. Truman could do the same this time. And we did get him
> as far as Aberdeen, Maryland. And it got good press and good motion picture
> newsreel coverage. But, as I said . . . he thought it was gimmickry and he wouldn't
> do it again.[22]

In addition to resisting staged events as "gimmickry," Truman would later decry the fundraising practices of his successors in the White House. Writing in December 1962, Truman expressed his indignation about President John F. Kennedy's fundraising activities:

> I have just been informed that the Democratic Party, of which I have been an
> active member since I was seventeen years old, has gone high hat and is charging
> one thousand dollars for the privilege of sitting with the president of the United
> States at a dinner! . . . When the Party of the People goes high hat on a cost basis,
> it no longer represents the common every day man—who is the basis of the
> Democratic Party.[23]

While Kennedy's fundraising practices incensed Truman, they pale in comparison to both the dollar amounts associated with and the frequency of fundraisers held by the most recent occupants of the Oval Office.

The aim of this discussion is not to argue that decisions made in the Truman White House were devoid of electoral considerations. The presidency has always been and always will be an inherently political office. Indeed, the West Coast trips in 1948 and 1950 showed that the administration was willing to engage in the kind of "subterfuge" suggested in the Clifford-Rowe memorandum to advance an electoral agenda under the guise of official presidential trips. Similarly, critics at the time claimed that Truman's journey to Wake Island to meet with General Douglas MacArthur in 1950 was timed to help the Democrats in the 1950 midterm elections, a charge that Truman aide Elsey denied.[24] But the record of the Truman administration does reveal dynamics markedly different from those of today. Because of both prevailing norms and the limited size and role of the White House staff, most political planning was done not by White House aides but instead by the Democratic National Committee.

THE ROLE OF WHITE HOUSE STAFF AND THE NATIONAL COMMITTEE IN THE REAGAN ADMINISTRATION

Examination of the dynamics of political planning in the Reagan administration reveals a picture quite different from that of Truman's presidency. The White House staff has grown tremendously since the 1940s and 1950s, becoming what Nelson Polsby famously dubbed "the presidential branch," which works to exert its influence on both the rest of the executive branch and the legislative branch.[25] John Hart, whose book of the same name extensively documents the expanding size and influence of the president's staff, argues that the emergence of a presidential branch has led to a concentration of power within the Executive Office of the

President.[26] One element of this trend has been the assumption by presidential staff of much political decision-making that used to be the province of the national party committee.

These dynamics are clearly evident in a contrast between the Truman White House and the Reagan White House, which created the White House Office of Political Affairs. Table 5.2 presents a summary of who authored and received political planning memos in the Reagan administration. I gathered these memos at the Ronald Reagan Presidential Library with the aid of archivists who provided direction about which staff members were most likely to have been involved with electoral planning. The memos detailed in table 5.2 are a sample, not the entire universe, of those related to political planning in the Reagan White House. But like those from the Truman Library, they present a clear picture about who was involved with electoral planning in the Reagan administration. The picture that emerges is one of a White House that, unlike Truman's, did not rely heavily on the national committee in making most political decisions.

Indeed, while two of the memos examined are from the Reagan-Bush '84 election committee and one is from a former White House aide, not one memo is from the Republican National Committee (RNC), and most are authored by and directed to White House staff. Only two—the memos from Reagan-Bush '84 pollster Richard Wirthlin—are directed to RNC officials in addition to White House aides. The memos reveal that the White House chief of staff, deputy chief of staff, and their assistants were at the heart of the political decision-making in the Reagan White House, as twenty-one of the twenty-seven memos found were directed to their attention. The offices of James Baker and Michael Deaver, two of the three aides who along with Edwin Meese were known as "The Troika" for their key roles in Reagan's first term, were the recipients of thirteen of the sixteen first-term memos examined. Many other White House offices are involved, including the Office of Political Affairs, Office of Appointments and Scheduling, Office of Legislative Affairs, Office of Planning and Evaluation, Office of Policy Development, Offices of the Chief of Staff and Deputy Chief of Staff, Office of Communications, Office of Intergovernmental Affairs, and Office of Political and Intergovernmental Affairs.

The memos paint a picture of a White House that was actively involved in nearly all aspects of partisan political planning. The emphasis during Reagan's first two years in office shows an early focus on the president's role in the midterm elections of 1982. A thirty-seven-page memo sent from Richard Beal in the Office of Planning and Evaluation to top White House aides Baker, Deaver, and Meese laid out a plan for the president to target key congressional races in order to minimize expected losses in the upcoming elections. The other documents from this period, dated as early as September 1981, focused on proposed plans for the president to

Table 5.2: Reagan Administration Political Planning Memos

Date	From (Person)	From (Office/Position)	To (Person)	To (Office/Position)	Title/Subject
9/29/81	Joseph Canzeri, Gregory Newell	Office of the Deputy Chief of Staff, Office of Appts. & Scheduling	Michael Deaver	Deputy Chief of Staff	Political Requests
9/30/81	Richard Williamson	Office of Intergovernmental Affairs	Lyn Nofziger	Office of Political Affairs	Senator Malcolm Wallop
9/30/81	Max Friedersdorf	Office of Legislative Affairs	James Baker	Chief of Staff	Congressional Requests for Presidential Campaign Appearances
4/1/82	Ed Rollins	Office of Political Affairs	Ronald Reagan	The President	Governor Thornburgh/ Senator Heinz, Political Event Requests—Background
4/9/82	Ken Duberstein	Office of Legislative Affairs	Michael Deaver	Deputy Chief of Staff	Senator Warner Invitation to Mrs. Reagan
8/18/82	Dan J. Smith	Office of Policy Development	Michael Deaver	Deputy Chief of Staff	Black Voter Plan
9/2/82	Richard S. Beal	Office of Planning and Evaluation	Edwin Meese, James Baker, Michael Deaver	Counselor to the President, Chief of Staff, Deputy Chief of Staff	1982 Presidential Targeting Strategy
12/15/82	Lyn Nofziger	No longer in White House	Michael Deaver	Deputy Chief of Staff	Presidential Travel Recommendation
2/4/83	Ed Rollins	Office of Political Affairs	James Baker, Michael Deaver, Ken Duberstein, Michael McManus, Bill Sadleir	Chief of Staff, Deputy Chief of Staff, Office of Legislative Affairs, Office of the Deputy Chief of Staff, Office of Appts. & Scheduling	Senate Fundraisers

Date	From	From Office	To	To Office	Subject
2/24/83	Frederick Ryan	Office of Appts. & Scheduling	Michael McManus	Office of the Deputy Chief of Staff	Constituency Oriented Events
4/6/83	Ed Rollins	Office of Political Affairs	James Baker	Chief of Staff	1984 Republican Senate Breakfast
10/18/83	James Baker	Chief of Staff	White House staff	N/A	Reassignment of Functions Performed by the Office of Political Affairs
3/14/84	James Baker	Chief of Staff	Michael Deaver	Deputy Chief of Staff	Ted Stevens Request for Presidential Resolution in Lieu of a Fundraiser
4/30/84	Frederick Ryan	Office of Appts. & Scheduling	Michael Deaver	Deputy Chief of Staff	Campaign Travel Recommendations
7/10/84	Richard Wirthlin	Reagan-Bush '84	James Baker, Frank Fahrenkopf, Paul Laxalt, Ed Rollins, Stu Spencer	Chief of Staff, RNC chair, Republican Party general chairman, Reagan-Bush '84, Reagan-Bush '84	Electoral Maps
7/26/84	Richard Wirthlin	Reagan-Bush '84	James Baker, Michael Deaver, Frank Fahrenkopf, Paul Laxalt, Ed Rollins, Stu Spencer	Chief of Staff, Deputy Chief of Staff, RNC chair, Republican Party general chairman, Reagan-Bush '84	Ballot Impact of the Democratic Convention
1/20/87	Frank Donatelli	Office of Political and Intergovernmental Affairs	Howard Baker, Ken Duberstein	Chief of Staff, Deputy Chief of Staff	The White House and Super Tuesday

Table 5.2, *continued*

Date	From (Person)	From (Office/Position)	To (Person)	To (Office/Position)	Title/Subject
7/17/87	Frank Donatelli	Office of Political and Intergovernmental Affairs	Howard Baker	Chief of Staff	1988 Presidential Campaigns—What We Need to Do
7/17/87	Frank Donatelli	Office of Political and Intergovernmental Affairs	Howard Baker	Chief of Staff	A Political Strategy for 1988
9/14/87	Frank Donatelli	Office of Political and Intergovernmental Affairs	Howard Baker	Chief of Staff	Political Plan for 1988
12/15/87	Tom Griscom	Office of Communications	Howard Baker	Chief of Staff	Reagan Political Activities for 1988
2/19/88	Frank Donatelli	Office of Political and Intergovernmental Affairs	Ronald Reagan	The President	Convention Program
2/24/88	Frank Donatelli	Office of Political and Intergovernmental Affairs	Howard Baker, Ken Duberstein	Chief of Staff, Deputy Chief of Staff	Political Programs and Projects
3/3/88	Frank Lavin	Office of Political Affairs	Rebecca Range	Office of Public Liaison	Target Groups
4/11/88	Frank Lavin	Office of Political Affairs	Frank Donatelli	Office of Political and Intergovernmental Affairs	Endorsement Plan
9/22/88	Frank Donatelli	Office of Political and Intergovernmental Affairs	Ken Duberstein	Chief of Staff	Campaign Coordination Meeting on September 23, 1988
11/7/88	Frank Donatelli	Office of Political and Intergovernmental Affairs	Ken Duberstein	Chief of Staff	The President's Political Involvement

Source: Data compiled by the author from the Ronald Reagan Presidential Library.

campaign with and raise money for Republican candidates for office, as well as one August 1982 memo titled "Black Voter Plan," which argued that Reagan could take steps to lower "the likelihood of a black voter backlash this November."[27]

The documents from 1983 and 1984 reveal a White House focused on President Reagan's reelection bid. Memos from the Office of Appointments and Scheduling discussed plans to reach out to key constituencies and recommendations on geographic targeting of the president's campaign efforts in advance of the upcoming election. Those from the Office of Political Affairs and the Office of the Chief of Staff detailed the dynamics of presidential support for Republican senators, with a focus on fundraising efforts. The two memos from the pollster for Reagan-Bush '84 were directed to the White House chief of staff, Republican National Committee officials, and campaign aides, and presented polling data and electoral maps.

The archival record from Reagan's second term demonstrates that the White House was still deeply involved with political planning, even with Reagan's reelection bid behind them. All but one of the memos examined come from the Office of Political and Intergovernmental Affairs or the recently subsumed Office of Political Affairs, which had been incorporated into the former office at the beginning of Reagan's second term. The lone exception originated in the Office of Communications.[28] Most focus on Reagan's political role in 1988, touching on dynamics from the question of a presidential endorsement in the Republican nominating race, to how often and for whom the president should campaign and attend fundraisers, to the president's plan for participating in the 1988 Republican National Convention. A January 20, 1987, memo advocating efforts to increase Republican voter turnout in nominating contests on Super Tuesday, which would take place more than a year later, on March 8, 1988, reveals the extent to which the White House not only planned but also planned ahead as it determined Reagan's electoral involvement in his second term.

Most of the Reagan administration memos, like those in Truman's day, were not directed to the president himself. One notable and interesting exception was a February 19, 1988, memo to Reagan from Frank Donatelli in the Office of Political and Intergovernmental Affairs regarding the president's participation in the 1988 convention. Reagan overruled his aide's recommendation that he speak on the second night of the convention and instead elected to speak on the convention's opening night. He approved a proposal that Nancy Reagan speak briefly that same night, and he chose to be introduced by former senator Paul Laxalt instead of being introduced with a documentary film or by Bob Hope. He accepted the recommendation that he spend one day and one overnight at the convention and approved the proposals for prominent Republican governors and former president Gerald Ford to have speaking roles.[29] This memo was one of the rare ones that showed the president determining his own political path.

Archival research clearly portrays a White House deeply involved in political planning in both of Reagan's two terms in office. The contrast with the activities of the White House in Truman's time is stark. A much larger White House staff has been organized into multiple units, some explicitly political, others not, that play central roles in recommending strategies about electoral matters that had formerly been outsourced to the national committee. This activity is not limited to election years but instead spans most of Reagan's time as president. The national committee appears to be a peripheral player at best. While the Reagan-Bush '84 campaign organization was created in October 1983 and the White House Office of Political Affairs was closed at the same time,[30] documents reveal that White House aides were still involved in political strategy in late 1983 and 1984.

Evolving Norms

Ronald Reagan, like Harry Truman, was concerned with seeming more political than was deemed proper. Understandably, presidents are quite sensitive about the suggestion that political calculations drive the ways they govern. On June 9, 1983, Ronald Reagan discussed these dynamics while on a visit to Minnesota. When a journalist asked him if he would seek a second term, he replied:

> It is far too early for anyone of my position to announce his intentions. And I can tell you why. If I did, and the answer was "no," then it wouldn't do me any good to ask Congress for anything. I'd be considered a lame-duck. And if I said the answer was "yes" at this point, the media—forgive me—but the media, very largely would be tagging everything I did, including a trip to Minneapolis, as political in nature.[31]

Reagan's concern led to a very odd event—an Oval Office ceremony to sign papers legally establishing his reelection committee in October 1983 at which he declared that he still had not decided whether to run for reelection. He commented that he would likely let the American people know whether he would be a candidate for another term as president "by the first of the year," referring to January 1, 1984. When reporters asked whether the papers he had signed establishing a reelection committee made him a candidate, he responded that they did so only "in the eyes of the law."[32] Reagan wanted to maintain the guise that he was not yet running for reelection.

The president's intentional ambiguity was not shared by his aides. Larry Speakes, his deputy press secretary, said, "He's running and the only thing that remains is the formal announcement." Senator Paul Laxalt, who would be the titular head of the reelection committee, declared, "As far as those of us on the campaign team are concerned, the Reagan-Bush campaign is off and running. As far as the committee is concerned, we're legal. We're legitimate. We can proceed to go into business. We can open a campaign headquarters. We can commence our fundraising efforts. We can encourage expenditures and do everything that is required in a campaign. We're legitimate from this moment on."[33]

Four years later, George H. W. Bush would engage in a similar Kabuki dance. When he submitted paperwork to the Federal Election Commission on October 11, 1991, creating the Bush-Quayle '92 committee, he wrote, "Although I am not yet formally declaring my candidacy for the Republican nomination for the office of president . . . I am hereby authorizing this organization as my principal campaign committee. . . . It is my hope that this committee will allow those people who have encouraged me to seek a second term as president a chance to express their support in a manner that fully complies with the federal election laws."[34] The support he hoped for was financial.

When Bush traveled to Texas on October 31, 1991, for two days of fundraisers in Houston and Dallas, he found himself in an odd position. The fundraisers, which sought to raise $2 million, included Bush's first events to fill the coffers of the Bush-Quayle '92 reelection committee, events that Harry Truman would likely have called "high hat." But the president still had not yet declared himself a candidate and did not plan to do so until after the State of the Union address at the end of January 1992.[35] In November 1991, press secretary Marlin Fitzwater offered this explanation for Bush's decision not to declare his candidacy for reelection until several months after both the establishment of his reelection committee and the start of his own fundraising: "Obviously, he would like to put that off as long as possible just because it makes life easier not to have to politicize everything."[36] When Bush finally proclaimed his candidacy for reelection on February 12, 1992, one journalist commented on the abundant indicators that he had already been running: "Never mind the Texas fund-raiser in October, or his telling an interviewer last month 'I will do what I have to do to be reelected,' or that he's already raised more than $11 million and put his name on the ballot in 26 states."[37] Bush, like Reagan and Truman, did not want to be seen as too political, but his efforts to give the impression that he was not yet an active candidate for reelection seemed to convince few observers. While presidents attempt to project an image of being above the political fray, Reagan, Bush, and other recent presidents sat atop a White House organization designed to make sure that political factors were taken into account throughout their terms in office.

Truman aide George Elsey attested that White House aides called in 1947 for the hiring of more staff at the Democratic National Committee to support campaign efforts because it would be inappropriate to put them on the government payroll. The role in the Reagan administration and other recent presidencies of the Office of Political Affairs and other White House offices similarly engaged in overtly partisan activities reveals how much prevailing norms have shifted. With more presidential aides involved in electoral activity, administrations still place an emphasis on drawing proper lines between campaigning and governing. Arguably, those lines are more necessary than ever, but their location has shifted.

While most federal government employees are prohibited by law from engaging in electoral activities at work, they can do so during their free time. The president and his senior White House aides are permitted to work on electoral matters at any time, but they must be sure that they do not use government equipment to do so. Consequently, both George W. Bush's and Barack Obama's White House aides who were involved with the 2004 and 2012 reelection campaigns had separate Blackberries, computers, and email accounts for official and campaign-related business. White House aides cannot solicit political funds, but they are allowed to give speeches at fundraising events. The president and vice president are allowed to solicit money on White House grounds, but only in parts of the White House considered part of the "private residence."[38]

When presidents travel, their events must be designated as either official or political by the White House staff. An official event, no matter how political it may appear, is paid for entirely by the taxpayer. When an event is political, aides on the trip are designated as "official travelers" or "political travelers." A December 1991 memo from White House counsel C. Boyden Gray advised that even on a trip that is classified entirely as political with no official events, Secret Service agents, military personnel, the president's doctor, staff focusing on logistics, a White House photographer, and a national security aide are among those staffers who are always considered to be "official travelers" whose travel costs will be paid for by government funds. Conversely, aides from the Office of Political Affairs are always considered "political travelers" whose expenses must be paid by an outside political organization, even if the purpose of the entire trip is designated as official, not political. The status of other aides is determined for each trip based on the roles they will perform in support of the president's travels.[39] Thus, even when a president embarks upon a campaign trip that is entirely political, the government funds many of the expenses that arise any time a president leaves the White House.

Both the Truman and Reagan administrations, like those of many other presidents, blurred the lines between official and partisan political business. Truman undertook two extensive taxpayer-funded train trips to the West Coast that were ostensibly nonpolitical but had decidedly partisan electoral objectives and fit the description in a key memo of travel that was subterfuge. Reagan and other recent presidents have taken part in such subterfuge far more often, traveling frequently to key electoral states and often pairing official events with campaign rallies or fundraisers so that the costs of their travel would be borne in large part by tax-payers.[40] Additionally, in an August 18, 1982, memo, Reagan aide Dan J. Smith laid out a plan to improve Reagan's standing with black voters. In it, he declared, "The estimated direct budget of $95,000 represents expenditures that would need to be carried on the White House budget. A larger amount (estimated at $200,000) would need to be *earmarked* among *existing RNC campaign budgets* to accomplish specific tasks directly related to Gubernatorial and Congressional elections."[41] This plan, which was aimed at improving the president's electoral prospects with a certain demographic group, would involve substantial taxpayer expense. While it is always difficult to separate official political presidential business from overtly partisan undertakings, the evidence presented here shows that the lines separating the two are far less distinct than they once were.

WHITE HOUSE ELECTORAL DECISION-MAKING IN THE PLEBISCITARY NOMINATING ERA

The contrast between electoral planning in the Truman and Reagan administrations provides a picture of just how much the role of the White House staff has changed. Aides within the walls of 1600 Pennsylvania Avenue now make decisions that once were outsourced to the Democratic or Republican National Committee. This transition happened gradually over the course of decades. The presidents who came to office via the plebiscitary nominating system were not the first to have electoral decisions handled by White House aides. Indeed, most modern presidents have had at least one person who fulfilled the role that Matt Connelly did under Truman as the White House point person for handling political concerns. Under recent presidents, however, the White House's role in these decisions has expanded and become institutionalized with the creation of offices within the White House dedicated to handling political concerns. These developments have made the perpetuation of the permanent campaign the path of least resistance for incoming White House staff.

As discussed earlier, in June 1978, the Carter administration became the first to designate a White House aide as an assistant to the president for political affairs, and the Reagan administration created the White House Office of Political Affairs in 1981. While the specific functions of the Office of Political Affairs have varied from administration to administration, its consistent purpose has been, in the words of former Reagan political affairs director Frank Donatelli, "to look after the personal political fortunes of the president and to try to bring a political dimension to all the decisions made at the White House."[42] Ed Rollins, who ran the political affairs office early in Reagan's term, discussed the office's role in more detail:

As the assistant to the president for political affairs, I was at the top level of the White House hierarchy and was included in all senior staff, cabinet and policy meetings. My office was involved in all personnel and scheduling meetings. We also served as the contact point inside the White House for the Republican National Committee and the 50 state party committees, along with the Congressional and Senate campaign committees. We approved and coordinated campaign appearances and fund-raising by the president, the vice president and the cabinet. But the most important part of the job was to keep the president informed about the ever-changing political environment. Presidents don't always make decisions based on politics, and they shouldn't. But they do need to understand the political climate. Believe it or not, most people in a White House are not from the world of politics. They are lawyers and experts on the budget and foreign policy. They are supposed to be the best and the brightest, counseling the president without regard to the political consequences. But they should never be so naïve that they think politics doesn't matter. There are 535 other major players in our government: 100 senators and 435 House members. Every one of them is a politician and every one of their jobs is affected by politics.[43]

The Office of Political Affairs is not the only place in the White House where decisions are made about electoral affairs, as senior staff members often play critical roles in these strategic choices as well, but it has functioned as an important part of the political nervous system of the White House, handling functions that were once thought to be more appropriately tackled by those outside of the administration and off the government payroll. It represents, in the words of presidential scholar Kathryn Dunn Tenpas, "institutionalized politics."[44]

Carter aides were involved with making decisions about electoral matters even before a staff member was specifically designated for that purpose in 1978. A year earlier, in June 1977, the White House decided that Carter's principal congressional liaison, Frank Moore, would lead a committee that would decide how to respond to petitions that the president, vice president, and other members of the first and second families attend electoral events. Other members of the group included the president's appointments secretary, one of top aide Hamilton Jordan's deputies, and members of the vice president's and Democratic National Committee's staffs. The choice of Moore to head the committee was designed in part to give him more clout with members of Congress. Said one White House aide, "The guy needs some leverage, he needs some coin, he needs something to deal with."[45] The committee was set up so far in advance of the midterm elections in part because the first pressing requests for Carter's political support would come in the races for governor in New Jersey and Virginia in the fall of 1977. In both cases, Carter would be called upon to lend a hand to two fellow Democrats who had backed the president early in his bid for the White House.[46]

When Carter embarked upon his reelection campaign, he followed in the footsteps of Nixon and Ford, becoming the third president to establish a reelection committee independent of the national party that would coordinate closely with the White House.[47] When Evan Dobelle was named in March 1979 to run Jimmy Carter's upcoming reelection campaign, he was given the unusual title of campaign coordinator, instead of campaign manager. This title reflected the reality that White House chief of staff Hamilton Jordan, who had headed Carter's successful 1976 bid, and other top White House aides would play a substantial role in shaping the strategy of the campaign. In the words of one White House staffer, "Let's face it, Hamilton is going to be in charge of strategy. He'll be in on all of the major decisions, and he'll be making them. But you don't have to spend every day working on the strategy for a candidate who is already the president of the United States. So Hamilton's role will be in an overall, an advisory, capacity. Not in a day-to-day operational role like it was last time."[48]

When Reagan established the Office of Political Affairs, he named Lyn Nofziger, who had worked on both of Reagan's gubernatorial bids in California, to head it. Political scientist Shirley Anne Warshaw attributes this decision to lingering tensions from Reagan's insurgent bid for the 1976 Republican presidential nomination. He had fought against the national party organization then and still did not fully trust it once he became president, so he installed a loyal aide to head a political affairs office inside the White House.[49] This decision fits in with Polsby's argument about the growth of the presidential branch and the centralization of power in the president's staff. In 1982, the Reagan White House put most of its cabinet secretaries and some senior administration aides, including White House chief of staff James Baker and counselor Edwin Meese, to work on the campaign trail. These efforts were planned jointly by the White House Office of Political Affairs and the Republican National Committee.[50] The memos detailed in table 5.2 show that the political affairs office was not the only one within the White House involved in decisions about electoral activities, but it did play an important role.

Indeed, in the Reagan administration, the Office of Political Affairs was such an unquestionably clear home for planning for Reagan's reelection bid and other political efforts that it was dissolved upon the creation of Reagan's formal reelection committee. On October 18, 1983, chief of staff James Baker sent a memorandum to all White House staff in which he wrote, "With the establishment of the reelection committee, Reagan-Bush '84, the White House Office of Political Affairs will go out of existence."[51] The office would be reestablished in Reagan's second term, when it was incorporated into the Office of Political and Intergovernmental

Affairs.[52] The director of the Office of Political Affairs, Ed Rollins, who had succeeded Nofziger, was named to lead the presidents' reelection committee, where he would be joined by his White House deputy, Lee Atwater.[53] According to press accounts, RNC chair Senator Paul Laxalt, White House chief of staff James Baker, and deputy chief of staff Michael Deaver would all be closely involved in decisions about the reelection campaign, holding strategy meetings every week at the White House in 1984.[54] The Office of Political Affairs had been the official governmental home for taking political concerns into account as a part of White House decision-making. That it was shut down a year before the 1984 election and its key personnel transitioned to the campaign committee as planning continued to take place inside the White House demonstrates the clear nature and purpose of the Office of Political Affairs.

The Office of Political Affairs played a similar, though slightly less prominent, role in the administration of George H. W. Bush, when its head was a deputy assistant to the president. In contrast, the aides in charge of political affairs under Reagan and Carter had held the title of assistant to the president. Ron Kaufman, who ran the office at the end of Bush's term, described its role this way: "In the first two years, your [the Office of Political Affairs'] major client, if you will, is the party in Congress and the states. The last two years . . . your client is the reelection campaign." The office was kept quite busy by all its clients. David Carney, who headed the office during the midterm election year of 1990, said, "In 1990, we scheduled over a thousand events, with the cabinet and the president, the vice president, Mrs. Bush, and Mrs. Quayle." The events he referred to were explicitly political ones, designed to help elect fellow Republicans to office.[55]

As was the case for Reagan, White House officials were deeply involved in the strategy for Bush's reelection bid. When the president convened thirty advisers at Camp David in August 1991 for a campaign planning retreat, deputy chief of staff Andrew Card, political office director Ron Kaufman, budget director Richard Darman, and top aide Sig Rogich were among the White House staffers in attendance.[56] The White House would assume an even more commanding role when James Baker left his position as secretary of state to become White House chief of staff in August 1992 with the dual charge of running both the White House and the president's reelection campaign.[57]

In the Clinton administration, political director Doug Sosnik and deputy chief of staff Harold Ickes were among the leading voices on political decisions in the White House during the president's first term. In September 1995, it was not a campaign official but Sosnik who briefed the media on campaign planning, saying, "We've raised a ton of money. We're moving into each state one by one, and we're moving quickly—not in a frenetic way—to set up for this re-election." Another White House aide made the case for why the White House would be the nerve center of the campaign even after the reelection committee had staffed up. "We've got the body. We've got the schedule. We've got the message. Anything else is little else."[58] Even when Clinton finally named a campaign manager in April 1992, the understanding was that the new chief, Peter Knight, would still report to Ickes, who would continue in his role at the White House.[59]

When George W. Bush assumed the presidency in 2001, he named Karl Rove, his chief political adviser from the campaign, to be a top White House aide who would oversee the Office of Political Affairs, the Office of Intergovernmental Affairs, the Office of Public Liaison, and the Office of Strategic Initiatives. This final office was created by Rove to serve as a long-term political planning operation, and it was nicknamed the "Office of Strategery," in tribute to Will Ferrell's portrayal on *Saturday Night Live* of then governor Bush during the 2000 campaign. This broad portfolio made Rove an influential figure who was almost always in the room during the president's "policy time" decision-making meetings. Bradley Patterson, one of the leading scholars on the organization of the White House staff who has also worked in several Republican administrations, wrote of Rove, "In George W. Bush's White House, politics and policy have been inextricably intertwined—in the person of senior adviser Karl Rove. Until his resignation in August 2007, Rove was de facto the agenda-setter for almost everyone in the White House."[60]

A *Washington Post* profile of Rove in 2004 described him as having "the broadest reach and most power of any official in the West Wing. But he also oversees every detail of the $259 million Bush-Cheney campaign. . . . [He] has cultivated an aura of mystery, rarely giving on-the-record interviews and doing little to undermine the myth that he is responsible for everything that occurs in the executive branch."[61] While some dispute the extent of Rove's influence, it was clear that the institutionalized structures within the White House devoted to electoral planning continued and were expanded during the Bush years.

Despite Barack Obama's criticism of what he called the politicization of the Bush White House, he did not adopt John McCain's promised plan to abolish the White House Office of Political Affairs. In addition to keeping the office, when Obama arrived at 1600 Pennsylvania Avenue, he brought with him David Axelrod, who had been one of his top political advisers during the campaign. After the surprise victory by Republican Scott Brown in the special election in January 2010 held to fill the Senate seat long occupied by Edward Kennedy, Obama moved to exert more influence on the Democrats' efforts for the upcoming midterm elections. He asked his 2008 campaign manager, David Plouffe, to work with the White House and the Democratic National Committee to coordinate the party's efforts in races across the country. While Plouffe remained off the government payroll at that point, he would work closely with White House aides tasked with focusing on political affairs.[62]

Two years into Obama's presidency, the White House announced in early 2011 that, like Reagan before him, Obama would shut down his Office of Political Affairs as his reelection bid formally began, and key White House aides would move to the campaign. Jim Messina, one of Obama's deputy chiefs of staff, was named to run the campaign, with White House social secretary Julianna Smoot as one of his deputies. Patrick Gaspard, who had headed the soon-to-be defunct Office of Political Affairs, would leave the White House to become executive director of the Democratic National Committee. Axelrod would leave the White House, returning to Chicago to help with the campaign, while Plouffe would join the White House staff.[63]

In an attempt to separate the campaign from the day-to-day politics of the nation's capital, Obama decided to base his reelection committee in Chicago, making him the first modern president to locate his campaign headquarters outside of the Washington, DC, area. White House press secretary Jay Carney made the case that having the reelection campaign's headquarters in Chicago would enable Obama to focus more on governing: "The President is focused on this work for the American people that he was elected to do, and that's what he does every day and that's what his staff here [at the White House] is doing. And he set up this structure . . . in Chicago, precisely or in part to allow him to focus on the work he needs to do from the White House for the American people."[64] According to Plouffe, "The philosophy of this campaign will not be that the White House is somehow running the campaign. The people running the campaign are in charge of the campaign. That's the way the president wants it. We'll do it in a coordinated way, but they're running this thing."[65] With Plouffe on the White House payroll, however, many observers predicted that the White House would be centrally involved in reelection planning, like its recent predecessors, in spite of the closure of the Office of Political Affairs.

CONCLUDING THOUGHTS

While this discussion of the role of White House staff in political decision-making could be expanded into an entire book in its own right, it is clear that the ways that presidents and their aides handle the political elements of their job have changed dramatically in the post–World War II era. Recent presidents have devoted increasing amounts of time to political fundraising and have targeted key electoral states throughout their terms in office. Many of these changes can be traced to developments within the White House itself. While the Truman administration, due both to practical necessity and to prevailing norms, relied on the Democratic National Committee to coordinate much of the political planning for the president, recent presidential administrations have made those decisions in offices within the White House itself throughout the president's term in office. These dynamics are part of a larger trend of the centralization of power within what has been called the presidential branch of government.

John Hart argues that the creation of the Office of Political Affairs can also be tied to the reforms of the 1970s that created the plebiscitary nominating process. According to Hart:

> The political affairs unit is a formal recognition of the need for first-term presidents to maintain an experienced and professional campaign organization during the first term to cope with the demands of the new rules of the nomination game. With the choice of the party's presidential nominee now beyond the control of party leaders, and with a system so open that it positively encourages challenges to the front-runner, incumbent presidents can no longer enjoy the luxury of automatic renomination after four years. Presidents who desire a second term in office must now give far more continuous attention to electoral politics during their first term than ever before.[66]

An entity that may have come into being to help advance a president's reelection has proved to be useful to presidents and their staffs in their second terms as well, when the Office of Political Affairs has played a key role in planning presidential party-building efforts.

The presidents who have followed Reagan, especially Bill Clinton, George W. Bush, and Barack Obama, have been the subject of much public discussion and criticism of their efforts to wage what has been termed a permanent campaign from the White House. At the start of this chapter, John McCain claimed that the permanent campaign had existed for sixteen years, dating to Bill Clinton's winning White House run in 1992, and promised that if he won, he would move the Office of Political Affairs to the RNC so that he could "have a White House that is without politics."[67] McCain identified the Office of Political Affairs as a key factor in the current politicization of the White House and called for a dynamic closer to that which existed during the Truman administration.

But former aide George Elsey, reflecting on Truman's presidency in 1964, expressed skepticism about taking the politics out of the presidency, regardless of where an office dealing with political affairs might be located:

> The White House has always been just a little jittery in recognizing that the President is a political leader and a politician 365 days of the year. The White House, in the Roosevelt and the Truman and the Eisenhower, the Kennedy Administrations, doesn't advertise the fact that it has continuing and close relations with the national party headquarters. Somehow, it's just not thought

to be very nice. As I say, this is part of the mythology of American life. We don't want to admit that a President has to be a good politician, if he's going to be halfway effective as a President.[68]

Elsey's point about effectiveness is worth emphasizing. The Carter White House designated an aide to focus on political affairs in 1978 not because it had been apolitical before then, but because of complaints that it had handled political questions and relationships poorly. If having a White House Office of Political Affairs is problematic, not having coordination of political concerns in White House decision-making can also lead to poor presidential leadership. Former Clinton political director Sosnik contended in 2004, "The notion that there's no politics in government, in the White House in particular in an election year, is laughable. It transcends political party, it transcends what year it is, it transcends who's in power because everything in government is a mix of policy and politics."[69]

The presidency is, has been, and will continue to be a political office. But the institutional arrangements designed to help political actors navigate the lines between campaigning and governing do indeed matter. Understandably, presidents want trusted advisers close to them who can advise them about the political dynamics of the decisions they make. But having White House aides whose sole job is to think about how political and electoral concerns should be taken into account has resulted in the increased blurring of the lines between campaigning and governing. No longer do presidential administrations outsource most political planning to the national committees. Instead, the handling of political questions has been institutionalized within the White House itself, which means that each new president inherits a White House where the path of least resistance is one that facilitates the perpetuation of the permanent campaign.

In the next chapter, I turn to the implications of the permanent campaign. What do the rise of presidential fundraising and strategic travel and the centralization of political decision-making in the White House mean for the nature and effectiveness of presidential leadership?

6. The Implications of the
Permanent Campaign

> But what frustrates the American people is a Washington where every day is
> Election Day. We can't wage a perpetual campaign where the only goal is to see who
> can get the most embarrassing headlines about the other side—a belief that if you
> lose, I win. . . . Washington may think that saying anything about the other side, no
> matter how false, no matter how malicious, is just part of the game. But it's precisely
> such politics that has stopped either party from helping the American people.
> Worse yet, it's sowing further division among our citizens, further distrust in our
> government. So, no, I will not give up on trying to change the tone of our politics.
> I know it's an election year. And after last week, it's clear that campaign fever has
> come even earlier than usual. But we still need to govern.
>
> *Barack Obama, State of the Union address, January 27, 2010*

As I conclude this book, the 2012 presidential election campaign is in full swing.
With the election still well over a year away, President Barack Obama has already
headlined more fundraisers for his reelection campaign committee than Jimmy
Carter, Ronald Reagan, George H. W. Bush, and Bill Clinton attended for their
campaign committee throughout their entire reelection bid. Obama has just concluded a bus trip through the Midwest that took him to rural communities that
was nominally an official presidential journey. This three-day sojourn carried him
to the battleground states of Minnesota and Iowa, as well as his home state of Illinois, earning him criticism for campaigning on the taxpayers' dime. Both the
nature of the trip and the negative reaction from the other side of the aisle have
many precedents in recent presidential administrations.

The aim of this book has been to systematically examine key elements of the
permanent campaign and offer an argument explaining the dynamics we have
seen. My goal is not to criticize any particular president for a focus on electoral
matters, but instead to better understand the ways in which political actors respond to the institutional incentives of our electoral system. No political system is
neutral. Each sets up a series of rules that help to structure the behavior of goal-
oriented politicians. While the term *permanent campaign* is often used broadly to
refer to presidential efforts to win public opinion, the use of extensive public opinion polling by presidential aides, and more, I have focused my analysis on actions
that relate directly to electoral questions—presidential fundraising, targeted travel

that corresponds to the incentives of the Electoral College and the presidential nominating system, and the key players in and outside the White House who help to make decisions about these matters. In this chapter, I will briefly review my key empirical findings and discuss their implications for presidential leadership.

Over the three and a half decades since Jimmy Carter's inauguration in 1977, presidents have devoted increasing amounts of time to electoral concerns throughout their time in office. The exigencies of campaigning have impinged more and more upon the demands of governing, as Barack Obama discussed in his 2010 State of the Union address, making it difficult to draw a line between when governing ends and campaigning begins. Presidential fundraising, which is an unambiguous indicator of presidential attention to electoral concerns, has increased sharply, and presidential travel has increasingly reflected the institutional incentives of both the Electoral College and the nominating process.

The frequency of presidential fundraising has steadily increased, with new presidents shattering the fundraising records of their predecessors. Jimmy Carter and Ronald Reagan each took part in an average of about two fundraisers per month. George H. W. Bush headlined about three fundraisers per month, as news accounts hailed him as the most prolific presidential fundraiser in history. Bill Clinton, George W. Bush, and Barack Obama outdid the first President Bush, averaging almost four fundraisers per month in their first terms, or about one per week. Clinton's second-term fundraising effort was unprecedented, as he attended a fundraiser every 3.1 days, or about ten per month, which was about five times the rate of fundraising by Carter and Reagan. Two and a half years into Obama's term as president, he is on pace to set a new record for the most first-term presidential fundraisers. To a greater and greater extent, the president is indeed the fundraiser-in-chief and party-builder-in-chief, and that activity is by no means confined to the traditional campaign season.

As presidents have spent increasing amounts of time headlining political fundraisers, they have done so both for themselves and for the benefit of their fellow party members. Of the presidents first elected via the plebiscitary nominating system and who have served during the evolving campaign finance regime created by the Federal Campaign Finance Act of 1974, all except Carter have been dedicated party builders. Most presidential fundraising has not benefited the president's own reelection campaign committee but instead has filled the coffers of the national committee and other party beneficiaries. While a president's reelection prospects might be directly strengthened by a well-funded national committee, they will benefit only indirectly from efforts to elect more senators, House members, governors, and other officials of their same party. While Reagan focused more on raising money for his party than for himself in his first term, George H. W. Bush, Clinton, George W. Bush, and Obama all devoted much time to their fellow party members in their first or only midterm election year and then shifted their efforts primarily to their own reelection committee and the national party in their third and fourth years in office. All three presidents since the mid-1970s who have served two terms committed substantial time and effort to party building in their second four years in office. The beneficiaries of presidential fundraising have varied by president, revealing the political priorities of a presidency and how presidents see their role as party-builder-in-chief. Two clear themes have been the consistent focus on Senate races and a rise in the importance of national party fundraising at the expense of state parties.

Presidential fundraising both for themselves and for their fellow Democrats and Republicans has been on the rise in large part because competitive presidential elections and narrow margins of party control of Congress have raised the importance of all federal and gubernatorial elections. The costs of presidential, congressional, and gubernatorial races have risen dramatically, and when presidents raise funds for their fellow party members, they must do so in the small increments prescribed by campaign finance legislation. Unregulated soft money in the 1990s and 2000s led to even more presidential fundraising for party committees, as presidents helped their parties to raise large sums of political cash in unlimited amounts, but its ban in 2002 did not lead to a slowdown in presidential fundraising. If anything, presidents pressured to raise increasing amounts of money have been incentivized to devote even more time to fundraising, as money now has to be gathered in smaller, regulated increments. Ironically, campaign finance legislation designed in part to limit the importance of money in politics has incentivized presidents to devote more time to fundraising throughout their term in office due to the combination of rising campaign costs and the limits on contribution amounts.

As presidents have devoted more and more of their time to fundraising, the incentives of the Electoral College and the presidential nominating process are increasingly reflected in the places where presidents travel throughout their term in office. While presidents do spend the most time in the most heavily populated states, population does not account for important variation in presidential attention, as certain states have been disproportionately favored. Battleground states—those electorally competitive states that are critically important in our winner-take-all Electoral College system, have been disproportionately favored throughout presidents' first terms in office over the three and a half decades since Carter's inauguration, and they have been so most markedly for our most recent presidents, especially George W. Bush. Presidents have increasingly visited greater percentages of battleground states in their first year in office, showing that electoral targeting starts soon after a president enters the Oval Office. Both Iowa and New Hampshire, the states whose early caucuses and primary, respectively, are central to any president's successful renomination, have been disproportionately visited by president after president. The states that presidents of both parties neglect to visit have much in common. They are overwhelmingly sparsely populated, noncompetitive states that were often carried by Republicans in the previous election. In the aggregate, states with greater numbers of Electoral College votes, smaller margins of victory or defeat in the previous election, and the interaction of these two factors—that is, larger states with more competitive elections—have been more likely to receive greater numbers of visits by the president.

Presidents are goal-oriented actors who respond to the incentives established by the rules of the game of the political system. Strategic presidents seek to win reelection in order to enact their policy priorities and secure their legacy. The evidence presented in this book shows that their efforts to win reelection are by no means confined to their fourth year in office. Why do we see an increasing prevalence of targeted presidential travel favoring key electoral states throughout a president's term in office? I contend that these dynamics are largely the consequence of the type of president produced in recent years by the rules structuring presidential nominating and general election campaigns. Presidents attain their high office by taking their case to the people in a way that responds to the strategic incentives of the nominating calendar and the Electoral College system. Once in office, presidents and their aides continue to employ the same strategies that landed them in the White House in the first place.

Presidents also respond to electoral incentives throughout their term in office because recent presidents are well aware that the chance of being frustrated in their bid for reelection is quite real. Before Jimmy Carter defeated Gerald Ford in 1976, a sitting president had not been beaten at the polls for forty-four years, since Franklin Roosevelt unseated Herbert Hoover in 1932. However, three of the four presidents between 1976 and 1992 lost their bid for another term in the White House, as Ford, Carter, and George H. W. Bush all were defeated by the other party's presidential nominee. Of the three presidents since 1976 who have been reelected, only Reagan won in a landslide. Bill Clinton earned his clear Electoral College victory in 1996 by carrying only 49.2 percent of the popular vote, as a slim majority of voters chose a candidate other than Clinton. George W. Bush won a popular majority in 2004, but his narrow Electoral College majority rested on his victory in Ohio, which he carried by just under 120,000 votes.[1] Additionally, Ford, Carter, and George H. W. Bush all faced significant intraparty challenges to their renomination, which left them politically weakened and likely contributed to their defeat at the polls in the general election. In short, presidents are keenly aware that they might fail in their efforts to secure a second term and are determined to do what they can to make sure they do not follow in the footsteps of the defeated Ford, Carter, and George H. W. Bush.

Another important factor in the rise of these key indicators of the permanent campaign has been changes in the organization and nature of the White House staff. While the Truman administration, responding to both practical necessity and the norms of the day, depended on the Democratic National Committee to coordinate much of the political planning for the president, recent administrations have had offices within the White House itself that were responsible for taking into account political and electoral considerations throughout the president's term in office. These developments are part of a larger trend of the centralization of power within the Executive Office of the President, creating what has been called the presidential branch of government. The result is a substantial political apparatus that has been institutionalized within the White House on the government payroll.

THE POTENTIAL PERILS OF THE PERMANENT CAMPAIGN

The prospective rewards of the permanent campaign are readily apparent. Presidents who raise sufficient funds for their own reelection campaign and for their fellow party members and who pay disproportionate attention to the states important in the Electoral College and the nominating process hope to be elected to a second term in the White House and to help their fellow party members to victory at the polls as well. Electoral success allows a president to work to realize his policy goals and leave a legacy that brings the country closer to his vision of a more perfect union. Placing trusted political advisers in the White House helps a president to achieve these aims. But there are potential perils that can result from the permanent campaign as well.

The Trade-offs of Allocating a President's Time to Electoral Concerns

Because time is a president's scarcest resource, the ways in which he allocates it can reveal a great deal about his priorities. When a president devotes so much time to fundraising, one must ask what he might have done had he not been raising money for himself or his party. In October 1982, White House deputy press secretary Larry Speakes made clear the trade-off inherent in a president focusing on electoral concerns when he gave a preview of Reagan's campaign schedule for the weeks leading up to Election Day: "The man will be out [campaigning] three days this week. The rest of the time he will govern."[2] Decades later, a spokesperson for Obama's reelection campaign made the case in May 2011 that Obama was at a competitive disadvantage because he "doesn't have the luxury of spending much time fundraising like the full-time GOP candidates."[3] Both spokespeople acknowledged that time spent campaigning takes away from time devoted to the task of governing.

The pressing concerns of governance often lead presidents to cancel plans to attend political fundraisers. Carter did so in late 1979 and 1980 after American citizens were taken hostage in Iran. Both George H. W. Bush and Obama did so when they were in the midst of difficult budget negotiations with the Congress. George W. Bush canceled fundraisers in the wake of the terrorist attacks of September 11, 2001. These decisions clearly indicated that when the nation's business was so urgent, the president could not spare time for political fundraising, or at least that he was sufficiently concerned about the perceived inappropriateness of fundraising at such a time. Even before the hostage crisis began in 1979, Carter's aides acknowledged these dynamics. In March 1979, Carter first set up his reelection campaign committee, which began laying the groundwork for the fundraising efforts necessary to reelect the president. The head of Carter's campaign, Evan Dobelle, indicated that Carter himself would not participate personally in any fundraising until he formally declared his candidacy later that year because he wanted to focus all his efforts on his responsibilities as president.[4]

When presidents do choose to fundraise, it means that they are not spending time tending to other pressing matters. A White House deputy chief of staff purportedly suggested in 1996 that Clinton's policy briefings be shorter so that he would have more time to spend with Democratic political contributors.[5] In December 1997, as Clinton was in the midst of a stretch in which he would headline thirty-two fundraisers in under two months, White House press secretary Mike McCurry said that the president "is confident that he can fulfill all the duties that he has been elected to pursue by the American people....I think he has a lot of regret that he has to spend as much time raising money."[6] Karl Rove, who is quite familiar with the demands of fundraising on a president's time, examined Obama's personal commitment to fundraising in the three months after he announced his reelection bid in the spring of 2011 and said, "Thirty-one fundraisers in a quarter is a big strain on any president's schedule. Mr. Obama can't keep that pace up and not just because he's got a day job. There are also just so many cities capable of producing $1 million and only so many times you can hold a million dollar fundraiser in them."[7] Obama's day job is one of the most challenging in the world. Presidents always have more demands on their time than they can oblige; when they give priority to political fundraising, attention to other priorities must, to a certain extent, suffer. Whether what suffers is time spent in meetings with advisers, reaching out to members of Congress, formulating policy positions, getting a sufficient amount of much-needed sleep, or something else is a question that merits further study.

Electoral Politics on the Taxpayers' Dime

Ronald Reagan, like many other presidents, often paired fundraisers with official travel, which meant that the campaign would not have to bear the entire cost of the trip. When, in 1981, Reagan took a week out of his monthlong vacation at his ranch in California to headline three fundraisers for the state party, the Republican National Committee announced that it would pay for the costs of the president's week in Los Angeles instead of charging the taxpayers for the trip. The RNC received about $50,000 raised at three fundraising cocktail parties, an amount sufficient to cover the expenses of presidential travel for the events.[8] In 1982, Reagan's director of the White House Office of Political Affairs, Ed Rollins, said that the Republican governor of Texas, William Clements, covered the cost of the president's journey to Houston to help Clement raise more than $3 million because the trip was entirely political. Said Rollins, "We always insist on the money up front because political people are the hardest to collect from."[9] In August 1982, Reagan planned to attend a fundraiser in Los Angeles for GOP gubernatorial hopeful George Deukmejian at the start of a two-week vacation at his ranch. When he decided to postpone the beginning of his vacation to remain in Washington while Congress debated a tax measure, he still planned a brief overnight trip to California to keep his commitment to Deukmejian. But because the Republican's campaign would have then had to foot a much greater share of the cost of Reagan's trip, the expense became more than Deukmejian's team could afford, and the fundraiser was postponed until Reagan would be in California again on official business.[10]

It is up to the White House to declare which trips and events are political and which are official. When clearly political events are deemed to be official, presidents are in an awkward position. Reagan directly addressed these dynamics when he declared at an official event in Ohio in 1982:

> This is a bipartisan meeting, so I'm not going to tell you how proud I am of Congressman Bud Brown and what an invaluable ally he's been in the fight against big government in Washington. And I'm certainly not going to tell you how he's won the respect of virtually everyone he's dealt with there, or of my confidence that he'll do a great job in any position the people of Ohio elect him to. And that goes for [Republican senatorial candidate] Paul Pfeifer, too. . . . But as I say, this isn't a political rally, so I won't say any of those things.

Reagan later delivered a similar speech at a fundraiser for Brown in another part of the hotel in which he gave the first speech.[11] In the eyes of the White House, the first event was nonpolitical, and was thus paid for by the taxpayer, while its doppelgänger fundraising event was a political affair.

Sometimes these official events are more substantive than others. In March 2002, George W. Bush traveled to Dallas, where he headlined a fundraiser for GOP Senate candidate John Cornyn. While there, he held an official event with local rescue workers, which allowed the White House to charge the taxpayers for much of the cost of the trip. This event, however, took a mere fifteen minutes, prompting a spokeswoman for the Democratic National Committee to comment, "The practice of adding political events to official travel for the purpose of saving candidates money seems to be of questionable merit."[12] She neglected to add that it was a common practice engaged in by Republican and Democratic presidents alike.

Even when the official events paired with fundraisers are substantive, they often have the feel of a campaign trip. When Bill Clinton headed to Florida in September 1995 for a fundraiser and several events deemed as official, only the fundraiser was designated as a political event. An event with police officers, a visit to a senior citizens' home, and an airport rally at which the crowd repeatedly chanted, "Four more years!" were all classified as official events, even though an Associated Press article covering the president's trip remarked, "The entire schedule resembled a day from Clinton's 1992 campaign."[13]

The financial advantage enjoyed by the commander-in-chief performing his official duties was made crystal clear when Reagan visited an auto assembly plant in Claycomo, Missouri, on April 11, 1984. Reagan used much of the same rhetoric that he did in his standard political stump speech, talking about the improving economy and the success of his policies. While Reagan made this official presidential trip, the cost of which was borne by taxpayers, Walter Mondale, the eventual Democratic nominee for the presidency, visited a Chrysler facility farther east, in Fenton, Missouri, in advance of that state's approaching Democratic caucuses, with the costs of his trip, of course, fully incurred by his campaign. Later in the day, Reagan traveled to Dallas, where he would hold an event at a construction site to highlight the recovering housing market. This trip would also be deemed nonpolitical.[14]

George H. W. Bush neatly summed up bipartisan presidential practice in this area in early 1990 when he discussed his itinerary for an upcoming trip in which he attended both official events and fundraisers in California, Nebraska, and Ohio. Bush met with the press corps flying with him aboard Air Force One and said, "This should be a very good trip, emphasizing some of our defense requirements, needs. And a little politics mixed in here. We'll be doing more of that this year."[15] Ellen Miller, the director of the Center for Responsive Politics, argued that the central question is if Bush would have traveled to take part in the official events had there been no fundraiser, or whether the official events were planned for the purpose of defraying the cost to the beneficiaries of the fundraisers. "It raises a serious question about abuse of taxpayer funds," she contended. Alixe Glen, a White

House press official, insisted that the official events come first. "He goes on trips to get his message out . . . on the flip side, the president is very committed to the Republican Party."[16] An official at Public Citizen, another government watchdog group, decried this practice as "a flagrant abuse."[17]

Crossing the Lines between Campaigning and Governing: Scandals

A politicized White House can lead to trouble for the president. In recognition that there should be lines between campaigning and governing, rules have been established to determine when and where it is proper for presidents and their aides to engage in electoral activity. Presidents and their staffs cross these lines at their political peril. In one prominent example, Bill Clinton's aggressive fundraising efforts in support of his reelection bid led to charges that he was renting out the White House's Lincoln Bedroom by offering an overnight stay there as a reward to big campaign contributors and that he was selling access to donors who were invited to events that were called White House coffees. Clinton argued that such gatherings were perfectly proper, saying that the planners followed "strict legal advice," and that "there was to be no price tag on the events. There was no solicitation at the White House."[18] Clinton's vice president, Al Gore, came under fire for soliciting campaign contributions from his White House office in spite of a law that prohibits political fundraising in federal buildings; he asserted, "I am proud of what I did. I do not feel like I did anything wrong, much less illegal." He famously declared, "My counsel advises me that there is no controlling legal authority or case that says that there was any violation of law whatsoever in the manner in which I asked people to contribute to our reelection campaign."[19] Gore's aggressive efforts to raise money for his and the president's reelection earned him the nickname among DNC officials as the "solicitor-in-chief," since Clinton reportedly refused to ask for contributions himself. Another anonymous Democrat close to Gore concluded, "Al could be the victim of his own success."[20]

These scandals brought to light the fact that many presidents had rewarded political donors with access to administration officials and visits to the White House. During the investigation of the Clinton reelection campaign's fundraising efforts, research at the Reagan Library turned up evidence that Reagan had made a number of calls from the White House to fundraising events, and while aides insisted that he did not directly solicit contributions, in one instance his "talking points" for a call to a gathering of donors called Eagles, who had given at least $10,000 to the Republican Party, suggested that he say, "We have the Eagles down to the White House quite often so I will be seeing you soon." Memos from the Reagan

White House showed that White House counsel had deemed these phone calls to be within the bounds of the law. Additionally, video surfaced of a 1987 event that Reagan had held in the East Room of the White House for a group of Eagles at which he said, "I'll campaign hard for the nominee of our party. And let me ask you now, I know this is silly, but can I count on you to help?" Campaign finance experts contended that this vague appeal might have violated campaign finance laws.[21]

Democrats, trying to show that the Clinton administration's practices were not a departure from those of its predecessors, made the case that George H. W. Bush held at least twenty-four events with donors at the White House during his four years as president, including ten functions for the so-called Eagles. Bush defended himself years after he left office, saying in 1997, "Some say having the Republican Eagles there was raising money. It was not." The former president made the case that inviting supporters to the White House was far different from actually soliciting money in the executive mansion. "I wouldn't do it. There was never any quid pro quo in terms of use of the White House, staying in the White House, anything to do with that, Air Force One, Camp David—you name it." While Bush declined to offer his opinion on the controversies surrounding Clinton at the time, he did say that the events in the nation's capital looked "awful and ugly."[22]

Republican donors in the first Bush administration were also rewarded with time with Vice President Dan Quayle. A 1990 letter from Republican senator Don Nickles to GOP contributors described an upcoming reception at the vice president's residence in which he wrote that "no other organization offers you the opportunity to meet the vice president and his wife at their home, participate in closed-door briefings with national and international figures, and then top the evening off by joining a senator, a Cabinet member or a U.S. Senate candidate for a private dinner." Quayle denied any wrongdoing, saying, "It was not the sleazy sale of a White House bedroom, or illegal dialing for dollars from government offices. I never solicited personal contributions on government property, either in person by telephone. Neither President Bush nor I would have tolerated it."[23]

Democrats pointed to these examples of Republicans holding events with donors to make the case that Clinton was merely continuing a long-standing Washington practice. But an official with the nonpartisan group Common Cause said that Clinton's efforts were different. "There has been for some time a pattern of using the White House for political fundraising. But I think the Clinton Administration has taken the game to a new level both in the amount of money that is being raised and in the aggressive use of the president and the White House as a key part of the fundraising. The image that is created is one of the White House being for sale." That image is one that can be tremendously damaging to the public's view of the presidency. Former president Gerald Ford agreed, saying that he was "deeply disturbed" by the controversy around the Clinton-Gore fundraising: "There is no question, across the board, it is unhealthy the way money is raised and the amount of money that is raised. There is no doubt this White House has abused that more than any White House in my memory."[24]

Bill Clinton explained the perils of a presidential reelection campaign working to raise so much money when he called for campaign finance reform legislation in 1997, saying, "A huge percentage, way, way over 90 percent," of campaign contributions is solicited "in a perfectly lawful fashion . . . [but] the problem is that the margins create great problems because of the sheer volume of money that is raised today." Clinton went on to contend that "no one is blameless here. It costs so much money to pay for these campaigns that mistakes were made here by people who either did it deliberately or inadvertently. Now others—it's up to others to decide whether those mistakes were made deliberately or inadvertently."[25]

The actions of George W. Bush's administration led to its own scandal about the blurring of lines between campaigning and governing when the Office of Special Counsel found that Bush's Office of Political Affairs had violated the 1939 Hatch Act, which forbids most federal workers from engaging in partisan politics on the job. The Office of Political Affairs was accused of having sponsored seventy-five meetings on political strategy for government employees, most of which took place at federal agencies during working hours and were aimed at helping the Republican cause at the ballot box. The Office of Special Counsel also concluded that some political travel by Bush administration officials had been wrongly deemed to be official, so the taxpayers improperly bore the costs of these trips. Because these findings were issued in January 2011, two years after Bush left office, they did not lead to criminal charges or other penalties.[26]

Most recently, the Obama administration came under fire in 2011 after the president met with Wall Street executives in the Blue Room of the White House about policies regulating the financial industry. While such meetings are commonplace, the invitations to this event came not from the White House but from the Democratic National Committee, and because a number of the executives invited had donated to the president's campaign and party in the past, the gathering was criticized as a donor maintenance event. White House press secretary Jay Carney justified the event, saying, "This was not a fundraiser. It is wholly understandable why the president would want to consult with business executives about their ideas about what to do in terms of economic policy and business policy going forward, including financial-sector policy. . . . Obviously, he would want to talk to his supporters about that, as well." Another White House spokesperson, Eric Schultz, explained, "This was an event with the president's political supporters in the residence. All presidents have meetings with their supporters." One executive who attended the meeting said, "It was policy-focused, but everyone knew why they were there," explaining that he had been invited by a DNC aide whose focus was fundraising. During the Carter administration, the Department of Justice held that the law that prohibits fundraising on federal property does not cover the White House residence, which includes not only the upper floors where the president and his family live but also the Blue Room and similar rooms on the main floor of the White House.[27]

At this writing, Republican congressman Darrell Issa, who chairs the House Committee on Oversight and Government Reform, is investigating the Blue Room gathering, as well as the activities of the White House Office of Political Affairs. Issa explained the investigation this way:

> President Obama's campaign promise to change politics as usual in Washington has been undermined by the continuing political campaign this White House has run through the White House Office of Political Affairs. During the previous administration, there was plenty of bipartisan criticism about the Office of Political Affairs as an institution, but many leading Democratic critics in Congress immediately went silent after the 2008 election. The change of administrations certainly hasn't resolved concerns that this office is being used by the Obama Administration to improperly coordinate with and help political campaigns rather than advancing specific policy initiatives being pushed by the president.[28]

Issa's efforts follow on the heels of those of former committee chairman Henry Waxman, a Democrat from California who investigated the activities of George W. Bush's Office of Political Affairs and advocated that it be abolished.[29]

Even trying to comply with the rules that aim to separate campaign activities from governing can land a White House in political hot water. Some aides to George W. Bush who were assigned separate computers, Blackberries, and email accounts on which they would transact campaign business in order to keep it separate from their official duties were accused of trying to subvert the 1978 Presidential Records Act, which requires that all presidential communications be preserved for the historical record. A White House aide said that administration staffers might have dealt with official government business on their campaign email accounts "out of an abundance of caution" not to violate the Hatch Act. When it was revealed that many email messages in the campaign accounts had been deleted, Democratic skeptics wondered if their actions had been intentional in an effort to conceal certain activities.[30] While it is difficult to discern intentions, this problematic situation resulted from the messy overlap of official and campaign duties performed by White House aides.

The lines between campaigning and governing have been drawn in part because it is both difficult and necessary to separate one from the other. Because it is so difficult, these lines often get crossed. Understandably, presidents feel that they need their trusted advisers to weigh in on questions with political and electoral ramifications. But it is often difficult to say exactly where the official duties of a presidential aide end and where his or her efforts to advance a president's electoral fortunes begin. These dynamics work against and often overcome the formal rules that are meant to separate the president's governing activities from his campaigning efforts. Indeed, the more these rules are necessary, the less they may be effective.

The Perception of a Politicized Presidency

A president who focuses on electoral gain can fuel the perception of a politicized presidency and heighten public cynicism. The controversy surrounding Clinton's and Gore's reelection fundraising efforts in the 1996 campaign is an illustrative example of the damage that such practices can do not just to one president's image but to the people's views of other presidents as well. Public opinion polling at the time indicated that a clear majority of Americans were troubled by the Democrats' practices, and that many questioned Clinton's honesty about the subject. In one April 1997 survey, 30 percent of respondents called the fundraising efforts of Clinton and his party "neither legal nor ethical," and another 55 percent deemed them to be "legal but ethically questionable."[31] In another poll that spring, 33 percent of respondents asked about the president's fundraising said that they thought he "broke the law and [was] covering it up," and an additional 33 percent labeled what Clinton had done to be "in bad taste, but legal."[32] In a survey conducted in April 1997, 51 percent of respondents indicated that they believed Clinton had "participated in a cover-up of his 1996 fundraising activities."[33] In October of that year, after months of media coverage of the controversy, the proportion of respondents who believed that Clinton was "not telling the truth about his involvement in political fundraising last year" reached 58 percent. Only 28 percent said that they thought Clinton had been honest about his fundraising efforts, a remarkably low number for a president who had been reelected just under a year before with more than 49 percent of the popular vote.[34]

The controversy affected people's assessments not just of Clinton's fundraising efforts but of his overall performance as president as well. In a January 1998 poll, a total of 71 percent of respondents indicated that "questionable political fundraising activities by the Clinton White House" were either very important (32 percent) or somewhat important (39 percent) "in judging Bill Clinton as president," while only 26 percent considered them to not be important.[35] What, specifically, were people concerned about? One April 1997 poll asked whether "elected officials spending too much of their time raising money for election campaigns" could impede the effective functioning of the national government. In response, 61 percent described the time devoted to fundraising as "a major problem," 30 percent deemed it "somewhat of a problem," and only 8 percent said it was "not much of a problem."[36] When another survey that month asked what in particular bothered respondents about political fundraising, 57 percent of respondents cited "the possibility that politicians make decisions based on who contributed money to their campaigns"; an additional 13 percent chose "the amount of time politicians have to spend raising money."[37] Two years later, an October 1999 poll found that "getting big money out of politics" was cited by 55 percent of respondents as being "one of the most important issues" that would affect their vote in the following year's presidential election.[38] In survey after survey, the public indicated that it saw a president's focus on fundraising as problematic in a number of respects.

Perhaps most important, the negative fallout from the fundraising controversy surrounding the 1996 election was not limited to Clinton and the Democrats. In a series of polls, the public indicated a clear belief that what Clinton and Gore had done was a common practice of other presidents and vice presidents, and the proportion of respondents who held this view increased throughout 1997. A poll in March of that year asked whether "it is a common practice for the president and vice president to be closely involved in campaign fundraising, or is this something that only Bill Clinton and Al Gore have done?" A full 70 percent of respondents called this a common practice, with only 12 percent believing that these activities were limited to just Clinton and Gore.[39] A similar question that July revealed that 74 percent of respondents believed that "many politicians have probably committed . . . [similar] political fundraising abuses."[40] In response to an identical question two months later, the percentage of respondents who thought that Clinton's practices were common among other politicians rose to 77 percent.[41] When the same question was posed in October 1997, 80 percent of respondents indicated that they believed other politicians engaged in similar questionable fundraising practices.[42] These polls were conducted against the backdrop of a steady stream of media stories about the controversy throughout the year. Presumably, continuing coverage of the scandal not only helped to fuel increasing public doubts about one particular administration but also led to heightened public cynicism about presidents and politicians in general.

Media coverage of targeted presidential travel can also fuel the perception of a politicized presidency. A presidential visit is a rare event in most parts of the country, and it generates a great deal of excitement and positive local news stories. The evidence presented here indicates that the incentives of the Electoral College and the nominating system are reflected in patterns of presidential travel. It is well known that electoral incentives structure the ways that presidents campaign. The United States does not hold a national presidential election; instead, the president is chosen via fifty-one subnational contests in the fifty states and the District of Columbia that determine the allocation of 538 Electoral College votes. In most years, the outcome in about thirty or more of these contests is not in question, so neither candidate spends time or other valuable resources there. They concentrate instead on the so-called battleground states where their campaigning could make a difference. Similarly, during the nominating process, not all states are equal. Iowa and New Hampshire, which hold the first two contests every four years, have disproportionate influence, as success in one of these two states is an all-but-necessary precursor to having a chance at winning the nomination.

It is not surprising to see key electoral states receive disproportionate attention from candidates during the closing months of a presidential campaign. In fact, a failure to target key Electoral College states can be seen as political malpractice, such as when Richard Nixon spent the final weekend of the 1960 campaign traveling to Alaska to fulfill his promise to visit every state he hoped to lead as president. While the visit arguably helped him carry that state's three Electoral College votes, critics assailed him for not campaigning in a more critical Electoral College state, as he ended up narrowly losing several battleground states to John F. Kennedy, which provided the Democrat with his slender margin of victory.[43]

Sitting presidents also devote disproportionate time to key electoral states throughout their terms in office. They do not travel exclusively to these states; indeed, they travel widely for a variety of reasons. But several measures indicate that the incentives of our electoral system manifest themselves in the patterns of attention paid by U.S. presidents to the fifty states. No electoral system is neutral. Any system sets up rules of the game that provide incentives that structure candidate behavior. Presidents concerned about the prospect of renomination and reelection might respond to these incentives not only in the months before an election but throughout a term in office. Indeed, the evidence here indicates that they do.

The practice of targeting key electoral states can lead to headlines like these, all of which ran outside of the traditional presidential campaign season: "Selling Stimulus, Obama Tours Battleground States"; "Obama's Travel Mixes Policy, Electoral Politics"; "Obama Makes Himself a Stranger in 12 (Mostly Red) States"; "Bush a Frequent Flyer to States That Could Decide 2004 Race"; "Bluest of the Blue: Vermont Doesn't Look Like Bush Country; It's Only State He Hasn't Visited While in Office"; and "President Mixes Politics and Business on the Road."[44] Responding to questions about Obama's early visits to battleground states, White House aide Dan Pfeiffer attested, "It is a coincidence. We'll certainly visit states of all shapes and sizes, regardless of who won."[45] In spite of White House denials, stories like these reinforce the notion that presidential travel and thus presidential attention are politically motivated, and that certain parts of the country that don't fit into a president's Electoral College calculus are likely to be ignored by the White House.

Similarly, the fundraising practices of Clinton and Gore in the 1990s demonstrated that such controversy can contribute to a growing perception of a politicized presidency.

The Difficulty of Problem-Solving in the Age of the Permanent Campaign

Political scandals, media coverage of targeted travel and taxpayer-funded political events, frequent fundraising, and the placement of key political advisers like Karl Rove and David Axelrod in the White House can lead to a focus on the president as a divisive figure with an eye on his party's interests instead of a unifying national leader working for the national interest. This frame is reinforced by criticism from the opposing party that the president is devoting too much time to electoral concerns. In 2011, the chairman of the Republican National Committee, Reince Priebus, offered this criticism of Obama's fundraising efforts and his travels to key electoral states: "The president is one of the most politically calculating people we've ever had in the White House. Almost all of his visits are political."[46] The criticism flows in both partisan directions, of course. When George W. Bush traveled to South Carolina, Georgia, and Texas in March 2002 to hold fundraisers for Senate candidates, Democrats criticized the practice of also holding official events, which meant that taxpayers would fund a greater portion of the trip. A spokesperson for congressional Democrats complained, "This is a clear example of the White House using people's hard-earned tax dollars to finance its partisan political activities." What he left unsaid, however, was that Bill Clinton had regularly engaged in the same practice for which the Democratic spokesperson was criticizing Bush.[47] Similarly, Republicans derided Clinton as a "part-time president" and "fund-raiser-in-chief" who traveled around the country on "Fund-raiser One" instead of tending to his official duties as president.[48] These criticisms are amplified by the media, which frequently focus on the political elements of anything presidents do, and can make the president look like just another politician.

Samuel Kernell argued that presidents who go public undermine the bargaining process with members of Congress and can actually make it more difficult at times for presidents to achieve their goals. Norman Ornstein and Thomas Mann contended that the zero-sum nature of campaigning is "antithetical" to the process of governing, which relies not on destroying the opposition but on negotiating an acceptable compromise.[49] Their arguments have resonance. How can presidents work well with members of Congress whom they have labored to defeat at the ballot box? In 2009, Ken Duberstein, who served as Ronald Reagan's final White House chief of staff, laid out the difference between campaigning and governing in a memorable fashion, saying, "In campaigning, you try to annihilate your opponent. Governing, you try to make love to your opponents, as well as your allies."[50]

Fundraising might help a president to build his party, but the costs to governing could be substantial. Republican Senator Lindsay Graham of South Carolina summed up the problem when he contended that the constant focus on regaining or retaining a congressional majority in the next election has a debilitating effect on the national government's abilities to tackle pressing problems. He argued, "Once you get in these battles where you break into camps, every vote is about the next election. As soon as the last election is over, those who lost are thinking, 'What can I do to get back in power?' and those who won are thinking, 'What can I do to stay in power?' When you try to solve problems from the perpetual campaign mindset, it's very difficult." One Democrat, then majority leader Steny Hoyer of Maryland, admitted that he had "demagogued" the issue of raising the federal debt ceiling in an effort to cast Republicans in a negative light in advance of the next congressional elections.[51]

Many contend that the change in the Congress came about in the 1990s, when Newt Gingrich encouraged Republicans not to cooperate with the Democratic majority in an attempt to draw clear distinctions between the parties that could be presented to the American people in a campaign. When the Republicans succeeded and, in 1994, retook the House of Representatives for the first time in forty years and the Senate for the first time in eight years, Democrats then followed suit when they became the minority party. When Democrats again took control first of both chambers of the Congress after the 2006 elections and then of the White House as well following the 2008 elections, many Republicans felt that their best strategy was to oppose the Democratic agenda en masse.[52] While this may be a winning political strategy employed at times by both parties, it is not one conducive to finding bipartisan solutions to many of the nation's most substantial problems.

We must be careful not to look nostalgically back to a mythical golden era when politics was a process in which well-meaning people who disagreed could reasonably reach mutually acceptable solutions without bitterness or rancor. Politics has been a contact sport throughout much of our nation's history. But in a permanent campaign, each side seeks electoral advantage in the hopes of using their newly acquired power to advance their particular vision of good public policy. The perpetual struggle for power means that the party in power finds it increasingly difficult to enact its policy preferences, as the opposition seeks to block and obstruct in an effort to win back power in the next election.

New York Times columnist Ross Douthat framed these dynamics around the political science theory of realigning elections—the sweeping, once-in-a-generation electoral victories that reconfigure the electoral map, leaving one party dominant for a sustained period and the other vanquished to the sidelines. These elections appeared to occur every thirty to forty years throughout American history, from the victory of Thomas Jefferson and the Democratic-Republicans over John Adams and the Federalists in 1800 up through the victory of Franklin Roosevelt and the Democratic Party in 1932. Douthat blames the "seductive dream of realignment" for much of the vitriol in American politics today. Because both parties hope for the possibility of winning a landslide victory in the next election that hands them control of all the levers of government, they are less inclined to compromise on policy issues. Instead, they stridently disagree with the opposition and plan to take their case to the people in the next election. As Douthat says, "After all, why cut a deal today if tomorrow you might overthrow your rivals permanently?"[53] This mentality, which is the mind-set of the permanent campaign, makes it much more difficult to address the most pressing public policy questions of the day.

THE PROSPECTS FOR THE PERMANENT CAMPAIGN

What, if anything, should be done to improve the American political system in light of the evidence presented in this book? Many of the dynamics of the permanent campaign are likely here to stay. Presidents are strategic actors who respond to institutional incentives and contextual factors. Because so many of their goals are more easily realized if they win reelection and more fellow party members are elected to Congress and other offices across the country, they work to achieve those aims. Several potential reforms might help to curb some of the elements of the permanent campaign, though we must be ever wary of the potential for unintended consequences that might make the cure worse than the disease.

Potential Reforms

The public interest might be better served if presidents did not devote so much time to fundraising. Simply wishing that this were so, however, will not make it so. The voluntary system of public financing for presidential campaigns succeeded in limiting the need for presidents to spend time raising money for their own campaigns until George W. Bush became the first sitting president to opt out of public financing at the nomination stage in 2004. Carter and Reagan attended four and zero fundraisers for their reelection committee, respectively, while George H. W. Bush and Clinton each took part in nineteen and fourteen fundraisers for their own reelection campaign committee, respectively. But when George W. Bush decided to forgo the matching funds of the public finance system at the nominating stage and the spending limits that come with the public money, he headlined fifty-seven fundraisers for the Bush-Cheney reelection committee—more than four times the number that either George H. W. Bush or Clinton had attended, and raised nearly $270 million, a total that dwarfed what had been raised by his predecessors.[54] In the two and a half months between the beginning of Obama's reelection fundraising in April 2011 and June 30 of that year, he took part in a re-markable thirty-one fundraisers for the Obama Victory Fund, a joint account that benefits both his reelection campaign and the Democratic National Committee. Both Bush and Obama started their reelection fundraising earlier than their pre-decessors because of the time necessary to raise large totals of money in the small increments regulated by federal contribution limits. Public funding for the general election has relieved past presidents of the need to spend their own time raising funds in the final months of the campaign. Because Obama has also made it clear that he will be the first sitting president not to take part in this program, following his decision to opt out as a candidate in 2008, the amount of fundraisers he will attend for his own reelection could easily surpass the combined totals of his five immediate predecessors in the White House as he heads what could be the first billion-dollar presidential campaign effort. So much time spent fundraising neces-sarily limits the time a president can devote to other matters.

George W. Bush and Obama both opted out of the public financing system because it was in their self-interest to do so. They determined that they could run a more effective campaign if they raised more financial resources than would be possible under the public system. Because of their choices, other leading candi-dates followed suit. Qualifying for federal matching funds in the nomination fight, which requires a candidate to raise at least $5,000 in each of twenty states in con-tributions of $250 or less, was once seen as the mark of a successful candidate with a broad base of financial support. Now, the leading candidates opt out of the matching funds program. Campaign finance legislation that modified the public funding program so that it provided more resources might offer a greater incen-tive for presidential aspirants to participate and thus accept the associated spend-ing caps, which limited both fundraising and spending by presidential campaigns for almost three decades. Legislation that provides more public funds for political candidates might not be popular in an era when so many elected officials are held in disdain by the public at large. But the alternative is a system in which public funding is no longer strategically appealing, and thus presidents and presidential candidates spend more and more time raising funds.

Perhaps raising the amount of the maximum individual contribution would relieve some of the pressure on presidents to fundraise, since they could then raise more money from fewer donors, but doing so would be at odds with the law's original goal of limiting contribution amounts to lessen the potential for corruption. Additionally, because presidents spend so much time raising money for their fellow party members, some sort of public funding system for congressional elections would relieve some pressure on both members of Congress and the president to devote so much time to fundraising. In a time of high budget deficits and with Congress's popularity at an all-time low, however, this idea is also unlikely to become law.

In 1997, White House press secretary Mike McCurry gave a blunt answer to a question about why Clinton was fundraising so much in the face of the investigations into his reelection fundraising efforts. "Wake up and see reality. Reality is that campaign spending is running somewhat out of control and that Republicans are outspending Democrats five-to-one. So just get used to it, because the president is going to have to do a lot more of it unless we secure campaign finance reform." McCurry continued, "People who are concerned about it or find [Clinton's continued fundraising] odd or peculiar ought to write their congressmen and assure that we get campaign finance reform enacted early next year."[55] But when campaign finance reform finally became law in 2002 and soft money contributions to national political parties were banned, presidents did not end up spending less time fundraising. Indeed, presidents attended more party fundraisers that raised less money after the ban than before, in part because the pressure to raise money had not eased, and they then were required to solicit funds in smaller increments. The Bipartisan Campaign Reform Act of 2002 may or may not have succeeded in achieving many of its goals, but it did not lead to presidents spending less time fundraising.

Some political actors have looked to reduce the pressure on presidents and other politicians to raise money by dealing with the factors related to the rising costs of campaigns. One of the biggest campaign expenses is money for television advertising. In the mid-1990s, Clinton put forth a proposal that would compel broadcasters to provide free airtime to political candidates. In exchange for their broadcast licenses, broadcasters agree to air a certain amount of public interest programming. The logic behind the legislation was that if the need to spend money on television ads were reduced, presidents and other officials would need to spend less time raising money and could spend more time on their official duties. Clinton summed up the logic behind his push, saying, "Free time for candidates can help free our democracy from the grip of big money." The president of the National Association of Broadcasters disagreed, arguing that free airtime would not lead to less political fundraising; instead, campaigns "would just buy twice as much."[56] The proposal was never enacted into law, so predictions about its potential consequences are speculative.

Some observers look at the targeted travel of presidents and presidential candidates and argue that the Electoral College must be abolished, as its incentives create classes of favored and neglected states. Political scientist Burdett Loomis of the University of Kansas writes evocatively about how his own state of Kansas is ignored by both parties in presidential election after presidential election because it is a reliably Republican state. But because he lives in the Kansas City media market, every four years he watches a competitive presidential campaign waged just miles away in the perennial battleground state of Missouri.[57] Over the three and a half decades of this study, Missouri was the most disproportionately visited state in the country, hosting presidential events on 101 days, or 39.9 more than its population would have predicted. Neighboring Kansas, meanwhile, was the ninth most disproportionately neglected state. It hosted presidents on just 15 days, or 14.4 days fewer than its population would have predicted. The incentives of the Electoral College not only make Missouri a more appealing presidential destination than Kansas during election campaigns; these dynamics also play out throughout a president's term in office.

If the Electoral College were abolished and replaced with a national popular vote, Loomis contends, his vote would count as much as his neighbor's vote in Missouri. The incentives that structure the attention of both presidential candidates and presidents would be fundamentally changed. Which states would get the most candidate attention in a system in which the president were elected via a national popular vote is unclear, and would not be known until presidents and candidates actually determine how best to allocate their scarce resources, but the distorting incentives of the Electoral College would be no longer. One potential consequence of such a reform, however, would be that the costs of a presidential campaign would rise substantially. In the current system, campaigns and parties raise funds to compete in battleground states; if every vote counted equally in every state, then the field of electoral competition would expand substantially, as would the costs of reaching voters all across the country. This, in turn, would likely increase the amount of time that presidents and candidates spend raising money to be able to wage this broader campaign. This trade-off might well be worth it, especially to people like Loomis who live in perennially neglected states like Kansas, but it is one worth considering.

Turning to the way political decisions are made, presidents might also want to consider the reform proposed by John McCain in 2008—permanently abolishing the White House Office of Political Affairs and moving most of its functions to the Democratic or Republican National Committee. As of this writing, Obama had recently shuttered the office upon the establishment of his reelection campaign, but if he wins a second term, he might follow Reagan's precedent and reestablish the office within the White House. The abolition of the Office of Political Affairs would likely be more symbolic than substantive. Presidential aides within the White House would still advise the president on the political ramifications of decisions he makes, and they would still closely coordinate to plan the president's campaign appearances and fundraising efforts for his fellow party members. But the symbolism of such a move might be important in and of itself, representing a commitment by the president and his staff to do their best to avoid the blurring of the lines between campaigning and governing.

Ted Sorensen, who was a top aide to President John F. Kennedy, supported Obama in the 2008 campaign. In October 2009, he offered this advice to the new president: "Stop campaigning. You've been campaigning for years, and of course you've been in perpetual campaign mode, and Clinton more than anyone else set that pattern of the permanent campaign. But once you're president you don't need to worry" about the media story of the moment. Instead a president must focus on the big picture and the long term.[58] Moving the Office of Political Affairs to the national committee might be one small step to help create the impression that a president has indeed stopped campaigning and turned his attention to governing.

CONCLUDING THOUGHTS

There is no silver bullet to deal with the negative elements of the permanent campaign. Politicking is tied to governing. Presidents campaign and raise funds for themselves and others and work to secure their own reelection and electoral victory for their fellow party members so that they can achieve their policy goals and do the people's business as they see it. They place trusted political advisers in the White House to help them achieve these aims. Bill Clinton addressed these dynamics when he spoke to staffers at the Democratic National Committee in early January 2001, with just weeks left in his presidency, and urged them to be proud of their political efforts:

> One other thing I want to say is that I think that the dividing line between politics and policy is not very clear. And most people say that in a pejorative way. I say it in a proud way. This is a political system we live in. The framers of the Constitution expected it to be and didn't think politics was a bad word. They thought it was a good word, and so do I. I am proud that I have spent my life in the American political system. So even though you have to worry about recruiting candidates and raising money and getting the talking points out there and answering the charges and doing all the things you have to do, the sort of nitty-gritty work of political life, you should never forget that it bears a direct relationship to the way the American people live.[59]

Politics and policy are indeed intertwined, and, arguably, in the American political system they are meant to be. The notion that a president can be above politics is a fiction. The last president who was seen as floating above the political fray was Dwight Eisenhower, who emphasized in public his role as a unifying national leader. But the research of political scientist Fred Greenstein has shown that behind the scenes, he was a skilled operator, very much involved in the hurly-burly of politics.[60] As Truman aide George Elsey said, "The White House has always been just a little jittery in recognizing that the President is a political leader and a politician 365 days of the year. . . . As I say, this is part of the mythology of American life. We don't want to admit that a President has to be a good politician, if he's going to be halfway effective as a President."[61]

Politics is the process through which we fight out disagreements over national priorities. The president is elected following a campaign in which he advocated certain policy prescriptions, and many members of Congress in his party share his political perspective. He works to enact those policy priorities, and to do so the president supports his fellow party members, helping to raise funds and framing his political stands in contrast to the political opposition. Presidents often devote much effort to winning the next election, for themselves or for their co-partisans, knowing that doing so will strengthen their ability to win other much-desired political victories.

A president must serve both as a uniting national leader and as the head of his political party. Clinton spokesperson Mike McCurry made the case in December 1997 that the two roles are tied together, arguing that Clinton "is also the leader of the Democratic Party and he has obligations in connection with that. As president, there are expenses incurred with his travel wherever he goes but I think most Americans understand that those are costs that are associated with fulfilling his duties as president."[62] Presidential scholar and former Eisenhower aide Stephen Hess concurred, saying, "The president is both president of all and at the same time, the titular elder of his party. It's sometimes hard to balance those two conflicting interests."[63] One Democrat argued that the more President Obama engaged in electoral activities, the better he would be able to perform the unifying, nondivisive presidential role. "Obama's ability to remain above the fray in the long term is directly tied to his success as campaigner-in-chief: a robust Democratic majority and strong coattails make it a lot easier for Obama to float above the ugly day to day politics that consumed Clinton and Bush 43," contended the unnamed strategist.[64] But too much focus on the president's role as partisan leader can create the perception that he is not focused on the national interest.

Ironically, Pat Caddell, the Carter aide often recognized for originating the concept of the permanent campaign, now argues that it has gone too far. In a column written with fellow Democratic pollster Douglas Schoen soon after the 2010 midterm elections, Caddell called on President Obama to announce that he would not seek a second term in the White House in order to dedicate himself to the issues facing the country instead of the politics of a reelection campaign. "Quite simply, given our political divisions and economic problems, governing and campaigning have become incompatible. Obama can and should dispense with the pollsters, the advisers, the consultants and the strategists who dissect all decisions and judgments in terms of their impact on the president's political prospects."[65] The merits of such advice, however, are debatable. In December 1982, Reagan, then at the same point in his term as Obama when Caddell and Schoen issued their recommendation, made the case that such a decision would leave him with limited ability to lead. When asked if he would run for a second term, he declined to answer, saying, "To make that decision too early or to make it public too early is to do one of two things. One way you're going to become a lame duck and have no authority to do anything you're trying to do. Or the other way, you're going to open yourself to the opposition charges that everything you do is political, based at the next election."[66] A president who announced he would not seek reelection would not be, as Caddell and Schoen predict, able to lead the nation to address the great problems of the day because he had been freed from electoral considerations. Instead, as Reagan contends, especially in the last two years of his term, he would be a lame duck, yesterday's news, with lessened potential for presidential leadership.

A president will continue to tend to electoral concerns throughout his, and someday her, term in office. As presidents do so, they and their staffs must be quite careful not to cross the lines that are supposed to divide their governing activities from their campaigning activities, as even the accusation of political wrongdoing can feed the cynicism of the media and the American people and undermine a president's ability to lead. Perhaps Alexander Hamilton was right when he defended the reelection of U.S. presidents in *The Federalist* No. 72, contending that "the desire of reward is one of the strongest incentives of human conduct; or that the best security for the fidelity of mankind is to make their interests coincide with their duty."[67] In this view, the reelection incentive would lead to better performance of official presidential duties. As citizens, we must be vigilant to ensure that it does, and when it does not, we must carefully consider whether we need to reform the system that incentivizes a perpetual focus on electoral concerns.

NOTES

CHAPTER I: PRESIDENTS AND THE PERMANENT CAMPAIGN

1. Clark Clifford, memorandum for Harry S. Truman, November 19, 1947, p. 29, Clifford Papers, Harry S. Truman Library.

2. Barack Obama, "Remarks at a Keep Indiana Blue Fundraiser Event in Indianapolis, Indiana," White House web site, May 17, 2009, http://www.whitehouse.gov/the-press-office/remarks-president-keep-indiana-blue-fundraiser-indianapolis-5172009 (accessed March 20, 2011).

3. Thomas E. Cronin and Michael A. Genovese, *The Paradoxes of the American Presidency* (New York: Oxford University Press, 2004); Fred I. Greenstein, *The Presidential Difference: Leadership Style from FDR to George W. Bush* (Princeton, NJ: Princeton University Press, 2004); Fred I. Greenstein, *The Hidden-Hand Presidency: Eisenhower as Leader* (New York: Basic Books, 1982).

4. Cited in Michael Nelson, *The Evolving Presidency: Landmark Documents, 1787–2008* (Washington, DC: CQ Press, 2008).

5. Quoted in Fareed Zakaria, "Obama Should Act More Like a President Than a Prime Minister," *Washington Post,* January 25, 2010.

6. Robert A. Dahl, *How Democratic Is the American Constitution?* 2nd ed. (New Haven, CT: Yale University Press, 2002).

7. Harry Truman, lecture at Columbia University, New York, New York, April 1959 (quotation displayed at the Truman Library, observed July 27, 2006).

8. George H. W. Bush, "Remarks at Dedication Ceremony of the Social Sciences Complex at Princeton University in Princeton, New Jersey," May 10, 1991, http://www.presidency.ucsb.edu/ws/?pid=19573 (accessed June 8, 2011).

9. See, for example, John R. Carter and David Schap, "Executive Veto, Legislative Override, and Structure-Induced Equilibrium," *Public Choice* 52, no. 3 (1987): 227–244; James A. Dearden and Thomas A. Husted, "Executive Budget Proposal, Executive Veto, Legislative Override, and Uncertainty: A Comparative Analysis of the Budgetary Process," *Public Choice* 65, no. 1 (1990): 1–19; Michael Fitts and Robert Inman, "Controlling Congress: Presidential Influence in Domestic Fiscal Policy," *Georgetown Law Review* 80, no. 5 (1992): 1737–1785; Robert P. Inman, "Local Interests, Central Leadership, and the Passage of TRA86," *Journal of Policy Analysis and Management* 12, no. 1 (1993): 156; Susanne Lohmann and Sharyn O'Halloran, "Divided Government and U.S. Trade Policy: Theory and Evidence," *International Organization* 48, no. 4 (1994): 595–632.

10. Nolan M. McCarty, "Presidential Pork: Executive Veto Power and Distributive Politics," *Political Science* 94, no. 1 (2000): 117–129.

11. See, for example, Scott L. Althaus, Peter F. Nardulli, and Daron R. Shaw, "Candidate Appearances in Presidential Elections, 1972–2000," *Political Communication* 19, no. 1 (2002): 49–72; Larry M. Bartels, "Resource Allocation in a Presidential Campaign," *Journal of Politics* 47, no. 3 (1985): 928–936; Steven J. Brams and Morton D. Davis, "The 3/2's Rule in Presidential Campaigning," *American Political Science Review* 68, no. 1 (1974): 113–134; Claude S. Colantoni, Terrence J. Levesque, and Peter C. Ordeshook, "Campaign Resource Allocations under the Electoral College," *American Political Science Review* 69, no. 1 (1975): 141–154; Darshan Goux, "Big State, Small State: The Shifting Nature of Electoral College Strategies" (paper presented at annual meeting

of the American Political Science Association, Washington, DC, September 2010), http://papers. ssrn.com/so13/papers.cfm?abstract_id=1644222 (accessed June 8, 2011).

12. Terence Hunt, "Gore: Made Fund-Raising Calls from Office, Won't Any More," Associated Press, March 3, 1997.

13. Richard Ellis, *Presidential Travel: The Journey from George Washington to George W. Bush* (Lawrence: University Press of Kansas, 2008).

14. Brendan J. Doherty, "The Politics of the Permanent Campaign: Presidential Travel and the Electoral College, 1977–2004," *Presidential Studies Quarterly* 37, no. 4 (2007): 749–773.

15. Memo, Fred F. Fielding to James A. Baker III, Michael K. Deaver, Edward J. Rollins, Michael A. McManus, John F. W. Rogers, and Fred Bush, October 19, 1982, Michael Deaver Files, Ronald Reagan Library.

16. Karlyn Bowman, "Polling to Campaign and to Govern," in *The Permanent Campaign and Its Future*, ed. Norman J. Ornstein and Thomas E. Mann (Washington, DC: American Enterprise Institute and the Brookings Institution, 2000), 62–63.

17. Sidney Blumenthal, *The Permanent Campaign: Inside the World of Elite Political Operatives* (Boston: Beacon Press, 1980).

18. Samuel Kernell, *Going Public: New Strategies of Presidential Leadership,* 4th ed. (Washington, DC: CQ Press, 2007).

19. George C. Edwards, *On Deaf Ears: The Limits of the Bully Pulpit* (New Haven, CT: Yale University Press, 2006).

20. Matthew Eshbaugh-Soha, *The President's Speeches: Beyond "Going Public"* (Boulder, CO: Lynne Rienner, 2006).

21. Brandice Canes-Wrone, *Who Leads Whom? Presidents, Policy, and the Public* (Chicago: University of Chicago Press, 2005); B. Dan Wood, *The Myth of Presidential Representation* (New York: Cambridge University Press, 2009).

22. Ornstein and Mann, *The Permanent Campaign.*

23. George C. Edwards, *Governing by Campaigning: The Politics of the Bush Presidency* (New York: Pearson Longman, 2007).

24. Kathryn Dunn Tenpas, *Presidents as Candidates: Inside the White House for the Presidential Campaign* (New York: Garland, 1997).

25. Scott C. James, *Presidents, Parties, and the State: A Party System Perspective on Democratic Regulatory Choice, 1884–1936* (New York: Cambridge University Press, 2006).

26. Matthew J. Dickinson, "The Executive Office of the President: The Paradox of Politicization," in *The Executive Branch*, ed. Joel D. Aberbach and Mark A. Peterson (New York: Oxford University Press, 2005), 135–173; John C. Hart, *The Presidential Branch: From Washington to Clinton,* 2nd ed. (Chatham, NJ: Chatham House, 1995); Stephen Hess and James P. Pfiffner, *Organizing the Presidency* (Washington, DC: Brookings Institution Press, 2002); Bradley H. Patterson, *To Serve the President: Continuity and Innovation in the White House Staff* (Washington, DC: Brookings Institution Press, 2008); Thomas J. Weko, *The Politicizing Presidency: The White House Personnel Office, 1948–1994* (Lawrence: University Press of Kansas, 1995); Kathryn Dunn Tenpas, "Institutionalized Politics: The White House Office of Political Affairs," *Presidential Studies Quarterly* 26, no. 2 (1996): 511–522.

27. Diane J. Heith, *Polling to Govern: Public Opinion and Presidential Leadership* (Stanford, CA: Stanford University Press, 2004); Robert M. Eisinger, *The Evolution of Presidential Polling* (New York: Cambridge University Press, 2003).

28. Ellis, *Presidential Travel.*

29. Blumenthal, *Permanent Campaign;* Scott McClellan, *What Happened: Inside the Bush White House and Washington's Culture of Deception* (New York: Public Affairs, 2008).

30. Kernell, *Going Public,* 122.

31. Untitled and undated document, Files of Ken Hechler, Harry S. Truman Library.

32. See, for example, Jeffrey E. Cohen, Michael A. Krassa, and John A. Hamman, "The Impact of Presidential Campaigning on Midterm U.S. Senate Elections," *American Political Science Review* 85, no. 1 (1991): 165–178; Luke J. Keele, Brian J. Fogarty, and James A. Stimson, "Presidential Campaigning in the 2002 Congressional Elections," *PS: Political Science and Politics* 37, no. 4 (2004): 827–832.

33. David R. Mayhew, *Congress: The Electoral Connection* (New Haven, CT: Yale University Press, 1975).

34. Ibid., 13.

CHAPTER 2: THE PRESIDENT AS FUNDRAISER-IN-CHIEF

1. George W. Bush, "Remarks at a Bush-Cheney Dinner in Denver, Colorado," August 11, 2003, http://www.presidency.ucsb.edu/ws/index.php?pid=64985&st=the+political+season+will+come+in+its+own+time&st1=#axzz1PN4IwsqF (accessed June 15, 2011).

2. For example, see Jeffrey E. Cohen, Michael A. Krassa, and John A. Hamman, "The Impact of Presidential Campaigning on Midterm U.S. Senate Elections," *American Political Science Review* 85, no. 1 (1991): 165–178; Luke J. Keele, Brian J. Fogarty, and James A. Stimson, "Presidential Campaigning in the 2002 Congressional Elections," *PS: Political Science and Politics* 37, no. 4 (2004): 827–832.

3. For example, the following studies examined activity from August through Election Day and from June to the end of the campaign, respectively: Matthew Hoddie and Stephen R. Routh, "Predicting the Presidential Presence: Explaining Presidential Midterm Elections Campaign Behavior," *Political Research Quarterly* 57, no. 2 (2004): 257–265; Matthew Eshbaugh-Soha and Sean Nicholson-Crotty, "Presidential Campaigning in Midterm Elections," *American Review of Politics* 30 (2009): 35–50.

4. Samuel Kernell, *Going Public: New Strategies of Presidential Leadership,* 4th ed. (Washington, DC: CQ Press, 2007), 126.

5. Paul S. Herrnson and Irwin L. Morris, "Presidential Campaigning in the 2002 Congressional Elections," *Legislative Studies Quarterly* 32, no. 4 (2007): 629–648; Gary C. Jacobson, Samuel Kernell, and Jeffrey Lazarus, "Assessing the President's Role as Party Agent in Congressional Elections: The Case of Bill Clinton in 2000," *Legislative Studies Quarterly* 29, no. 2 (2004): 159–184; Patrick J. Sellers and Laura M. Denton, "Presidential Visits and Midterm Senate Elections," *Presidential Studies Quarterly* 36, no. 3 (2006): 410–432.

6. Michael J. Malbin, *The Election after Reform: Money, Politics, and the Bipartisan Campaign Reform Act* (Lanham, MD: Rowman & Littlefield, 2006); David B. Magleby and Anthony Corrado, *Financing the 2008 Election: Assessing Reform* (Washington, DC: Brookings Institution Press, 2011); Wendy K. Tam Cho, "Contagion Effects and Ethnic Contribution Networks," *American Journal of Political Science* 47, no. 2 (2003): 368–387; Raymond J. La Raja, *Small Change: Money, Political Parties, and Campaign Finance Reform* (Ann Arbor: University of Michigan Press, 2008); James G. Gimpel, Frances E. Lee, and Joshua Kaminski, "The Political Geography of Campaign Contributions in American Politics," *Journal of Politics* 68, no. 3 (2006): 626–639;

Wendy K. Tam Cho and James G. Gimpel, "Prospecting for (Campaign) Gold," *American Journal of Political Science* 51, no. 2 (2007): 255–268.

7. Terence Hunt, "Bush Defends Reagan Policies before Black Audience," Associated Press, April 12, 1981; Maureen Santini, "Reagan Bids Farewell to Secret Service Protector, Talks to FBI," Associated Press, April 7, 1981.

8. William Clairbourn, "Carter, Celebrities Sell Out Democratic Dinner," *Washington Post*, June 24, 1977.

9. Maureen Santini, "Reagan Campaign Strategy: From Black Tie to Hard Hat," Associated Press, July 15, 1982.

10. "Briefing by White House Press Secretary Robert Gibbs," White House web site, March 25, 2009, http://www.whitehouse.gov/the-press-office/briefing-white-house-press-secretary-robert-gibbs-32509 (accessed June 17, 2011).

11. Deb Riechmann, "Bush Debuts as Fund-Raiser-in-Chief," Associated Press, April 26, 2001.

12. Sharon Theimer, "Bush Style Seeks to Avoid 'Fund-Raiser in Chief' Label," Associated Press, July 4, 2001.

13. Ibid.; Sandra Sobieraj, "Bush Hangs Back in Fund Raising While Clinton Returns for Another Big-Money Season," Associated Press, August 18, 2001.

14. Frank Cormier, Associated Press, December 28, 1977.

15. Jay Perkins, "The Money Man: Filling GOP Coffers and Winning IOUs," Associated Press, July 25, 1982.

16. W. Dale Nelson, "President Can Raise Big Money for Candidates; Votes More Questionable," Associated Press, July 5, 1986.

17. Walter R. Mears, "Reagan Makes Unprecedented Effort for Bush," Associated Press, August 15, 1988.

18. Rita Beamish, "Bush Hits the Campaign Trail for GOP Candidates," Associated Press, December 9, 1989.

19. Tom Raum, "Bush Hits the Hot Dog Circuit for Fellow Republicans," Associated Press, April 4, 1990.

20. Rita Beamish, "President Stumping for GOP Candidates in Two-Day Trip," Associated Press, June 7, 1990.

21. Tom Raum, "Bush Hits Campaign Trail after Rough Domestic Month," Associated Press, July 18, 1990.

22. Walter R. Mears, "Bush on Campaign Trail: Filling Those GOP Coffers," Associated Press, October 20, 1990; Tom Raum, "Bush: 'Get Out and Vote,'" Associated Press, November 5, 1990.

23. Tom Raum, "Bush Hoping to Tap Texas for $2 Million in Two Days," Associated Press, October 31, 1991.

24. Rita Beamish, "Huge Contributions Roll In as GOP Holds Biggest Fundraiser Ever," Associated Press, April 28, 1992.

25. Connie Cass, "Democratic Fund-Raiser Pulls In $4.2 Million," Associated Press, June 29, 1993.

26. John King, "A Lesson from Defeat Echoes in 1996 Fund-Raising Focus," Associated Press, February 1, 1997.

27. Kevin Galvin, "Democrats Look to Raise $12.3 Million at Gala," Associated Press, May 9, 1996; Connie Cass, "Democrats and Republicans, Nearly Broke, Still Raising Money," Associated Press, December 6, 1996.

28. Kevin Galvin, "GOP Continues to Out-raise Democrats," Associated Press, October 27, 1998.

29. Jonathan D. Salant, "Unions, Lobbyists Help Democrats Break Money Record," Associated Press, May 23, 2000.

30. Terence Hunt, "Clinton's King of Presidential Fund-Raising, Analysts Say," Associated Press, September 4, 1999.

31. Scott Lindlaw, "White House Takes Credit for GOP Gains, Looks to Move Bush Agenda Ahead," Associated Press, November 6, 2002.

32. Sharon Theimer, "Republican National Committee on Pace to Break Clinton-Gore Fund-Raising Record at Presidential Gala," Associated Press, May 13, 2002; Sharon Theimer, "GOP, Bush Set Fund-Raising Record at Party Gala," Associated Press, May 5, 2004.

33. "Table 3-29," CQ Press Electronic Library, Vital Statistics on the American Presidency Online Edition, originally published in Lyn Ragsdale, *Vital Statistics on the Presidency,* 3rd ed. (Washington, DC: CQ Press, 2009), http://library.cqpress.com/vsop/vsop3e-1078–47643–2086100 (accessed May 15, 2009).

34. "Inflation Calculator: Bureau of Labor Statistics," n.d., http://www.bls.gov/data/inflation_calculator.htm (accessed June 27, 2011).

35. Quoted in Christopher Connell, "'Professionalization of Politics' Proving Costly," Associated Press, October 9, 1984.

36. King, "A Lesson from Defeat Echoes in 1996 Fund-Raising Focus."

37. La Raja, *Small Change,* 163.

38. Ibid., 79, 153.

39. Nelson W. Polsby, Aaron B. Wildavsky, and David A. Hopkins, *Presidential Elections: Strategies and Structures of American Politics* (Lanham, MD: Rowman & Littlefield, 2008); "Table 3-30," Ragsdale, Vital Statistics.

40. Tom Raum, "Bush Aides Anxious to Get Campaign in Gear," Associated Press, September 4, 1991.

41. Chuck Todd et al., "First Read—First Thoughts: He's In," April 4, 2011, http://firstread.msnbc.msn.com/_news/2011/04/04/6405441-first-thoughts-hes-in (accessed April 6, 2011).

42. Gary C. Jacobson, *The Politics of Congressional Elections,* 7th ed. (New York: Longman, 2008).

43. La Raja, *Small Change,* 79.

44. Ibid., 78; "Table 2-9," Ragsdale, *Vital Statistics.*

45. Pete Yost, "Despite Reform Talk, Big Checks Continue to Flow to Political Parties," Associated Press, October 11, 1994.

46. "Democrats Collecting Bonanza in 'Soft Money,' Group Says," Associated Press, June 21, 1994.

47. Jonathan D. Salant, "Democrats' New Level of Giving: $500,000," Associated Press, May 3, 2000.

48. La Raja, *Small Change,* 79, 107; Julie Pace, "Obama Hits Broadway Looking for Campaign Cash," Associated Press, June 24, 2011.

49. Adam Liptak, "Supreme Court Blocks Ban on Corporate Political Spending," New York Times, January 21, 2010.

50. Sharon Theimer, "Congressional Republicans Raise $22 Million at Gala Headlined by Bush," Associated Press, May 22, 2003.

51. David Jackson, "Obama vs. Bush—'More Fundraisers, Less Funds,'" USAToday.com, July 8, 2010, http://content.usatoday.com/communities/theoval/post/2010/07/obama-vs-bush—more-fundraisers-less-funds/1 (accessed June 16, 2011).

52. "Table 2.4," CQ Press Electronic Library, Vital Statistics on American Politics Online Edition, originally published in Harold W. Stanley and Richard G. Niemi, *Vital Statistics on American*

Politics 2007–2008 (Washington, DC: CQ Press, 2008), http://library.cqpress.com/vsap/ (accessed May 15, 2009); "Table 3-29," Ragsdale, *Vital Statistics*.

53. John King, "Dole Complains of Clinton Financial Edge, Suggests Returning Money," Associated Press, April 12, 1996; Sharon Theimer, "Kerry, Bush Start Spring at Different Points on Election Money Trail," Associated Press, March 29, 2004.

54. Sharon Theimer, "Convention Timing Gives Bush Money Advantage," Associated Press, September 21, 2004.

55. Evans Witt, "May Not Taking Matching Money for Primary Campaigns," Associated Press, January 30, 1984.

56. Christopher Connell, "Reagan Nomination Fund Shows Big Surplus," Associated Press, September 21, 1984.

57. "Table 3-30," Ragsdale, *Vital Statistics*.

58. "Presidential Spending Limits 2008," n.d., http://www.fec.gov/pages/brochures/pubfund_limits_2008.shtml (accessed July 7, 2011); "Table 2.4," Stanley and Niemi, *Vital Statistics;* Nelson W. Polsby et al., *Presidential Elections: Strategies and Structures of American Politics,* 13th ed. (Lanham, MD: Rowman & Littlefield, 2011).

59. Beth Fouhy, "Goodbye to Federal Funding for 2012 Candidates," Associated Press, March 31, 2001, http://news.yahoo.com/s/ap/20110331/ap_on_el_ge/2012_spurning_campaign_money (accessed June 10, 2011).

60. John King, "From Clinton on Down, a White House Heavy Hand in Party Fund-Raising," Associated Press, February 25, 1997.

61. Sonya Ross, "President Picks Up Support, Cash and Otherwise, in New York," Associated Press, October 13, 1998.

62. Jeff Zeleny, "Obama's Fund-Raising, in His Best Interest," New York Times, October 27, 2009, http://www.nytimes.com/2009/10/27/us/politics/27obama.html (accessed June 3, 2010).

CHAPTER 3: THE PRESIDENT AS PARTY-BUILDER-IN-CHIEF

1. "Press Briefing by Mike McCurry," January 31, 1996, http://www.presidency.ucsb.edu/ws/index.php?pid=48893#axzz1RthyJDzE (accessed July 12, 2011).

2. Nelson W. Polsby, *Consequences of Party Reform* (Berkeley: Institute of Governmental Studies Press, 1983); Nelson W. Polsby, Aaron B. Wildavsky, and David A. Hopkins, *Presidential Elections: Strategies and Structures of American Politics* (Lanham, MD: Rowman & Littlefield, 2008).

3. Samuel Kernell, *Going Public: New Strategies of Presidential Leadership,* 4th ed. (Washington, DC: CQ Press, 2007), 54.

4. Sidney M. Milkis, *The President and the Parties: The Transformation of the American Party System since the New Deal* (New York: Oxford University Press, 1993), 10, 300–301.

5. Daniel J. Galvin, *Presidential Party Building: Dwight D. Eisenhower to George W. Bush* (Princeton, NJ: Princeton University Press, 2009), 2, 246.

6. Ibid., 262.

7. V. O. Key Jr., *Politics, Parties, and Pressure Groups* (New York: Crowell, 1942).

8. Luke J. Keele, Brian J. Fogarty, and James A. Stimson, "Presidential Campaigning in the 2002 Congressional Elections," *PS: Political Science and Politics* 37, no. 4 (2004): 827–832; Paul S. Herrnson and Irwin L. Morris, "Presidential Campaigning in the 2002 Congressional Elections," *Legislative Studies Quarterly* 32, no. 4 (2007): 629–648; Gary C. Jacobson, Samuel Kernell, and Jef-

frey Lazarus, "Assessing the President's Role as Party Agent in Congressional Elections: The Case of Bill Clinton in 2000," *Legislative Studies Quarterly* 29, no. 2 (2004): 159–184; Jeffrey E. Cohen, Michael A. Krassa, and John A. Hamman, "The Impact of Presidential Campaigning on Midterm U.S. Senate Elections," *American Political Science Review* 85, no. 1 (1991): 165–178; Patrick J. Sellers and Laura M. Denton, "Presidential Visits and Midterm Senate Elections," *Presidential Studies Quarterly* 36, no. 3 (2006): 410–432; Matthew Hoddie and Stephen R. Routh, "Predicting the Presidential Presence: Explaining Presidential Midterm Elections Campaign Behavior," *Political Research Quarterly* 57, no. 2 (2004): 257–265; Matthew Eshbaugh-Soha and Sean Nicholson-Crotty, "Presidential Campaigning in Midterm Elections," *American Review of Politics* 30 (2009): 35–50.

9. Gary C. Jacobson, *The Politics of Congressional Elections,* 7th ed. (New York: Longman, 2008).

10. U.S. Senate Historical Office, "Party Division in the Senate, 1789–Present," n.d., http://senate.gov/pagelayout/history/one_item_and_teasers/partydiv.htm (accessed August 17, 2011); Office of the Clerk of the U.S. House of Representatives, "Party Divisions of the House of Representatives (1789 to Present)," n.d., http://artandhistory.house.gov/house_history/partyDiv.aspx (accessed August 17, 2011).

11. Personal communication with Mark Knoller, CBS News, July 1, 2011.

12. Liz Sidoti, "Obama Enters Campaign, Fundraising Fray," Associated Press, March 26, 2009.

13. Herrnson and Morris, "Presidential Campaigning in the 2002 Congressional Elections."

14. Ibid.; "EMILY's List: About EMILY's List," n.d., http://emilyslist.org/about/ (accessed June 16, 2011).

15. Sidoti, "Obama Enters Campaign, Fundraising Fray."

16. Office of the Clerk of the U.S. House of Representatives, "Party Divisions of the House of Representatives"; U.S. Senate Historical Office, "Party Division in the Senate."

17. Jack McWethy, "Carter's Drive to Woo His Own Party," *U.S. News & World Report,* July 3, 1978.

18. Jeff Greenfield, *Then Everything Changed: Stunning Alternate Histories of American Politics JFK, RFK, Carter, Ford, Reagan* (New York: Penguin, 2011).

19. "President Jimmy Carter Oral History, Carter Presidency Project, University of Virginia Miller Center," November 29, 1982, http://millercenter.org/scripps/archive/oralhistories/detail/3260, pp. 42–43 (accessed July 12, 2011).

20. Dom Bonafede, "The Personal Touch," *National Journal,* July 16, 1977.

21. Walter Pincus, "Democrats Fall Way Behind Money-Making GOP," *Washington Post,* December 18, 1977.

22. David S. Broder, "Carter Takes Complete Control of Democratic Party Machinery," *Washington Post,* January 22, 1977.

23. Bonafede, "Personal Touch."

24. Lou Cannon, "Ford Says 'Mess' Still in Washington," *Washington Post,* May 20, 1977.

25. David S. Broder, "State Democratic Chairmen Upset at White House Relations," *Washington Post,* April 1, 1977.

26. Hal Bruno, "Democrats in Distress," *Newsweek,* December 19, 1977.

27. McWethy, "Carter's Drive to Woo His Own Party."

28. Pincus, "Democrats Fall Way Behind Money-Making GOP."

29. Frank Cormier, Associated Press, May 9, 1978.

30. "Preview of '78 Voting; Carter: Help or Hindrance?" *U.S. News & World Report,* October 9, 1978.

31. Roger H. Davidson, Walter J. Oleszek, and Frances E. Lee, *Congress and Its Members,* 13th ed. (Washington, DC: CQ Press, 2011); Office of the Clerk of the U.S. House of Representatives,

"Party Divisions of the House of Representatives"; U.S. Senate Historical Office, "Party Division in the Senate."

32. Associated Press, November 27, 1979.

33. Don McLeod, "Carter Campaign Off and Running," Associated Press, December 5, 1979; Associated Press, November 30, 1979.

34. Jimmy Carter, "Interview with the President: Remarks and a Question-and-Answer Session with Editors and News Directors," The American Presidency Project, January 15, 1980, http://www.presidency.ucsb.edu/ws/index.php?pid=33040&st=&st1=#axzz1KGPwoGUh (accessed April 22, 2011).

35. W. Dale Nelson, "Carter Speaks at Partisan Dinner but Remains Mum on Campaign Plans," Associated Press, March 27, 1980.

36. "Carter Makes First, and Last, Primary Campaign Trip," Associated Press, May 30, 1980.

37. "Carter Oral History," 44.

38. Office of the Clerk of the U.S. House of Representatives, "Party Divisions of the House of Representatives"; U.S. Senate Historical Office, "Party Division in the Senate."

39. Maureen Santini, "Reagan Campaign Strategy: From Black Tie to Hard Hat," Associated Press, July 15, 1982.

40. Richard S. Beal, "Memorandum to Edwin Meese, James Baker, and Michael Deaver re: 1982 Presidential Targeting Strategy," April 2, 1982, Ronald Reagan Presidential Library.

41. Terence Hunt, "Reagan Heads for Peoria to See If His Program Still Plays," Associated Press, October 19, 1982.

42. Maureen Santini, "President Says Democrats Try to Scare People for Political Gain," Associated Press, October 26, 1982; James Gerstenzang, Associated Press, October 26, 1982.

43. Terence Hunt, "Cabinet Members Are Roving for Ronnie This Year," Associated Press, September 27, 1982.

44. James Gerstenzang, "Reagan Ready to Go Public in Final Weeks of Campaign," Associated Press, October 10, 1982.

45. Santini, "Reagan Campaign Strategy."

46. Maureen Santini, "Reagan Campaign Scorecard: About 50-50," Associated Press, November 4, 1982.

47. Beal, "Memorandum to Edwin Meese, James Baker, and Michael Deaver."

48. Evans Witt, "Political Pros See GOP Congressional Losses," Associated Press, June 30, 1982.

49. Office of the Clerk of the U.S. House of Representatives, "Party Divisions of the House of Representatives"; U.S. Senate Historical Office, "Party Division in the Senate."

50. Christopher Connell, "Reagan Nomination Fund Shows Big Surplus," Associated Press, September 21, 1984.

51. Office of the Clerk of the U.S. House of Representatives, "Party Divisions of the House of Representatives"; U.S. Senate Historical Office, "Party Division in the Senate."

52. Donald Rothberg, "GOP Concerned about Change in Tone at White House," Associated Press, March 20, 1985.

53. Susanne M. Schafer, "Reagan Heads South to Work for GOP Candidates," Associated Press, July 23, 1986.

54. Walter R. Mears, "Bush on Campaign Trail: Filling Those GOP Coffers," Associated Press, October 20, 1990.

55. Office of the Clerk of the U.S. House of Representatives, "Party Divisions of the House of Representatives"; U.S. Senate Historical Office, "Party Division in the Senate."

56. "Iran Contra Report; Arms, Hostages and Contras: How a Secret Foreign Policy Unraveled," *New York Times,* November 19, 1987, http://www.nytimes.com/1987/11/19/world/iran-contra-report-arms-hostages-contras-secret-foreign-policy-unraveled.html (accessed August 17, 2011).

57. Walter R. Mears, "Reagan Makes Unprecedented Effort for Bush," Associated Press, August 15, 1988.

58. Walter R. Mears, "Clinton Campaigns, Not Quite Unleashed," Associated Press, November 3, 2000.

59. Sidney M. Milkis and Michael Nelson, *The American Presidency: Origins and Development, 1776–2007,* 5th ed. (Washington, DC: CQ Press, 2007).

60. Office of the Clerk of the U.S. House of Representatives, "Party Divisions of the House of Representatives"; U.S. Senate Historical Office, "Party Division in the Senate."

61. Tom Raum, "Bush Hits Campaign Trail after Rough Domestic Month," Associated Press, July 18, 1990.

62. Tom Raum, "Bush Hits the Hot Dog Circuit for Fellow Republicans," Associated Press, April 4, 1990.

63. William M. Welch, "Reapportionment Puts Focus on Three Sunbelt Governors Races," Associated Press, January 11, 1990.

64. Rita Beamish, "President Heads Out on Behalf of GOP Candidates," Associated Press, September 18, 1990.

65. Tom Raum, "Bush Tells Hungary He Will Press on Soviet Troops," Associated Press, May 18, 1990.

66. Mears, "Bush on Campaign Trail."

67. Tom Raum, "Clinton to Test Length of His Coattails," Associated Press, March 2, 1994.

68. Mears, "Bush on Campaign Trail."

69. Tom Raum, "Bush: 'Get Out and Vote,'" Associated Press, November 5, 1990.

70. Office of the Clerk of the U.S. House of Representatives, "Party Divisions of the House of Representatives"; U.S. Senate Historical Office, "Party Division in the Senate."

71. "The Governor Years," Lawton Chiles Foundation, n.d., http://chilesfoundation.org/lawton-chiles/the-governor-years/ (accessed August 18, 2011); Roberto Suro, "Fierce Election for Governor Is Narrowly Won by Richards," *New York Times,* November 7, 1990; "Governors of California," The Governors' Gallery, n.d., http://governors.library.ca.gov/36-wilson.html (accessed August 18, 2011).

72. George H. W. Bush, "Remarks at a Republican Party Fundraising Luncheon in North Kingstown, Rhode Island," August 20, 1990, http://www.presidency.ucsb.edu/ws/index.php?pid=18776&st=&st1=#axzz1NNjkq303 (accessed May 25, 2011).

73. Rita Beamish, "Bush Says No Reason Politicking Should Stop," Associated Press, September 19, 1990.

74. Hans Nichols and Jonathan D. Salant, "Obama to Test Fundraising Skills Amid 'Donor Fatigue,' Crisis," *Bloomberg,* March 16, 2009, http://www.bloomberg.com/apps/news?pid=20601087&sid=aBcmH5_wa8Jo&refer=home.

75. "Candidates Request Fresh Helping of Federal Campaign Funds," Associated Press, February 4, 1992.

76. Tom Raum, "Bush Hoping to Tap Texas for $2 Million in Two Days," Associated Press, October 31, 1991.

77. Office of the Clerk of the U.S. House of Representatives, "Party Divisions of the House of Representatives"; U.S. Senate Historical Office, "Party Division in the Senate."

78. Office of the Clerk of the U.S. House of Representatives, "Party Divisions of the House of Representatives"; U.S. Senate Historical Office, "Party Division in the Senate."

79. James W. Ceaser and Andrew Busch, *Losing to Win: The 1996 Elections and American Politics* (Lanham, MD: Rowman & Littlefield, 1997), 124; John King, "He Raises Money Galore for Dems, but Often Skips Plug for Congress," Associated Press, June 13, 1996.

80. "Clinton Fundraisers Will Reopen to Media," *New Orleans Times-Picayune,* October 13, 1993.

81. Office of the Clerk of the U.S. House of Representatives, "Party Divisions of the House of Representatives"; U.S. Senate Historical Office, "Party Division in the Senate."

82. Jonathan D. Salant, "Despite One-Day Record, Democrats Outraised by GOP," Associated Press, July 14, 2000.

83. Terence Hunt, "Clinton's King of Presidential Fund-Raising, Analysts Say," Associated Press, September 4, 1999.

84. Laura Myers, "Clinton Does the Hamptons, Raising Cash for Democrats," Associated Press, August 1, 1998; Hess and Common Cause official quoted in Hunt, "Clinton's King of Presidential Fund-Raising, Analysts Say."

85. Terence Hunt, "Clinton Will Work Harder to Help Democrats Raise Money," Associated Press, March 27, 1997.

86. Ron Fournier, "Clinton Strategy for Democratic Victory in November: Money, Money, Money," Associated Press, June 11, 1998.

87. Office of the Clerk of the U.S. House of Representatives, "Party Divisions of the House of Representatives"; U.S. Senate Historical Office, "Party Division in the Senate."

88. Ronald Powers, "Clinton's Primary-Eve Fund-Raiser Irks State Democrats," Associated Press, September 4, 1998.

89. Mears, "Clinton Campaigns, Not Quite Unleashed"; Ron Fournier, "National Democrats Hope to Raise Enough Millions to Help Nominee," Associated Press, December 10, 1999; Deb Riechmann, "Bush Still Raking In Cash for GOP," Associated Press, August 15, 2008.

90. Office of the Clerk of the U.S. House of Representatives, "Party Divisions of the House of Representatives"; U.S. Senate Historical Office, "Party Division in the Senate."

91. Sharon Theimer, "The Greening of Washington—With Party Fund-Raisers," Associated Press, May 17, 2001; Scott Lindlaw, "New Campaign Finance Law Doesn't Stop Bush from Fund Raising," Associated Press, March 28, 2002.

92. Walter R. Mears, "Bush Sprouts Coattails," Associated Press, November 6, 2002; Scott Lindlaw, "White House Takes Credit for GOP Gains, Looks to Move Bush Agenda Ahead," Associated Press, November 6, 2002; Office of the Clerk of the U.S. House of Representatives, "Party Divisions of the House of Representatives"; U.S. Senate Historical Office, "Party Division in the Senate."

93. Office of the Clerk of the U.S. House of Representatives, "Party Divisions of the House of Representatives"; U.S. Senate Historical Office, "Party Division in the Senate."

94. David Espo, "Talking War and Change, Democrats Challenge GOP for Control of Congress, Governorships," Associated Press, November 8, 2006.

95. Office of the Clerk of the U.S. House of Representatives, "Party Divisions of the House of Representatives"; U.S. Senate Historical Office, "Party Division in the Senate."

96. "Press Briefing by Dana Perino," September 18, 2008, http://georgewbush-whitehouse. archives.gov/news/releases/2008/09/20080918–3.html (accessed June 8, 2010).

97. George W. Bush, "Remarks Following a Lunch with Senator John McCain of Arizona and

an Exchange with Reporters," March 5, 2008, http://www.presidency.ucsb.edu/ws/index.php?pid=76576&st=&st1=#axzz1S6PfU9bs (accessed July 14, 2011).

98. "Bush Travels to Illinois for Private Fundraiser," Associated Press, July 25, 2008.

99. Riechmann, "Bush Still Raking In Cash for GOP."

100. Office of the Clerk of the U.S. House of Representatives, "Party Divisions of the House of Representatives"; U.S. Senate Historical Office, "Party Division in the Senate."

101. R. G. Ratcliffe, "Some Dems Fear More of Same after Obama Visit," *Houston Chronicle,* August 9, 2010, http://www.chron.com/disp/story.mpl/metropolitan/7145208.html.

102. Davidson, Oleszek, and Lee, *Congress and Its Members;* U.S. Senate Historical Office, "Party Division in the Senate."

103. Personal communication with Mark Knoller, CBS News, July 1, 2011.

104. "Obama Raises More Than $86M for Campaign, DNC," *USAToday.com,* July 13, 2011, http://www.usatoday.com/news/politics/2011–07–13-obama-fundraising_n.htm (accessed August 18, 2011).

105. Sandra Sobieraj, "Bush Shares Stage with Senate Democratic Leader, the Man He Hopes to Replace with a Republican," Associated Press, April 24, 2002.

106. Evan Bayh, "Why I'm Leaving the Senate," *New York Times,* February 21, 2010, http://www.nytimes.com/2010/02/21/opinion/21bayh.html (accessed July 14, 2011).

CHAPTER 4: STRATEGIC TRAVEL AND THE PERMANENT CAMPAIGN

1. Public Papers of William J. Clinton, The American Presidency Project, December 8, 2000, http://www.presidency.ucsb.edu/ws/index.php?month=12&year=2000#axzz1jpq9AXlm (accessed July 8, 2011); Dan Eggen, "With Nebraska, Clinton Makes It 50-50," *Washington Post,* December 9, 2000; Marc Lacey, "Nebraska, at Last, Gets a Visit," *New York Times,* December 9, 2000; Ken Herman, "Bluest of the Blue: Vermont Doesn't Look Like Bush Country; It's Only State He Hasn't Visited While in Office," *Houston Chronicle,* August 17, 2008, http://www.chron.com/CDA/archives/archive.mpl?id=2008_4610725.

2. Ben Fox and Laura Wides-Munoz, "Obama Courting Puerto Ricans at Home and Abroad," *MiamiHerald.com,* June 14, 2011, http://www.miamiherald.com/2011/06/13/2264851/obama-courting-puerto-ricans-at.html#storylink=misearch (accessed June 15, 2011).

3. Frances Robles, "Obama Visit to Puerto Rico: It's All about Florida," *MiamiHerald.com,* June 12, 2011, http://www.miamiherald.com/2011/06/07/v-fullstory/2263438/obama-visit-to-puerto-rico-its.html#ixzz1PGRa6w6K (accessed June 16, 2011); Carrie Budoff Brown and Glenn Thrush, "Barack Obama Goes in Quest of Hispanic Votes," *Politico,* June 12, 2011, http://www.politico.com/news/stories/0611/56787.html (accessed June 16, 2011); Lizette Alvarez, "In Visit to Puerto Rico, Obama Has Eye on Mainland," *New York Times,* June 9, 2011, http://www.nytimes.com/2011/06/10/us/politics/10rico.html (accessed June 16, 2011).

4. George W. Bush, *Decision Points* (New York: Crown, 2010).

5. Mike Allen, "Bush Capitalizes on Travel Bargain; President Uses Air Force One for Price of 1st Class," *Washington Post,* March 5, 2004; Mike Allen, "On the Way to the Fundraiser; Stopovers Let Bush Charge Taxpayers for Political Trips," *Washington Post,* May 20, 2002; Charles R. Babcock, "Campaigning via Air Force One: Public Foots Much of Bill," *Washington Post,* December 31, 1991; Charles R. Babcock, "Flying Political Class on Air Force One; Commercial Rates Make Every Trip an Incumbent Advantage," *Washington Post,* October 19, 1992; Dana Milbank,

"The Cost of Presidential Travel Is Anyone's Guess," *Washington Post,* October 29, 2002; Ellen Nakashima, "White House Travel Bill: $292 Million; Republican Senator Says Clinton's Air Transport Expenses Are 'Exorbitant,'" *Washington Post,* August 18, 2000; Edward Walsh, "U.S. Spent over $100,000 on Trip Carter Postponed," *Washington Post,* November 9, 1977.

6. Ronald Reagan, *The Reagan Diaries* (New York: HarperCollins, 2007), 448.

7. George Stephanopoulos, *All Too Human* (New York: Back Bay Books, 2000), 317.

8. Matthew Eshbaugh-Soha and Jeffrey S. Peake, "'Going Local' to Reform Social Security," *Presidential Studies Quarterly* 36, no. 4 (2006): 689–704; Andrew W. Barrett and Jeffrey S. Peake, "When the President Comes to Town: Examining Local Newspaper Coverage of Domestic Presidential Travel," *American Politics Research* 35, no. 1 (2007): 3–31.

9. Tom Raum, "Bush a Frequent Flyer to States That Could Decide 2004 Race," Associated Press, September 20, 2003.

10. Sig Rogich, "Memorandum for President George H. W. Bush," January 24, 1990, George Bush Presidential Library.

11. Jeffrey E. Cohen and Richard J. Powell, "Building Public Support from the Grassroots Up: The Impact of Presidential Travel on State-Level Approval," *Presidential Studies Quarterly* 35, no. 1 (2005): 11–27.

12. Richard Simon, "Presidential Visits, Once 'Hail to the Chief,' Now More Like 'Hiya,'" *Los Angeles Times,* March 18, 2009, http://www.latimes.com/news/nationworld/nation/la-na-obama-california18–2009mar18.0.7920725.story.

13. Larry Rulison and Irene Jay Liu, "Many Call, but Few Are Chosen," *Albany Times Union,* September 20, 2009.

14. Bill Buell, "Presidential Visits Rare, Especially by Republicans," *Schenectady Daily Gazette,* September 20, 2009.

15. Lyn Ragsdale, *Vital Statistics on the Presidency: The Definitive Source for Data and Analysis on the American Presidency,* 3rd ed. (Washington, DC: CQ Press, 2008).

16. See, for example, Scott L. Althaus, Peter F. Nardulli, and Daron R. Shaw, "Candidate Appearances in Presidential Elections, 1972–2000," *Political Communication* 19, no. 1 (2002): 49–72; Larry M. Bartels, "Resource Allocation in a Presidential Campaign," *Journal of Politics* 47, no. 3 (1985): 928–936; Steven J. Brams and Morton D. Davis, "The 3/2's Rule in Presidential Campaigning," *American Political Science Review* 68, no. 1 (1974): 113–134; Claude S. Colantoni, Terrence J. Levesque, and Peter C. Ordeshook, "Campaign Resource Allocations under the Electoral College," *American Political Science Review* 69, no. 1 (1975): 141–154; Darshan Goux, "Big State, Small State: The Shifting Nature of Electoral College Strategies" (paper presented at the American Political Science Association Annual Meeting, Washington, DC, 2010), http://papers.ssrn.com/s013/papers.cfm?abstract_id=1644222 (accessed June 8, 2011).

17. Roderick P. Hart, *The Sound of Leadership: Presidential Communication in the Modern Age* (Chicago: University of Chicago Press, 1987), 178.

18. Ibid., 182.

19. Brendan J. Doherty, "The Politics of the Permanent Campaign: Presidential Travel and the Electoral College, 1977–2004," *Presidential Studies Quarterly* 37, no. 4 (2007): 749–773; Brendan J. Doherty, "Hail to the Fundraiser in Chief: The Evolution of Presidential Fundraising Travel, 1977–2004," *Presidential Studies Quarterly* 40, no. 1 (2010): 159–170; Emily Jane Charnock, James McCann, and Kathryn Dunn Tenpas, "Presidential Travel from Eisenhower to George W. Bush: An 'Electoral College' Strategy," *Political Science Quarterly* 124, no. 2 (2009): 323–339.

20. A. Colin Cameron and Pravin K. Trivedi, *Regression Analysis of Count Data* (New York:

Cambridge University Press, 1998); J. Scott Long, *Regression Models for Categorical and Limited Dependent Variables* (Thousand Oaks, CA: Sage, 1997).

21. This model was run using STATA's xtnbreg function, which estimates negative binomial models for longitudinal data.

22. This distance is the number of air miles between Andrews Air Force Base, just outside of Washington, DC, which is the president's usual point of departure for air travel, and each state capital. Data were gathered from a company named Frequent Flyer Services.

23. Richard M. Nixon, "Address Accepting the Presidential Nomination at the Republican National Convention in Chicago," The American Presidency Project, July 28, 1960, http://www.presidency.ucsb.edu/ws/index.php?pid=25974#axzz1Ux0XTVpS (accessed August 14, 2011).

24. Theodore H. White, *The Making of the President 1960* (New York: Harper Perennial, 2009).

25. Herman, "Bluest of the Blue."

26. George H. W. Bush, "Remarks at a Republican Fundraising Breakfast in Burlington, Vermont," October 23, 1990, http://www.presidency.ucsb.edu/ws/index.php?pid=18954&st=&st1=#axzz1NHsTkCHo (accessed May 24, 2011).

27. Steve Kraske and Dave Helling, "Missouri, the Bellwether, Backed the Loser: What Happened?" *Kansas City Star,* November 6, 2008, http://www.mcclatchydc.com/2008/11/06/55406/missouri-the-bellwether-backed.html.

28. Darshan Goux, "The Battleground State: Conceptualizing Geographic Contestation in American Presidential Elections, 1960–2004" (PhD diss., University of California, Berkeley, 2010); Daron R. Shaw, "The Methods behind the Madness: Presidential Electoral College Strategies, 1988–1996," *Journal of Politics* 61, no. 4 (1999): 893–913; Daron R. Shaw, *The Race to 270: The Electoral College and the Campaign Strategies of 2000 and 2004* (Chicago: University of Chicago Press, 2006).

29. "Paths to 270 Electoral College Votes," Obama for America web site, December 29, 2011, http://www.barackobama.com/news/entry/paths-to-270-electoral-votes?utm_source=HP&utm_medium=Content&utm_term=20120102&utm_campaign=270 (accessed December 29, 2011).

30. Jimmy Carter, "Democratic Congressional Campaign Dinner Remarks at the Dinner," The American Presidency Project, May 9, 1979.

31. Ron Fournier, "Election Time: Clinton Lays Down Roots in Iowa," Associated Press, April 25, 1995.

32. William J. Clinton, "Remarks on the Issuance of Final Regulations on Protection of Medical Records Privacy," The American Presidency Project, December 20, 2000, http://www.presidency.ucsb.edu/ws/index.php?pid=1272&st=&st1=#axzz1UqRN25xk (accessed August 11, 2011).

33. Matthew Mosk, "Hawaii Rare for Obama; Swing States Top His Itinerary," *Washington Times,* December 28, 2009, http://www.washingtontimes.com/news/2009/dec/28/swing-states-still-top-sway-of-hawaii-palms/.

34. Scott Wilson, "Obama's Travel Itinerary Mixes Policy, Electoral Politics," *Washington Post,* June 21, 2009, http://www.washingtonpost.com/wp-dyn/content/article/2009/06/20/AR2009062001837.html (accessed August 2, 2011).

35. Ibid.

36. Tom Raum, "Bush Ignored Political Storm Warnings," Associated Press, November 3, 1992.

37. For election data, see "Dave Leip's Atlas of U.S. Presidential Elections," n.d., http://uselectionatlas.org/RESULTS/ (accessed August 9, 2011).

38. Adam Nagourney, "Kerry Says bin Laden Tape Gave Bush a Lift," *New York Times,* January

31, 2005, sec. Washington, http://www.nytimes.com/2005/01/31/politics/31kerry.html (accessed August 9, 2011).

39. Nelson W. Polsby, *Consequences of Party Reform* (Berkeley: Institute of Governmental Studies Press, 1983); Samuel Kernell, *Going Public: New Strategies of Presidential Leadership,* 4th ed. (Washington, DC: CQ Press, 2007).

40. Peter Goldman and Eleanor Clift, "The New/Old Jimmy," *Newsweek,* May 15, 1978.

41. James Gerstenzang, Associated Press, May 26, 1978.

42. Karl Rove, "Obama and the Permanent Campaign," *wsj.com,* August 13, 2009, sec. Commentary (U.S.), http://online.wsj.com/article/SB10001424052970203863204574346512956227346 .html (accessed June 3, 2010).

43. Diane Sawyer, "Interview with Barack Obama," *ABC World News,* January 25, 2010, http://abcnews.go.com/WN/Obama/abc-world-news-diane-sawyer-diane-sawyer-interviews/ story?id=9659064 (accessed January 26, 2010).

CHAPTER 5: THE EVOLVING ROLE OF WHITE HOUSE STAFF IN
ELECTORAL DECISION-MAKING

1. Glenn Thrush and Josh Gerstein, "Campaigning from the White House," *Politico,* July 22, 2011, http://www.politico.com/news/stories/0711/59631.html (accessed July 25, 2011).

2. John McCain, "Remarks in New Orleans, Louisiana," June 3, 2008, http://www.presidency. ucsb.edu/ws/index.php?pid=77410&st=&st1=#axzz1U7GIA61c (accessed August 5, 2011).

3. John McCain, "Interview with Scott Pelley of CBS News' '60 Minutes,'" September 21, 2008, http://www.presidency.ucsb.edu/ws/index.php?pid=84345&st=&st1=#axzz1U7GIA61c (accessed August 4, 2011).

4. Kathryn Dunn Tenpas, "Institutionalized Politics: The White House Office of Political Affairs," *Presidential Studies Quarterly* 26, no. 2 (1996): 511–522.

5. Interview with George Elsey, September 27, 2006.

6. John C. Hart, *The Presidential Branch: From Washington to Clinton,* 2nd ed. (Chatham, NJ: Chatham House, 1994).

7. Oral history interview, Matthew J. Connelly, November 28, 1967, pp. 129–130, Harry S. Truman Library.

8. Oral history interview, George M. Elsey, July 17, 1969, pp. 241–242, Truman Library.

9. Oral history interview, George M. Elsey, February 17, 1964, pp. 57–58, Truman Library.

10. Oral history interview, Clark M. Clifford, May 10, 1971, p. 240, Truman Library.

11. Elsey, interview.

12. David Bell to Charles Murphy, March 6, 1950, Hechler Papers, Truman Library; David Bell to Charles Murphy, March 8, 1950, Hechler Papers, Truman Library.

13. Oral history interview, Matthew J. Connelly, August 21, 1968, pp. 393–394, Truman Library.

14. Elsey, interview.

15. Oral history interview, Charles S. Murphy, June 3, 1963, p. 57, Truman Library.

16. Oral history interview, George M. Elsey, February 17, 1964, pp. 57–58, Truman Library.

17. Clark Clifford, memorandum for Harry S. Truman, November 19, 1947, p. 29, Clifford Papers, Truman Library.

18. George M. Elsey, "Summary of Remarks in Politics 203, Princeton University," 1949, George M. Elsey Papers, Box 32, Truman Library.

19. Oral history interview, Charles S. Murphy, May 2, 1963, p. 21–22, Truman Library.

20. Stephen Spingarn to Charles Murphy, November 18, 1948, Clifford Papers, Truman Library.

21. David G. McCullough, *Truman* (New York: Simon & Schuster, 1992).

22. Elsey, interview.

23. Robert H. Ferrell, ed., *Off the Record: The Private Papers of Harry S. Truman* (New York: Harper & Row, 1980), 406–407.

24. McCullough, *Truman;* Elsey, interview.

25. Nelson Polsby, "Some Landmarks in Modern Presidential-Congressional Relations," in *Both Ends of the Avenue: The Presidency, the Executive Branch, and Congress in the 1980s,* ed. Anthony King (Washington, DC: American Enterprise Institute, 1983).

26. Hart, *Presidential Branch.*

27. Memorandum, Dan J. Smith to Mike Deaver, August 18, 1982, Michael Deaver Files, Ronald Reagan Presidential Library.

28. Ronald Reagan Presidential Library, "White House Offices," http://www.reagan.utexas.edu/archives/textual/whodesc.html (accessed April 8, 2010).

29. Memorandum, Frank J. Donatelli to the President, February 19, 1988, Frank J. Donatelli Files, Reagan Library.

30. Memo, James A. Baker III to White House Staff, October 18, 1983, James A. Baker Files, Reagan Library.

31. Ronald Reagan, "Interview with Stan Turner of KSTP-TV in Minneapolis, Minnesota," The American Presidency Project, June 9, 1983, http://www.presidency.ucsb.edu/ws/index.php?pid=41450&st=&st1=#axzz1jpq9Axlm (accessed June 22, 2011).

32. James Gerstenzang, Associated Press, October 17, 1983.

33. Ibid.

34. Tom Raum, "Bush Triggers Re-election Fund Raising," Associated Press, October 11, 1991.

35. Tom Raum, "Bush Hoping to Tap Texas for $2 Million in Two Days," Associated Press, October 31, 1991.

36. Tom Raum, "Fitzwater Says Bush Won't Be Rushed into Action by GOP Critics," Associated Press, November 18, 1991.

37. Harry F. Rosenthal, "You Can't Miss This Candidate; He's Already Got the Job," Associated Press, February 12, 1992.

38. Thrush and Gerstein, "Campaigning from the White House"; Judson Berger, "Obama Aides Defend Use of White House Room for Campaign Pitch," *Foxnews.com,* June 28, 2011, http://www.foxnews.com/politics/2011/06/28/obama-aides-defend-use-white-house-room-for-campaign-pitch/ (accessed June 28, 2011); Scott Lindlaw, "Delicate Balance between Official White House Duties, Campaign Operation," Associated Press, March 1, 2004.

39. C. Boyden Grey, "Memorandum: Presidential Travel: Designation of Official Travelers," December 6, 1991, Papers of C. Boyden Grey, George Bush Presidential Library.

40. Brendan J. Doherty, "The Politics of the Permanent Campaign: Presidential Travel and the Electoral College, 1977–2004," *Presidential Studies Quarterly* 37, no. 4 (2007): 749–773.

41. Memo, Dan J. Smith to Mike Deaver, August 18, 1982, Michael Deaver Files, Ronald Reagan Library.

42. Quoted in Tenpas, "Institutionalized Politics."

43. Edward J. Rollins, "Yes, Play Politics in the White House," *New York Times,* November 21, 2008, http://www.nytimes.com/2008/11/21/opinion/21rollins.html?th&emc=th (accessed August 10, 2011).

44. Tenpas, "Institutionalized Politics."

45. Edward Walsh, "New Unit to Determine Carter Election Aid Role," *Washington Post,* June 24, 1977.

46. Ibid.

47. Tenpas, "Institutionalized Politics."

48. Martin Schram, "The President's Man Out Front: Evan Dobelle to Coordinate President's Reelection Campaign," *Washington Post,* March 4, 1979.

49. Shirley Anne Warshaw, personal communication, April 23, 2010.

50. Terence Hunt, "Cabinet Members Are Roving for Ronnie This Year," Associated Press, September 27, 1982.

51. Memo, James A. Baker III to White House Staff, October 18, 1983, James A. Baker Files, Ronald Reagan Library.

52. Ronald Reagan Presidential Library, "White House Offices," http://www.reagan.utexas.edu/archives/textual/whodesc.html (accessed April 8, 2010).

53. Gerstenzang, Associated Press, October 17, 1983.

54. Maureen Santini, Associated Press, January 30, 1984.

55. Quoted in Tenpas, "Institutionalized Politics."

56. Rita Beamish, "Bush, Political Advisers Meet to Discuss '92 Campaign," Associated Press, August 3, 1991.

57. "Mosbacher Moves to Party Office to Raise Money," Associated Press, August 27, 1992.

58. Ron Fournier, "Clinton Re-election Team Off to Smooth Start—For Now," Associated Press, September 20, 1995.

59. Ron Fournier, "Clinton Selects Campaign Head," Associated Press, April 24, 1996.

60. Bradley H. Patterson, *To Serve the President: Continuity and Innovation in the White House Staff* (Washington, DC: Brookings Institution Press, 2008), 160.

61. Quoted in ibid., 160.

62. Jeff Zeleny and Peter Baker, "Obama Moves to Centralize Control over Party Strategy," *New York Times,* January 24, 2010, http://www.nytimes.com/2010/01/24/us/politics/24union.html (accessed June 3, 2010).

63. Anne E. Kornblut and Aaron Blake, "Obama Shifts Political Staff, Will Launch Campaign in March or April," *WashingtonPost.com,* January 20, 2011, http://voices.washingtonpost.com/thefix/eye-on-2012/obama-shifts-political-staff-0.html?wpisrc=nl_pmpolitics (accessed January 20, 2011).

64. "Press Briefing by Press Secretary Jay Carney," White House web site, April 4, 2011, http://www.whitehouse.gov/the-press-office/2011/04/04/press-briefing-press-secretary-jay-carney-442011 (accessed April 6, 2011).

65. Jeff Zeleny, "Obama Campaign Picks Headquarters in Chicago," *NYTimes.com,* March 28, 2011, http://thecaucus.blogs.nytimes.com/2011/03/28/obama-campaign-to-be-run-from-chicago/?hp (accessed March 28, 2011).

66. Hart, *Presidential Branch,* 128.

67. McCain, "Interview with Scott Pelley of CBS News' '60 Minutes.'"

68. Oral history interview, George M. Elsey, February 17, 1964, pp. 55–56, Truman Library.

69. Lindlaw, "Delicate Balance between Official White House Duties, Campaign Operation."

CHAPTER 6: THE IMPLICATIONS OF THE PERMANENT CAMPAIGN

1. For election data, see "Dave Leip's Atlas of U.S. Presidential Elections," n.d., http://uselectionatlas.org/RESULTS/ (accessed August 9, 2011).

2. James Gerstenzang, Associated Press, October 26, 1982.

3. Fredreka Schouten, "Obama Doubles as DNC Fundraiser in Chief," *USA Today,* May 23, 2011.

4. Don McLeod, Associated Press, April 24, 1979.

5. John King, "From Clinton on Down, a White House Heavy Hand in Party Fund-Raising," Associated Press, February 25, 1997.

6. Terence Hunt, "Clinton to Raise Money in New York, Florida," Associated Press, December 8, 1997.

7. Karl Rove, "I'm Impressed by Your Fundraising, Mr. Obama—But Not as Much as I Thought I'd Be," *Foxnews.com,* July 18, 2011, http://www.foxnews.com/opinion/2011/07/18/im-impressed-by-your-fundraising-mr-obama-but-not-as-much-as-thought-id-be/ (accessed July 25, 2011).

8. "RNC to Pay for Reagan Expenses in Los Angeles," Associated Press, August 9, 1981.

9. "In Politics, Get the Money Up Front," Associated Press, June 15, 1982.

10. "Reagan Drops Fundraiser Appearance for Tax Fight," Associated Press, August 9, 1982.

11. Michael Putzel, "As Election Nears, Who Pays Reagan's Tab on the Road?" Associated Press, October 24, 1982.

12. Scott Lindlaw, "New Campaign Finance Law Doesn't Stop Bush from Fund Raising," Associated Press, March 28, 2002.

13. Tom Raum, "Clinton Paints Bleak Picture of GOP Cuts as He Seeks Florida Support," Associated Press, September 19, 1995.

14. Michael Putzel, "Reagan Tells Autoworkers Economy Recovered Because They 'Hung Tough,'" Associated Press, April 11, 1984.

15. Tom Raum, "President Mixes Politics and Business on the Road," Associated Press, February 7, 1990.

16. Ibid.

17. Ibid.

18. James Rowley, "Clinton Says Having Donors at the White House Was 'Entirely Appropriate,'" Associated Press, February 26, 1997.

19. Terence Hunt, "Gore: Made Fund-Raising Calls from Office, Won't Any More," Associated Press, March 3, 1997.

20. "Post: Gore Was 'Solicitor-in-Chief' for 1996 Re-election Campaign," Associated Press, March 2, 1997.

21. Eun-Kyung Kim, "Video Shows Reagan Asking Donors: 'Can I Count on You to Help?'" Associated Press, October 9, 1997; John Solomon, "Reagan Made Fund-raising Calls from the White House, Hosted Donors," Associated Press, September 4, 1997.

22. "Bush: No White House Fund Raising in His Administration," Associated Press, March 28, 1997.

23. "Quayle Denies Raising Funds at Vice Presidential Residence," Associated Press, March 4, 1997.

24. "Former President Ford Says Republicans Need to Move to Center," Associated Press, March 30, 1997.

25. Terence Hunt, "Clinton: 'Mistakes Made' but White House Not for Sale," Associated Press, January 28, 1997.

26. Eric Lipton, "Bush White House Broke Elections Law, Report Says," *New York Times,* January 24, 2011, sec. U.S. / Politics, http://www.nytimes.com/2011/01/25/us/politics/25ethics.html?_r=1&ref=politics (accessed August 9, 2011).

27. Josh Gerstein, "Donor Meeting at White House Draws Fire," *Politico,* June 20, 2011, http://www.politico.com/news/stories/0611/57389.html (accessed August 9, 2011).

28. Carrie Budoff Brown, "Issa Presses W.H. for Travel Answers," *Politico*, June 3, 2010, http://www.politico.com/news/stories/0610/38100.html (accessed August 9, 2011).

29. Carrie Budoff Brown, "Obama Faces Test on WH Political Office," *Politico*, November 13, 2008, http://dyn.politico.com/printstory.cfm?uuid=93F0867A-18FE-70B2-A83286FC31EF06CB (accessed June 19, 2009).

30. Jennifer Loven, "A Look at Questions about White House Staffers Using Political E-Mail Accounts," Associated Press, April 13, 2007.

31. NBC News/Wall Street Journal Poll, April 1997, retrieved from the iPOLL Databank, Roper Center for Public Opinion Research, University of Connecticut, http://www.ropercenter.uconn.edu/data_access/ipoll/ipoll.html (accessed September 22, 2011).

32. Fox News/Opinion Dynamics Poll, March 1997, retrieved from the iPOLL Databank, Roper Center for Public Opinion Research, University of Connecticut, http://www.ropercenter.uconn.edu/data_access/ipoll/ipoll.html (accessed September 22, 2011).

33. Gallup/CNN/USA Today Poll, April 1997, retrieved from the iPOLL Databank, Roper Center for Public Opinion Research, University of Connecticut, http://www.ropercenter.uconn.edu/data_access/ipoll/ipoll.html (accessed September 22, 2011).

34. NBC News/Wall Street Journal Poll, October 1997, retrieved from the iPOLL Databank, Roper Center for Public Opinion Research, University of Connecticut, http://www.ropercenter.uconn.edu/data_access/ipoll/ipoll.html (accessed September 22, 2011); for election data, see "Dave Leip's Atlas of U.S. Presidential Elections."

35. PSRA/Newsweek Poll, January 1998, retrieved from the iPOLL Databank, Roper Center for Public Opinion Research, University of Connecticut, http://www.ropercenter.uconn.edu/data_access/ipoll/ipoll.html (accessed September 22, 2011).

36. Center for Responsive Politics Money and Politics Survey, April 1997, retrieved from the iPOLL Databank, Roper Center for Public Opinion Research, University of Connecticut. http://www.ropercenter.uconn.edu/data_access/ipoll/ipoll.html (accessed September 22, 2011).

37. CBS News/New York Times Poll, April 1997, retrieved from the iPOLL Databank, Roper Center for Public Opinion Research, University of Connecticut, http://www.ropercenter.uconn.edu/data_access/ipoll/ipoll.html (accessed September 22, 2011).

38. PSRA/Newsweek Poll, October 1999, retrieved from the iPOLL Databank, Roper Center for Public Opinion Research, University of Connecticut, http://www.ropercenter.uconn.edu/data_access/ipoll/ipoll.html (accessed September 22, 2011).

39. CBS News Poll, March 1997, retrieved from the iPOLL Databank, Roper Center for Public Opinion Research, University of Connecticut, http://www.ropercenter.uconn.edu/data_access/ipoll/ipoll.html (accessed September 22, 2011).

40. NBC News/Wall Street Journal Poll, July 1997, retrieved from the iPOLL Databank, Roper Center for Public Opinion Research, University of Connecticut, http://www.ropercenter.uconn.edu/data_access/ipoll/ipoll.html (accessed September 22, 2011).

41. NBC News/Wall Street Journal Poll, September 1997, retrieved from the iPOLL Databank, Roper Center for Public Opinion Research, University of Connecticut, http://www.ropercenter.uconn.edu/data_access/ipoll/ipoll.html (accessed September 22, 2011).

42. NBC News/Wall Street Journal Poll, October 1997, retrieved from the iPOLL Databank, Roper Center for Public Opinion Research, University of Connecticut, http://www.ropercenter.uconn.edu/data_access/ipoll/ipoll.html (accessed September 22, 2011).

43. Theodore H. White, *The Making of the President 1960* (New York: Harper Perennial, 2009).

44. Jeff Zeleny, "Selling Stimulus, Obama Tours Battleground States," *New York Times*, February 19, 2009, sec. U.S. / Politics, http://www.nytimes.com/2009/02/19/us/politics/18web-

zeleny.html?hp (accessed August 10, 2011); Scott Wilson, "Obama's Travel Itinerary Mixes Policy, Electoral Politics," *Washington Post,* June 21, 2009, http://www.washingtonpost.com/wp-dyn/content/article/2009/06/20/AR2009062001837.html (accessed August 2, 2011); Erin McPike, "Obama Makes Himself a Stranger in 12 (Mostly Red) States," *RealClearPolitics.com,* May 10, 2011, http://www.realclearpolitics.com/articles/2011/05/10/obama_makes_himself_a_stranger_in_12_mostly_red_states_109803.html (accessed May 10, 2011); Tom Raum, "Bush a Frequent Flyer to States That Could Decide 2004 Race," Associated Press, September 20, 2003; Ken Herman, "Bluest of the Blue: Vermont Doesn't Look Like Bush Country; It's Only State He Hasn't Visited While in Office," *Houston Chronicle,* August 17, 2008, http://www.chron.com/CDA/archives/archive.mpl?id=2008_4610725 (accessed June 12, 2011); Raum, "President Mixes Politics and Business on the Road."

45. Zeleny, "Selling Stimulus, Obama Tours Battleground States."

46. Richard Wolf, "Obama's Travels Favor 2012 'Swing' States," *USA Today,* July 17, 2011, http://www.usatoday.com/news/politics/2011-07-17-obama-travel-visits_n.htm (accessed July 30, 2011).

47. Scott Lindlaw, "Traveling to South Carolina and Georgia, Bush to Stump for One-time McCain Backer Graham," Associated Press, March 25, 2002.

48. Sonya Ross, "President Picks Up Support, Cash and Otherwise, in New York," Associated Press, October 13, 1998.

49. Samuel Kernell, *Going Public: New Strategies of Presidential Leadership,* 4th ed. (Washington, DC: CQ Press, 2007); Norman J. Ornstein and Thomas E. Mann, eds., *The Permanent Campaign and Its Future* (Washington, DC: American Enterprise Institute and the Brookings Institution, 2000), 225.

50. Peggy Noonan, "There Is No New Frontier," *Wall Street Journal,* October 16, 2009.

51. Carl Hulse, "As Aisle Gets Wider, Arms Get Shorter," *New York Times,* December 28, 2009.

52. Ibid.

53. Ross Douthat, "Waiting for a Landslide," *New York Times,* August 7, 2011, sec. Opinion, http://www.nytimes.com/2011/08/08/opinion/waiting-for-a-landslide.html?_r=2&nl=todaysheadlines&emc=tha212 (accessed August 9, 2011).

54. "Table 3-29," CQ Press Electronic Library, Vital Statistics on the American Presidency Online Edition, originally published in Lyn Ragsdale, *Vital Statistics on the Presidency,* 3rd ed. (Washington, DC: CQ Press, 2009), http://library.cqpress.com/vsop/vsop3e-1078-47643-2086100 (accessed May 15, 2009).

55. Ron Fournier, "Clinton Seeks More Donations for Democrats," Associated Press, December 1, 1997.

56. Carolyn Skorneck, "Broadcasters Fighting Free-Ad Proposal in Congress," *Associated Press,* May 29, 1997.

57. Burdett Loomis, "Resolved, The President Should Be Elected Directly by the People," in *Debating the Presidency: Conflicting Perspectives on the American Executive,* ed. Richard J. Ellis and Michael Nelson, 2nd ed. (Washington, DC: CQ Press, 2009).

58. Noonan, "There Is No New Frontier."

59. William J. Clinton, "Remarks to the Democratic National Committee Staff," The American Presidency Project, January 8, 2001, http://www.presidency.ucsb.edu/ws/index.php?pid=640 11&st=&st1=#axzz1UXyjRGmI (accessed August 9, 2011).

60. Fred I. Greenstein, *The Hidden-Hand Presidency: Eisenhower as Leader* (New York: Basic Books, 1982).

61. Oral history interview, George M. Elsey, February 17, 1964, pp. 55–56, Harry S. Truman Library.

62. Hunt, "Clinton to Raise Money in New York, Florida."

63. Raum, "President Mixes Politics and Business on the Road."

64. Chris Cillizza, "The Fix—White House Cheat Sheet: Obama the Fundraiser," *Washington Post.com,* May 26, 2009, http://voices.washingtonpost.com/thefix/cheat-sheet/052609white-house-cheat-sheet.html?wprss=thefix (accessed March 3, 2011).

65. Douglas E. Schoen and Patrick H. Caddell, "One and Done: To Be a Great President, Obama Should Not Seek Reelection in 2012," *WashingtonPost.com,* November 14, 2010, http://www.washingtonpost.com/wp-dyn/content/article/2010/11/12/AR2010111202846.html (accessed May 18, 2011).

66. Ronald Reagan, "Remarks in an Interview with Independent Radio Network Correspondents on Domestic and Foreign Policy Issues," The American Presidency Project, December 18, 1982, http://www.presidency.ucsb.edu/ws/index.php?pid=42130&st=&st1=#axzz1MuOJU8jv (accessed August 10, 2011).

67. Cited in Michael Nelson, *The Evolving Presidency: Landmark Documents, 1787–2008* (Washington, DC: CQ Press, 2008).

INDEX

MANEW

3-30-16
02/04/2016   **$34.95**